Ozark Mountain Humor

Ozark Mountain Humor

*Jokes on Hunting, Religion,
Marriage and Ozark Ways*

Edited by W. K. McNeil

August House / Little Rock
PUBLISHERS

Printed in the United States of America

10 9 8 7 6 5 4 3 2 1

LIBRARY OF CONGRESS CATALOGING-IN-PUBLICATION DATA

Ozark Mountain humor: jokes on hunting,
religion, marriage, and Ozark ways /
edited by W. K. Neil. — 1st ed.
p.   cm. — (The American folklore series)
Bibliography: p. 202
ISBN 0-87483-085-0 : $18.95. — ISBN 0-87483-086-9 (pbk.) : $8.95
1. American wit and humor—Ozark Mountain region.
2. Ozark Mountains region—Social life and customs—Humor.
3. Mountain life—Ozark Mountains Region—Humor.
I. McNeil, W. K.   II. Series.
PN6162.093   1989
818'.5402'0897671—dc19   89-400
                                                      CIP

First Edition, 1989

Cover illustration by Wendell E. Hall
Production artwork by Ira Hocut
Typography by Lettergraphics, Memphis, TN
Design direction by Ted Parkhurst
Project direction by Hope Norman Coulter

This book is printed on archival-quality paper which meets the
guidelines for performance and durability of the Committee on
Production Guidelines for Book Longevity of the Council on
Library Resources.

AUGUST HOUSE, INC.   PUBLISHERS   LITTLE ROCK

To the memory of Hubert Wilkes (1905-1984),
who knew how to bring the "big stories" to life

Acknowledgments

It is a rite of passage for authors to say that their book could not have been produced without the help of numerous friends and colleagues. That is a very nice tradition and one I am happy to continue here, because this volume would have been incomplete without the selfless help of a number of people. These include Barbara Allen, Laura Bullion, Bill Clements, Michael Dabrishus, Michael Glenn, Max Hunter, George Lankford, Guy Logsdon, Betty Lombardi, Gordon McCann, Norma Ortiz, and Ellen Shipley. Although this brief notice is their only mention in this book, I do not consider their contributions small. Yet they should not be held responsible for any interpretations or errors herein; for those I am solely responsible.

W. K. McNeil
The Ozark Folk Center
Mountain View, Arkansas

Contents

Introduction

This book deals with folk humor from the Ozark Mountains, a well-known but poorly defined region. Ask any two
experts to tell where the geographical boundaries of the
Ozarks are and you are likely to receive two different answers. The most exclusive definition is that the region is
composed of most of northern Arkansas and southern Missouri; the most inclusive holds that it consists of those two
areas plus portions of eastern Oklahoma, eastern Kansas,
and southern Illinois. If one opts for this larger drawing of
the boundary lines, as is done in the present volume, then
one can say that the Ozarks are bounded in a rough way by
major rivers. On the south is the Arkansas, on the north the
Missouri, on the east the Mississippi, and on the west the
Neosho. These four waterways provide a convenient means
of orientation.

"Ozark" is an unusual name that is not encountered in
English other than in reference to the mountain range. A
question that often arises is, where did the name come
from? That query is easily answered because no one knows;
most explanations suggest that it is an anglicization of a
French phrase. Since at this late date it is unlikely that a
definitive explanation can be offered, it is helpful to present
some of the theories previously advanced. According to one
hypothesis the term is derived from the French phrase *bois
aux arcs,* supposedly referring to a wood used for bows.
When the first Europeans—Frenchmen—came into the

Ozarks, they noted that the Indians used bows and arrows that were unusually strong. These were made from the wood of the bois d'arc tree (also known as the Osage orange and hedge apple) and, upon learning this fact, the French trappers called the entire region "Bois Aux Arcs." After some time the term was shortened to "Aux Arcs" and eventually anglicized to the present "Ozarks."[1]

A second theory holds that the name is derived from the tendency of early French settlers to abbreviate long Indian tribal names by merely using their first syllables. For example, documents might refer to a hunting expedition of fur-traders as "aux Kans," meaning that it was made into the territory of the Kansas tribe of Indians. According to this thesis the French used the terms "aux Arks" and "aux Os" to refer to expeditions into the territory of the Arkansas and Osage Indians—the region now known as the Ozarks—and the two terms were eventually anglicized to the present word.[2]

A third theory is connected to a geological thesis popular around the time of the American Revolution. This concept was the work of Abraham Gottlob Werner (1750–1817), a German scientist, who suggested that there were two kinds of rock formations found in the earth: aqueous rock formed by the action of water and containing fossils, and azoic rock formed by fire and containing no living organisms. Several of the Europeans who first came into the region that came to be known as the Ozarks were aware of Werner's ideas and called the granite rocks found throughout the area azoic. On a map this territory roughly resembles an arc, especially if one accepts the more inclusive set of geographical boundaries, and so this became the "Azoic Arc," a name that evolved into the present "Ozark." Ideas such as this sound farfetched but, in lieu of any better arguments, they are as valid as any other explanation.[3]

While there is dispute about the origins of the name "Ozark," there is no argument about when it first gained widespread acceptance. By the 1820s the name was in popular usage, for in 1821 Henry Rowe Schoolcraft

(1793–1864), a famous nineteenth-century explorer and writer, published a book in which he referred to the region as the Ozarks. This volume, *Journal of a Tour into the Interior of Missouri and Arkansas in 1818 and 1819,* recounted a journey undertaken in search of lead mines but it also included some of the earlier recorded examples of Ozark humor.[4] Over three decades later, in 1853, Schoolcraft produced *Scenes and Adventures in the Semi-Alpine Regions of the Ozark Mountains of Missouri and Arkansas,* which gave further details about his 1818–1819 explorations, but by the 1850s the name "Ozark" was in common usage, with Schoolcraft deserving some of the credit for popularizing the name outside the region.

How can the Ozarks be characterized? What are the cultural traits that distinguish the area? The major one is that the region is rural. One recent authority suggests that this "is the least argumentative and perhaps the most important cultural fact relating to the Ozarks."[5] There are, of course, some urban sections—for example, Springfield and Joplin in Missouri and the Fayetteville-Springdale area in Arkansas—but the general nature of daily life in the Ozarks is rural. Even most of the tourist-oriented communities, such as Eureka Springs, Arkansas, and Branson, Missouri, are small towns as far as population, most being well under ten thousand. A second distinctive feature is the Ozarker's sense of place. While experts may not agree on exactly where the Ozarks are, the people who live in the region have no hesitation in identifying themselves as Ozarkers and recent arrivals as outsiders. In many communities natives always consider those persons not born in the Ozarks outsiders even though they may have spent all but a few years of their life in the Ozarks.

Another cultural trait characteristic of the Ozarks is a relatively stable social system, especially when compared with that found in most parts of the United States. As one cultural geographer puts it,

Things are relatively uncomplicated. There are

strong and stable kinship relations that extend back generations. Social activities focus on schools and churches, and these institutions are dependable and predictable. Ozarkers know who their friends are and who their enemies are and what to do about it. There are few ego problems or questions about belonging. The rigors of making a living in a region blessed with only modest resources have built character, or at least the idea is widely accepted, and a kind of kinship or bond forms from a shared experience in an Ozarks understood by all.[6]

One final aspect of Ozark culture merits mention here, namely the dominant role that Upland South immigrants have played in shaping the traditional heritage of the Ozarks. Immigrants from eastern Tennessee, southeastern Kentucky, southwestern Virginia, and other parts of southern Appalachia were not the earliest settlers in the Ozarks but they have been the largest and most influential group. Most of them moved into the Ozarks during the period 1820 to 1850, motivated in part by land bounties granted to soldiers of the Revolutionary War and the War of 1812. One cannot honestly deny the importance of these Appalachian immigrants in forming Ozark history and folklore, but one should not overestimate their significance either. Despite the claims of many authors, Ozark traditional heritage is not solely derived from the white Anglo-Saxons who moved west from the major mountain chain of the eastern United States.

Briefly characterizing any region is, to some extent, always an exercise in futility, but it is hardly less so than providing a brief description of folklore. As I have noted elsewhere, folklore "is a complex area of intellectual study that does not easily lend itself to a brief description."[7] Even so, because the present work deals with an aspect of folklore, some general words of definition are in order. Folklore is material passed on orally and, usually, informally; it is traditional, in the sense that it is passed on repeatedly in relatively fixed form and circulates among members of a group; it exists in variants and versions; it is frequently formulaic; and it is anonymous, in the sense that the original authorship is not important to the people passing the item of folklore on because their concern is with the text, not the creator.[8]

Folklore, then, covers a wide variety of material ranging from folk speech to folk gestures and what folklorists refer to as material culture (meaning such items as fences, cabins, and barns which are built according to traditional, informal guidelines). The table of contents of one of the most popular textbooks on folklore gives a good idea of the numerous topics folklorists typically study. These include proverbs and proverbial phrases, riddles, rhymes and folk poetry, myths, legends, folktales, folksongs, ballads, superstitions, customs, festivals, folk dances, folk dramas, folk games, folk music, folk crafts, folk art, folk costumes, and foodways.[9] This lengthy list is misleading, however, for until relatively recent times most folklorists have been preoccupied mainly with folksongs and narratives. More specifically, much folklore scholarship has been concerned with ballads and folktales. Through the first half of the twentieth century a majority of ballad collectors occupied themselves with seeking out versions and variants of the 305 songs included in Francis James Child's ten-volume *The English and Scottish Popular Ballads* (1882–1898). At the same time most folktale studies concerned what folklorists call *Märchen*, a German term for which there is no exact English equivalent. In popular parlance these stories are sometimes referred to as fairy tales, but that is a very poor substitute for the German word, because the "little people," or fairies, of European legend rarely figure in these narratives. Such terms as "nursery tales" and "wonder tales" are also sometimes used, but they also distort and misrepresent the meaning of the German original. There is another reason why folklorists prefer *Märchen* to any substitute, namely that it was used by the fathers of folklore scholarship, Jakob and Wilhelm Grimm, for their *Kinder-*

und Hausmärchen (Children's and Household Stories) (1812).

Marchen have been the prize plums for folktale scholars for various reasons. One, the first folklorists concerned themselves with them, so many of those who followed naturally dealt with the same subject. Perhaps a more important reason, though, is that Märchen are among the most complex of folk narratives. Stith Thompson, America's most famous folktale specialist, defines a Märchen as "a tale of some length involving a succession of motifs or episodes. It moves in an unreal world without definite locality or definite characters and is filled with the marvelous."[10] A third reason why Märchen have proven so fascinating to folklorists is that they are in a state of decline. Frequently, scholars become most interested in studying those materials that are in immediate danger of extinction, or are perceived to be in such peril. American folklorists studying Märchen is akin to linguists doing research on Latin, for they are no longer part of a living folk tradition in most parts of the United States. True, they are occasionally recorded, but in a majority of instances the texts collected are a part of "memory culture."

Another type of folk narrative, however, is very much part of a living tradition. Indeed, it is, along with the legend, the most vital and vibrant form of folk narrative in America today. This form, the joke, has received relatively little attention from folklorists, its widespread popularity being one of the reasons for its general neglect. Most twentieth-century Americans know and tell jokes, so they are commonplace, but this statement should not be interpreted as meaning that everyone who tells such narratives is a skillful or "star" joketeller. Nevertheless, because jokes seem to be on everyone's lips they lose much of their appeal to folklorists. In other words, they are simply not exotic or obscure enough to merit much consideration. There are other possible reasons why jokes have not received the scholarly attention they deserve. Jokes usually lack the multi-episodic structure of Märchen and by contrast seem simple and thus unworthy of extensive investigation. This appearance is deceptive, for the simplicity is only relative when compared with more complex forms. Undoubtedly, some folklorists shy away from studying jokes because they are afraid that such research would be perceived as not being serious. Others probably are deterred by the idea that many jokes are "dirty" and a great interest in them might soil their careers. Perhaps the most important reason for the general inattention to jokes, though, is merely the mental conditioning of folklorists. Most researchers are, for better or worse, to some extent controlled by their intellectual predecessors. Because most previous folklorists *did* not study jokes, it was tacitly suggested they *should* not. But, as with all restrictions of this type, eventually some researchers broke away from the previous trend. With the lowly joke this situation has happened in very recent years, most of the important works on the genre having been completed since 1950.[11]

Some of the characteristics of jokes are alluded to in the preceding discussion, but to prevent confusion a definition is offered here: Jokes are short narratives, usually consisting of a single episode, which have relatively simple plots and realistic settings and are perceived by the group in which they circulate as being humorous. Sometimes one must have inside knowledge even to understand why a joke is funny, a fact acknowledged by one woman from Flat River, Missouri, who told Vance Randolph the following joke in August 1950:

> The mayor of Potosi, Missouri, once put up a sign: LET US CEASE OUR FEVERISH ACTIVITY, AND SUSPEND BUSINESS DURING THE NOON HOUR ON GOOD FRIDAY.

She concluded the tale with the statement, "This is a lot funnier if you've seen Potosi, Missouri."[12] Sometimes anecdotes—short personal legends, supposedly true but usually apocryphal, dealing with an episode in the life of an individual, sometimes a famous personality but more often a local character—are also humorous. Several of the selections in the present book are anecdotes.

Jokes told in the Ozarks are, like those heard in other parts of the United States, either indigenous or imported. The joke about Potosi given above is an example of the former, while the following tale is an instance of the latter:

> There was a soldier that his girl has run off with another fellow, so he was fixing to kill himself. He went down to the river and tied a rope round his neck, and he tied the other end to the bridge. Also he poured gasoline on his clothes, and swallowed a dose of rat poison. Then he set himself afire, and drawed his pistol. It looks like he was a goner for sure. But the bullet missed his head, and cut off the rope. So he fell in the river, and put the fire out. Also he swallowed a lot of muddy water, and throwed up the poison. Pretty soon he crawled out on the bank, and walked back to camp. If he hadn't of been a good swimmer, the damn fool might have got drownded, at that.[13]

Although the narrator, E.J. Ferris, heard this story at Camp Pike, Arkansas, during World War I, it was a widely known yarn even then. Earlier reports said it happened to "a young French officer at St. Malo" in the 1860s. It is also reported from North Carolina, Oklahoma, and Colorado, and evidence suggests that it is known in Mexico as well.[14]

Seemingly, to be funny jokes would have to be timely—that is, of relatively recent vintage—and, of course, a few jokes told in the Ozarks can be so characterized. The following yarn told by a Eureka Springs, Arkansas, resident seems to be such a story:

> Lots of the old-timers here don't like tourists, and they say that city people are no better than hogs. Several years ago a man here in town built a rail fence around his hotel, to make it look kind of quaint and old-fashioned. "I see they've put a hogpen round the

tavern," says one of the old residents. After a long silence he added, "It ain't a bad idea, neither."[15]

Most of the tales related by the hillfolk have lengthier histories, although perhaps not extending as far back in time as do the following two items:

> They used to tell about the time old Dunk Hargrove's wife fell in the river, and everybody come out to help find the corpse. They was dragging the blue holes and shooting off dynamite down below the bridge. Pretty soon somebody seen old Dunk poking around brushpiles, away up above the place where she fell in. They thought he was just drunker than common, and turned around, but that wasn't it. He figgered that Elsie was so contrary she wouldn't float downstream, no matter if she *was* dead.[16]

> There was two drummers went to bed in the hotel. One was bald-headed and smooth-shaven, the other one had long hair and whiskers, but both of 'em was drunk. Pretty soon the long-haired fellow passed out, and some fool boys cut off his whiskers and shaved his head. When they got him up to catch the early train the fellow was still pretty drunk, but he knowed something was wrong. He felt of his head and rubbed his chin awhile. "By God," he says, "they've woke up old Baldy instead of me!"[17]

The first story was told in 1936 by a resident of Branson, Missouri, who had recently heard it from friends in Springfield, Missouri. Although this informant regarded it as a new joke, it is at least seven centuries old. In his edition of the *Exempla of Jacques de Vitry* (1890), which dates from the thirteenth century, Thomas Crane published what is generally considered the oldest version. The tale also appeared in many later English jest books such as *Mery Tales and Quicke Answeres* (1535) and *Pasquils Jests mixed with*

Mother Bunche's Merriments (1604), in Italian popular literature, in stories about the Oriental trickster Nasreddin
Hodja, and such American folklore collections as Harold
Thompson's *Body, Boots and Britches* (1939). Will Rice of St.
Joe, Arkansas, told the second story in July 1934, but it is a
version of a tale that can be traced back to a fifteenth-
century manuscript. The item also appeared in a number of
nineteenth-century jokebooks and in such folklore collections as W.A. Clouston's *The Book of Noodles*, Arthur Huff
Fauset's *Folklore from Nova Scotia* (1931), and Juan B.
Rael's *Cuentos Espanoles de Colorado y de Nuevo Mejico*
(n.d.). Found in the British Isles, Canada, the Orient, and the
United States, this joke is both ancient and widespread.

Most Ozark jokes and humorous anecdotes can be
traced back only to the nineteenth century. That is the case
with the following joke, which was told in the 1890s about
Kansas politician "sockless Jerry" Simpson, later about
turn-of-the-century Arkansas governor Jeff Davis, and
about several other politicians, including Harry Truman.

> You know old "Give-'em-Hell" Harry was well-
> known for his "blue" language. Bess was always trying
> to cure him from cussing, and one day some impor-
> tant guests were at the White House. And somebody
> said the lawn didn't look too good and needed some-
> thing done to it or it would get out of hand. Harry said,
> "Oh, it'll be all right, I'll just have 'em put some horse
> manure on it." Margaret acted real shocked and said,
> "Mother, you ought to get Dad to say fertilizer rather
> than manure." But Bess said, "I ain't goin' to worry
> about it 'cause I've had a hard enough time gettin' him
> to say manure."[18]

Although most jokes told by the hillfolk did not originate in
the Ozarks, they are localized and made to seem indigenous
in various ways. For example, the story about Harry Truman might be told substituting a local politician's name. A
yarn that originated in Europe might be given an Ozark

twist by replacing Old World place names for regional ones. This is what happened with the following narrative that migrated to America from the British Isles:

The traveler asked, "Is this the road to Harrison?" and an old man setting in front of the tavern says yes. So the traveler drove on, getting farther away from Harrison every minute. After while he come back, and he was pretty mad. The old man was still setting in front of the tavern. "I thought you told me this was the road to Harrison?" shouted the traveler. "Yep, it's the right road," said the old man calmly, "but this is the wrong end of it."[19]

Sometimes, as in the tale cited earlier about the obstinate wife sought upstream, an ancient yarn is transformed into an Ozark joke by assigning it to a person well-known locally. Of course, many other techniques are used to make old material over so that it seems new. Such change is the nature of jokes, and all folklore, which are constantly being adapted to fit new situations and times. Some jokes, however, do not undergo such change and they are the ones that pass out of general usage.

A central requirement of any definition of jokes is that the stories told be regarded as funny. This brings up the question, what makes a joke funny? Very few folklorists, or other scholars, have spent time asking informants about such matters, so most statements on this subject are speculative and largely based on assumptions. Those who have attempted to answer the question are almost unanimous in stating that a joke's success depends upon a sudden alteration, or incongruity, in point of view. For instance,

One time there was a couple of guys talking and Joe said, "At her request you gave up drinking?"
Jim said, "Yep."
Joe said, "At her request you gave up smoking?"
Jim said, "Yep."

Joe said, "For the same reason you gave up danc-
ing, poker, and gambling?"

Jim said, "Yes."

Then Joe said, "Well, then why in the world didn't
you marry her?"

Jim said, "Well, I felt that after I'd improved myself
so much I could probably do better."[20]

A census-taker stopped at the house of an old
farmer in the Arkansas hills.

"How many children have you got?"

"Nineteen."

"Big family!"

"Yes. The first thirteen of 'em was born before I
found out the cause of 'em."[21]

Each of the two examples above was chosen because the
alteration is extreme and, thus, fairly obvious. Jim gives up
his favorite vices for love of a girl but then decides, after
improving his character, that she is his inferior. This is
probably the last thing the listener expects from him, having been led in the rest of the joke to believe Jim is more
interested in pleasing the girl than anything else. Such
dramatic change is not impossible in reality but is highly
improbable. In fictitious narratives, such as jokes, however,
they are not only probable but usual. Although some people
may have children without really comprehending how
they are made, it is ludicrous to think that anyone would
have thirteen children and not know "the cause of 'em."
Here the incongruity is of a different order than that of the
first joke because the yarn plays on stereotypes about hillbillies that hold them to be both moronic and very fertile.
Even those who don't agree with the stereotype are aware
that it exists. Yet the denouement is successful in provok-
ing laughter because it takes the hillbilly of caricature and
places in his mouth an answer that is unexpected even in
this special case. To put it another way, both jokes go from a
point of view that the listener can take seriously to one that

must be taken much less seriously.

A second requirement for a joke to be funny is that it must involve a topic about which one can laugh or be playful about. Some subjects, such as the ludicrous actions of a local character, will be suitable matter for jokes to most audiences. For example,

> ———— had a girlfriend and they were both plumb illiterate. They got these welfare checks but since neither of them could write they had to sign them with an X. ———— got to feeling romantic and decided he would marry his girlfriend. So, one day he goes in the bank with his girl when her check came. While she was putting her X on it he said real proudly, "The next time you see that name on the check it'll be changed."[22]

Most audiences would probably find this anecdote humorous, but probably not the relatives of the man and woman who are the protagonists. In fact, the person who told the story was aware of that possibility and requested that the names of the source, the protagonist, who is a well-known local character, and the community not be mentioned just in case anyone reacted adversely.[23]

Other topics are more clearly not humorous to most audiences. Few people find tales about deaths of loved ones and other major personal tragedies funny, no matter how comic their intent. Instead, they are more likely to find such jokes in poor taste. Yet if the tragedy is not too close, a person may find jokes about it humorous. Consider, for example, the following riddle jokes about the *Challenger* space shuttle tragedy of January 1986 that were popular in the Ozarks and elsewhere in the United States:

> What were the last words of the *Challenger* crew?
> "No, no. I mean a Bud light."

> Where did Christa McAuliffe take her vacation?
> All over the Caribbean.[24]

Many people obviously found these jokes funny—after all they were told and were popular—but it is doubtful that anyone related to the *Challenger* crew would find anything humorous in them. Thus, one must have some familiarity with the joke topic but at the same time be distanced from it in order for it to be funny. When it strikes too close to things one regards seriously, a joke loses its humor.

Surprise is also an essential ingredient in making a joke funny. Without the unexpected, or surprise, ending there is no laughter. With jokes the surprise often involves a ludicrous denouement, as in the following example:

> Somebody told Aunt Molly that a local girl had turned out to be a poet. The old woman was horrified. "My God, who'd a thought it! And she had as good a mother as ever walked!" Pretty soon the old lady leaned forward, all curiosity. "Did you find out *who with?*" she whispered.[25]

One of the main reasons jokes fall out of fashion is that through repeated tellings they lose the element of surprise and as a result no longer amuse listeners.[26] This happened with the following joke, which was a big laugh-getter a century ago:

> "Who was that lady I saw you with last night?"
> "That was no lady, that was my wife."[27]

Now this is just a worn-out joke, with its punch line one of the best known in the United States. This very familiarity will likely prevent this joke from becoming popular as humor again, except in a reverse sense, but traditional jokes often do return to popularity after enough time has passed that they can seem fresh again.

Incongruity, laughability, and surprise are the most important, but by no means only, elements that make jokes funny. To discuss the numerous possibilities fully would exhaust far more space than can be devoted to this brief introduction. Like most aspects of folklore, this is a very complicated subject, and to cover it comprehensively requires consideration of a multitude of variables. In other words, there are no simple answers to the question of what makes a joke funny. The comments offered here are only tentative, beginning attempts to understand folk reactions to narratives told in jest.

Undoubtedly the main reason jokes are told is because they are considered funny by the teller and, most importantly, by the audience. Without someone to listen to humorous stories they quit being told because, unlike some genres, jokes require an audience of at least one person other than the narrator. Moreover, this is a tacitly understood rule governing the communication of jokes in most Western cultures, a fact that can be demonstrated by contrasting two hypothetical situations. Folksingers commonly sing songs for their own enjoyment, an action that is not considered unusual in most American communities. However, someone who goes off alone and tells jokes to himself will be immediately considered at best odd and at worst a prime candidate for a mental institution.If being funny is the most obvious reason why jokes are told, an attempt to be entertaining is the second major reason. Most people find it enjoyable to amuse their friends and acquaintances, and some personalities find it essential. These are the men and women about whom it is said, "He, or she, likes to be the center of attention." Being known as a skillful joketeller gives these people a place of prominence or local renown. But there are many other reasons why jokes are told. Sometimes, as in the following two examples, jokes and humorous anecdotes are kept alive because they are part of family lore:

When Dad was a schoolboy he had to walk several miles to school. Not only did the walk take time but he had to rise early enough to help my granddad in the dairy, milking twenty-three cows. This work caused him to be late several mornings at school. According to

Dad, his teacher was very hard-nosed and unreasonable about his tardiness. She threatened him by telling him that she was going to send him to the principal if it happened again.

Dad strived pretty hard for a few days to get to school on time, but one morning he just couldn't make it. His teacher met him at the door of the classroom, intending to send him down to the principal's office, which was at that time a fate worse than death. He pleaded his case, explaining that he had to help milk and then walk all the way to school. His teacher, who was a very tall, lanky person, told him that when she was a little girl she used to walk five miles across country—crawling over fences, walking through fields, and so on—and that she never was tardy a day in her life. Dad never was long on patience and at this point he couldn't resist saying, "Well, Miss ———, if my legs were as long as yours are I could straddle those fences and get here on time myself."

He was immediately sent to see the principal.[28]

When we were little kids, I was about six, I guess, three covered wagons went to Oklahoma. We got down to the Arkansas River—it was up real good. We had to stay there three days and nights, I think, and during that time we had to pick cotton and wait for the river to go down. So when the river went down, so the ferryboat could ferry us across, we drove our wagons on the ferryboat and they told us kids to get in the wagon and not get out nowhere. So we got back in the wagon and our mothers got down on the ferryboat, sat down on the ferryboat, and held the little kids. So me and my brother slips out and gets up on the wagon seat and all the rest of them, the other two wagons had kids and they did the same thing. My dad said, "I want you to look at them damn little Democrats. I told them to stay in the wagon."[29]

Such yarns are among those that never grow old even though most of the people hearing them, usually members of one's immediate family or relatives, know the story and, thus, are not surprised by the ending. Generally, these tales also circulate among smaller groups than is true of most other humorous anecdotes.

Some jokes are told because they are considered part of local history. This is one of the factors sustaining stories about local characters. Often jokes are told to indicate how witty locals are, especially when contrasted with outsiders. The following joke, told by a fishing guide near Branson, Missouri, in the 1920s, is one of those in which locals jestingly advance their superiority to those from outside the region:

> Some tourists was crossing White River on the ferryboat, and the current was pretty swift, also the water was pretty deep. So one of the women says it looks kind of dangerous, and she wants to know if any passengers was ever lost here. "No, ma'am," says the fellow that was running the ferry. "They get drownded sometimes, but we always find 'em in a day or two."[30]

Philosophers and writers since the time of Plato and Aristotle have recognized that feelings of superiority, such as those advanced in the above joke, are important in maintaining humor.[31] Depicting someone else's weaknesses raises one's own level of esteem and also contributes to establishing a sense of identity. For example, the guide's joke depicts tourists as naive, gullible, and inexperienced, while Ozarkers are pictured as the exact opposite.

Frequently jokes are used as an acceptable means of openly criticizing a person or group. Most of the humorous tales about preachers are told partly for this reason. Consider also the following jokes, all of which poke fun at an individual or group:

> Some people say that boys don't learn nothing at

college, but I know better. Why, my boy hadn't been at the University more than two weeks till he learned how to open beer-bottles with a silver dollar. It's the slickest thing you ever seen![32]

There was a Spanish War veteran come a-limping through the Basin Park hotel. "What's the matter, Zeke?" says I, "you got a touch of the rheumatism?" The old soldier considered for a moment. "No," he says, "it was a fat woman stepped on my foot." Then there was a long silence. "She was from Chicago," the old man added gently.[33]

A Negro woman lost patience when her lighter son bullied her black son. "Rastus," she exclaimed, "you'd be jest as dark as yo' brother if I hadn't got *so* far behind in my house rent!"[34]

A Yankee officer said to an ex-Confederate, "Well, we fit against each other once, but we're all Americans now. Comes another war, we'll both be in the same army, a-fighting for the old flag." The southerner shook his head. "Us Confederates will be there, all right, but you Federals won't." The Yankee was puzzled. "What do you mean by that?" The Confederate laughed. "Why," said he, "the pension rolls show that you-uns was all totally disabled!"[35]

Old Buster Packenham was kind of foolish, and he had got pretty drunk besides. "There sure is a lot of liars in this town," says he. "I been here all day, and I asked seven respectable businessmen what time it is. Would you believe it, every goddamn one of 'em has give me a different answer!"[36]

When they built the railroad through here in 1882, there was a freight car on the siding at Beaver. The folks all come down to look at it, because lots of 'em never seen a freight car before. One of them Walters boys spelled out the word CAPACITY painted on the car. "Cape City," says he, "is a big town, and it is a long ways off." Later on somebody found out what CAPACITY means, and the folks all figured it was a great joke. They called that boy "Cape City Walters" all the rest of his life.[37]

Another important reason jokes are told in the Ozarks is to make fun of popularly held stereotypes about hillfolk. That is one of the motives jokers in Joplin, Missouri, have for telling this story:

A fellow from Neosho took his fourteen children to the county fair, and there was a big bull in the tent which some folks said the critter was worth ten thousand dollars. The fellow wanted to see the bull, but you had to pay fifty cents to get in. "Is these kids all your'n?" says that man that was selling the tickets. The fellow from Neosho says yes. "Well, you can all go in the tent free," says the ticket-seller, "I want that bull to take a look at *you!*"[38]

These few suggestions, of course, do not exhaust the list of possible reasons why people tell jokes and humorous anecdotes. A complete catalogue of motives would be almost limitless; no single explanation adequately covers the topic. Those suggestions offered thus far are functions that the joketeller is conscious of, but there are other functions of an unconscious nature. Several writers have suggested that humorous yarns release sexual and aggressive impulses, release tensions, serve as a form of social control, and provide for communication.[39] Jokes told in the Ozarks probably serve all of these functions and others yet unnoticed by folklorists. Unfortunately, for most texts reported to date one must rely on speculation to determine how a joke functions for the simple reason that few collectors provide anything more than the text. Often an informant's name is given but contextual data is rarely provided. One needs more than just a text to determine how a joke, or any item of folklore, functions. Biographical information, the informant's understanding of a joke's meaning, the audiences to whom it is told and not told, and similar details are important to have because "even a single tale may not have the same meaning and same function for all who tell and listen to it in different contexts or even in the same context."[40] With only the content to examine, folklorists can only guess about the various meanings and functions; such speculation is not useless, but neither is it ideal.

There are numerous books containing Ozark folk anecdotes and jokes, but few of these volumes are studies. Most of the material included is not the result of systematic collecting, nor do most of the authors have scholarly or folklore pretensions. Still, at least four types of publications that are not written from a folklore viewpoint contain material of interest to anyone concerned with Ozark folk humor. Earliest of these are the writings of explorers and travel writers such as Schoolcraft, George William Featherstonhaugh, and Friedrich Gerstäcker. Featherstonhaugh (1780–1866) was employed by the United States War Department to report on the geological resources of several frontier states. In 1834 and 1835 he visited Arkansas, and nine years later, in 1844, published *Excursion Through the Slave States*, a book that is still valuable for its discussion of life in the antebellum South. Included among Featherstonhaugh's remarks are several tall tales that he heard in the Ozarks.[41] Gerstäcker (1816–1872) was a writer of romances and travel books who came to the United States in 1837, when he was twenty-one, and spent the next six years traveling throughout the West. During most of the years from 1838 to 1842 he lived in Arkansas. Though he received small remittances from home, he earned his living primarily by farm labor, hunting, and trapping. While this meant much hard work that most other travel writers in the region did not engage in, it also meant that Gerstäcker became more intimate with the settlers than did most other travelers. A large number of tall tales were set down faithfully as heard in his loosely kept diary, published as *Streif- und Jadzüge durch die Vereinigten Staaten Nordamerikas* (Expeditions and Hunting-Parties Through the United States of North America) (1844). This book is now usually known by the title chosen for an 1859 translation of the more lurid sections of the diary, *Wild Sports in the Far West.*[42]

A second group important among the incidental collectors of Ozark jokelore are the compilers of jokebooks. Some, such as Thomas W. Jackson, whose *On a Slow Train through Arkansaw* (1903) became a best-seller enabling him to resign his job as a railroader and go into full-time publishing of jokebooks, have been very successful.[43] Most, though, are like Zeek Zinderman, whose undated *A Pig in a Poke and The Vanishing Outhouse* (1977) is sold primarily in tourist traps in Missouri and Arkansas, and who has enjoyed much less prosperous results.[44] Among the most significant of the numerous jokebooks are Jackson's *Slow Train,* his *Through Missouri on a Mule* (1904), Marion Hughes's *Three Years in Arkansaw* (1904), Jim Owen's *Hillbilly Humor* (1970), and Bill Ring's *Tall Tales Are Not All from Texas* (1980). All of these volumes indicate that the authors had more than a passing familiarity with folk narratives, and Ring, whose book was compiled from entries in a tall tale contest he held on radio, includes extended discussions of a few tall tale tellers.[45]

Novelists and writers of fiction are a third group who have unsystematically collected and published traditional Ozark jokes. Some, such as Charles Fenton Mercer Noland, who used the pseudonym Pete Whetstone, wrote exclusively in the humorous vein.[46] Most, however, were like Amos R. Harlin, who said his intent was "to entertain and to give a fair picture of a people living in the Ozark mountains."[47] In attempting to achieve such goals the authors frequently present traditional jokes and anecdotes and discuss activities pertaining to them. For example, in his novel *For Here Is My Fortune* (1946) Harlin provides the only description in print of a colorful organization that flourished in Howell County, Missouri, from 1900 to 1918. This was a group of storytellers and practical jokers known as the "Post," after the phrase "Every man to his post."[48] Having all the trappings of a regular lodge, including secret signs, grips, passwords, and rituals, the "Post" existed for the sole purpose of playing jokes on strangers and making them believe outrageous tall tales. Harlin's account of this group is substantially accurate, although he toned down some of the pranks and did not provide exact names of people involved.[49] When used with proper caution, works such as Harlin's can be valuable sources of information for students of traditional Ozark jokes and anecdotes.

Writers of local histories and nostalgic reminiscences also frequently give much information on folk humor, often providing both texts and contexts. Some worthwhile publications in this category include E.J. Hoenshel and L.S. Hoenshel's *Stories of the Pioneers* (1915), Jesse Russel's *Behind These Ozark Hills* (1947), Evelyn Milligan Jones's *Tales about Joplin . . . Short and Tall* (1962), and Mary Frances Harrell's *History and Folklore of Searcy County, Arkansas* (1977). Two of the most important Ozark books in this vein are Wayman Hogue's *Back Yonder, an Ozark Chronicle* (1932) and John Quincy Wolf's *Life in the Leatherwoods* (1974), both dealing with the Arkansas Ozarks. While Hogue's book does have several anecdotes, it contains very little of a humorous nature. Wolf's book, originally written as a series of articles for a Batesville, Arkansas, newspaper, does include a number of funny anecdotes and stories. Moreover, the volume benefits from skillful editing by the author's son, who was very knowledgeable about folklore.[50]

It is when one comes to books on jokes and humorous anecdotes written from a folklore viewpoint that one finds very little to choose from. Even some works with promising titles prove to be disappointing. For example, Fred W. Allsopp's two-volume *Folklore of Romantic Arkansas* (1931) does contain a few jokes and humorous items but is a poorly edited mishmash of material garnered mostly from newspaper clippings. Even knowledgeable commentators like Otto Ernest Rayburn generally offer little more than highly "improved" versions of traditional jokes in their writings. In *Ozark Country* (1941), however, Rayburn does provide contextual data and information on how the rewritten jokes he includes are used in the Ozarks. Charles Morrow Wilson's *Backwoods America* (1934), a study of the southern mountain way of life, does have some perceptive comments about rural humor, but they are scattered throughout a book that is primarily devoted to other aspects of folk tradition. Much the same assessment applies to Joseph Medard Carriere's *Tales from the French Folklore of Missouri* (1937), which includes several jokes and anecdotes collected primarily from Frank Bourisaw and Joseph Ben Coleman of Old Mines, Missouri. Carrier's emphasis, however, is on animal tales, novelle, and farces, in other words essentially the same type of material that has occupied most American folktale specialists.

Ultimately, then, the major scholarly publications on Ozark jokelore are the work of two men, and one of them wasn't exclusively concerned with the Ozarks. At the time he wrote *Tall Tales of Arkansaw* (1943), James R. Masterson was a faculty member of Hillsdale College in Michigan. His book was an outgrowth of a seminar paper written at Harvard while he was working on a Ph.D. in English. Masterson's subject is the whole field of Arkansas humor, a subject he covers superbly. He courageously presents unexpurgated discussions of bawdy as well as "clean" humor, thereby backing up his claim that "I have included every report or rumor of 'Arkansaw' that I have seen in print."[51] Masterson's account of the fiddle-tune-dialogue "The Arkansas Traveler" has been called "the first adequate study of this masterpiece,"[52] but he also gives significant attention to many less prominent jokes, anecdotes, and folktales. Although most of Masterson's texts are taken from old books and magazines rather than oral tradition, *Tall Tales of Arkansaw* is required reading for anyone interested in folk humor or jokelore.

Even more important for present purposes are the works of Vance Randolph, the premier student of Ozark folklore. Author of over two hundred articles and pamphlets and twenty books, Randolph included jokes and anecdotes in most of his folklore publications, but three are specifically devoted to such material. *We Always Lie to Strangers* (1951) is entirely concerned with one genre of jokes, tall tales, collected by Randolph. The narratives are broken down into nine categories based on subject matter, and the characteristics of Ozark yarns are discussed extensively. While some Ozark raconteurs are mentioned by name, most of the informants are not so identified. The reasons for this omission are spelled out in Randolph's preface:

> Several old friends and neighbors who helped me in this enterprise do not wish to be mentioned here, and there are other reasons for omitting many informants' names. Whenever it has seemed permissible to identify the teller of a particular story, I have done so in the text. In case such identification was not advisable, I have named the village or the county where I heard the tale and let it go at that.[53]

Randolph's experience is not unique, for I have encountered the same attitude when collecting humorous material in the Ozarks and elsewhere. Even without such data as informant names, places of residence, other biographical details, and circumstances of the collecting situation, *We Always Lie to Strangers* is important for a variety of reasons, two of the most important being that it is the lengthiest study to date of the genre and it covers the field broadly.

In 1965 Randolph scored another first with *Hot Springs and Hell and Other Folk Jests and Anecdotes from the Ozarks.* This collection of 460 texts recorded by Randolph over a forty-year period is to date the only book exclusively devoted to Ozark jokes that also includes detailed scholarly annotations. For those jokes gathered while Randolph was collecting folksongs for the Library of Congress there are verbatim transcriptions. Most of the entries, however, are the result of recall, being written down in longhand and typed up a few hours later "while the details were fresh in my mind."[54] Although the resulting texts are not given exactly in the informants' words they are not conscious attempts at "improvement." *Hot Springs and Hell* contains much more than just texts; indeed in many respects it is a model of how a collection of folk jokes should be presented. Randolph includes names of people he collected material from, their place of residence, date of collection, notes tracing the jokes through a wide range of published sources, and, where applicable, type and motif numbers that indicate the narratives are part of international folk tradition. In addition, he provides information about where informants heard the jokes and, occasionally, some discussion of how the tales are used. For example, in the notes for an ancient joke told by a Pineville, Missouri, narrator he says, "He heard it near Noel, Mo., about 1895. 'The feller that told me that story,' said he, 'told it pretty near every day for twenty years. It was his favorite story.'"[55]

A third relevant volume by Randolph, *Pissing in the Snow and Other Ozark Folktales* (1976), has a curious history. The 101 bawdy tales were originally included in manuscripts published by Columbia University Press from 1952 to 1958 but were deleted at the publisher's request.[56] Although Randolph considered the move unwise he had no choice but to bow to the wishes of those who found the texts obscene and, hence, unprintable. Ironically, when the University of Illinois Press published the "unprintable" volume two decades later Randolph received letters from Columbia asking him to submit a similar manuscript because they would be very interested in publishing such a book.[57] All of the items were collected between 1921 and 1953. The value of the texts is increased by Randolph's usual excellent notes on informants, comments about when and where they heard the tales, and several other features. One of these is Rayna Green's lengthy introduction explaining the significance of the collection and tracing the history of the manuscript. Frank A. Hoffmann, a specialist in bawdy lore, provides annotations that indicate how these Ozark narratives compare with similar material in other parts of the country and the world. Ironically, *Pissing in the Snow,* which is a volume of material culled from other publications, is the finest collection of traditional bawdy Ozark jokes, anecdotes, and humorous narratives yet published. It is also one of the outstanding works on American ribald folklore. Not bad for a book that its author originally envisioned as merely parts of several other volumes.

The present book includes jokes and anecdotes told in the Ozarks during the past sixty years. All but the items from Jimmie Wilson were collected from oral tradition, and his texts were derived from folklore. Obviously, not every humorous Ozark narrative is represented here, nor do the book's nine categories exhaust all those used by the region's joketellers. They are some of the major themes found in humorous yarns told by the hillfolk; the texts included here were chosen because they are representative of such material. Several of the items come from my own fieldwork, but a majority are from other collectors. The material from outside sources was selected because it was demonstrably folk. As a result most of the tales given here are widely traveled and, even though relatively short, are known to exist in several variants and versions. A few texts that seem to have little or no variation from one rendering to another are included, *but only where evidence suggests that they are ensconced in Ozark folk tradition.*

One question remains concerning this collection and deserves consideration even though, admittedly, it can't be satisfactorily answered. That query is, Is there anything distinctly Ozark about these narratives? This is a reasonable matter to speculate about, and some features, such as settings in Ozark communities and the use of local personalities in the case of these tales, suggest the possibility that there are numerous uniquely Ozark aspects to these jokes. To know what they are, though, requires knowledge not only of Ozark jokelore but of similar traditions in other parts of the United States and the world. Unfortunately, so few studies of this genre of folklore exist that the necessary information needed to establish what is unusual to the Ozarks doesn't exist. Thus, one is left with the few tentative comments offered in this introduction and in the notes. To go further at the present time would be foolhardy.

And now, appropriately, this introduction ends with an anecdote. According to an apocryphal story a departed wit in an Ozark town had inscribed on his tombstone, "What now?" Readers of this introduction are probably asking the same question. The answer is one word—jokes. If any book was ever intended to be fun reading it is this one. So, read on and enjoy.

Notes

[1]Otto Ernest Rayburn, *Ozark Country* (New York: Duell, Sloan & Pearce, 1941), pp. 16–17.

[2]Robert L. Ramsay, *Our Storehouse of Missouri Place Names* (Columbia: University of Missouri Press, 1973; reprint of a work originally issued in 1952), p. 10. Also see Ernie Deane, *Arkansas Place Names* (Branson, Missouri: The Ozarks Mountaineer, 1986), pp. 8–9.

[3]Rayburn, *Ozark Country*, pp. 17–18.

[4]Henry Rowe Schoolcraft, *Journal of a Tour into the Interior of Missouri and Arkansaw . . . Performed in the Years 1818 and 1819* in *New Voyages and Travels: Consisting of Originals and Translations* (London: Sir Richard Phillips & Co., 1821), vol. 4, separately paginated, p. 64. A few other tall tales are scattered throughout the volume.

[5]Milton D. Rafferty, *The Ozarks: Land and Life* (Norman: University of Oklahoma Press, 1980), p. 4.

[6]Ibid., p. 6.

[7]W.K. McNeil, *The Charm Is Broken: Readings in Arkansas and*

Missouri Folklore (Little Rock: August House, Inc., 1984), p. 11.

[8]Ibid., pp. 11–13. The definition is treated in greater detail here.

[9]Jan Harold Brunvand, *The Study of American Folklore: An Introduction* (New York: W.W. Norton & Company, Inc., 1968).

[10]Stith Thompson, *The Folktale* (New York: Holt, Rinehart and Winston, 1946), p. 8.

[11]It is worth iterating here that I am not saying that no one worked on the genre of jokes prior to 1950. Most of the earlier works, such as Sigmund Freud's *Der Witz und seine Beziehung zum Unbewussten* (Jokes and Their Relation to the Unconscious) (1905), were by psychologists. There were, however, several studies of tall tales by folklorists, one example being Richard M. Dorson, *Jonathan Draws the Long Bow* (1945). A few of the important works on jokes produced in the past forty years include Martha Wolfenstein, *Children's Humor: A Psychological Analysis* (1954); Gershon Legman, *Rationale of the Dirty Joke* (1968–1975); William M. Clements, *The Types of the Polack Joke* (1969); and Ronald L. Baker, *Jokelore: Humorous Folktales from Indiana* (1986). While there are not huge numbers of books on jokelore there are, of course, many more than the four cited here.

[12]This is item 64 in Vance Randolph, *Hot Springs and Hell and other Folk Jests and Anecdotes from the Ozarks* (Hatboro, Pennsylvania: Folklore Associates, Inc., 1965), p. 23. Potosi, the seat of Washington County, has a population of 2,528.

[13]This is item 222 in Randolph, *Hot Springs and Hell*, p. 79.

[14]Ibid., p. 219.

[15]Ibid., p. 94.

[16]Ibid., p. 22.

[17]Ibid., p. 114.

[18]Collected in March 1976 from a woman in Cabool, Missouri, who agreed to be interviewed only if her name was not mentioned in any resultant publications.

[19]Randolph, *Hot Springs and Hell*, p. 68.

[20]From the Max Hunter Collection, Greene County Public Library, Springfield, Missouri. The joke was apparently collected from a man in Springfield.

[21]James R. Masterson, *Arkansas Folklore: The Arkansas Traveler, Davy Crockett, and Other Legends* (Little Rock: Rose Publishing Co., Inc., 1974; reprint and retitling of a work originally issued in 1943), p. 390.

[22]Compare the following tale given in Randolph, *Hot Springs and Hell*, p. 84:

> There was a woman in the south end of the county that couldn't read or write, so she just marked a cross on her pension checks. After a while she went and got married to some old farmer, and the next time she got a check she marked it with a circle. A fool boy that worked in the bank made some crack about it. But the woman said that her name was changed now, so naturally the check has got to be signed different.

The joke in the form reported by Randolph has been popular at least since the turn of the century.

[23]The community is in northern Arkansas.

[24]Heard many times from several joketellers in northern Arkansas and southern Missouri in 1986. Now, over two years later, jokes about the *Challenger* tragedy seem to have passed out of common usage.

[25]Randolph, *Hot Springs and Hell*, p. 127.

[26]There are, of course, a number of jokes that do not depend on the element of surprise for their survival, those that are considered part of family lore, for example.

[27]This joke was most commonly associated with Joe Weber and Lew Fields but was also told by other comics popular in the late nineteenth and early twentieth centuries.

[28]Collected in 1958 by James McClain Stalker from John M. Stalker, Batesville, Arkansas.

[29]Collected November 1982 by W.K. McNeil from Nola Treat, Big Flat, Arkansas. She explained that her father was a "hidebound" Republican who held a grudge against Democrats.

[30]Randolph, *Hot Springs and Hell*, p. 11.

[31]See Patricia Kieth–Spiegel, "Early Conceptions of Humor," in Jeffrey Goldstein and Paul E. McGhee, eds., *The Psychology of Humor* (New York: Academic Press, 1972), pp. 3–13.

[32]Randolph, Hot Springs and Hell, p. 131.

[33]Ibid., p. 116.

[34]Masterson, *Arkansas Folklore*, p. 391.

[35]Randolph, *Hot Springs and Hell*, pp. 132–33.

[36]Ibid., p. 107.

[37]Ibid., pp. 21–22.

[38]Randolph, *Hot Springs and Hell*, p. 39. As already noted one of the popularly held stereotypes about hillbillies is that they are very fertile.

[39]Mahadev L. Apte, *Humor and Laughter: An Anthropological Approach* (Ithaca, New York: Cornell University Press, 1985), pp. 60–61.

[40]Ronald L. Baker, *Jokelore: Humorous Folktales from Indiana* (Bloomington: Indiana University Press, 1986), xxvii.

[41]George William Featherstonhaugh, *Excursion Through the Slave States* (New York: Harper & Brothers, 1844), pp. 42, 81–82, 99.

[42]Friedrich Gerstäcker, *Wild Sports in the Far West* (Boston: Crosby, Nichols & Co., 1859). See pages 126–374. This volume was reprinted in 1968 by Duke University Press.

[43]W.K. McNeil, ed., Thomas W. Jackson, *On a Slow Train Through Arkansaw* (Lexington: The University Press of Kentucky, 1985), includes the text of the 1903 edition along with a preface, introduction, and extensive notes on the numerous jokes.

[44]Zeek Zinderman, *A Pig in a Poke* (West Plains, Missouri: Quill Print, n.d.) and *The Vanishing Outhouse* (Raynesford, Montana: Janher Publisher, 1977).

[45]Bill Ring, *Tall Tales Are Not All from Texas* (Point Lookout, Missouri: School of the Ozarks Press, 1980), pp. 3–12.

[46]The most recent selection of the Whetstone letters is Leonard

Williams, *Cavorting on the Devil's Fork: The Pete Whetstone Letters of C.F.M. Noland.*

[47]Amos R. Harlin, *For Here is My Fortune* (Branson, Missouri: The Ozarks Mountaineer, 1979: reprint of a work originally issued in 1946), Author's Note.

[48]Ibid., pp. 34, 54–59.

[49]This is according to information supplied by several people interviewed by Vance Randolph. See his *We Always Lie to Strangers: Tall Tales from the Ozarks* (New York: Columbia University Press, 1951), p. 10.

[50]John Quincy Wolf, *Life in the Leatherwoods* (Memphis: Memphis State University Press, 1974), the book was reprinted in 1988 by August House, Inc., the main addition being new drawings.

[51]Masterson, *Arkansas Folklore*, vii.

[52]Randolph, *We Always Lie to Strangers*, p. 282.

[53]Ibid., Preface, vii.

[54]Randolph, *Hot Springs and Hell*, xxvi.

[55]Ibid., p. 223.

[56]The four books are *Who Blowed Up the Church House? and Other Ozark Folk Tales* (1952); *The Devil's Pretty Daughter, and Other Ozark Folktales* (1955); *The Talking Turtle, and Other Ozark Folktales* (1957); *Sticks in the Knapsack, and Other Ozark Folktales* (1958).

[57]This information was conveyed in several conversations with Randolph between 1976 and 1980.

Tall Tales

In the Ozarks the art of spinning tall tales is known by many names, including "telling big stories," "stretching the blanket," "letting out a whack," "sawin' off a whopper," or "spinnin' a windy," among others. Although folklorists, and others who classify and study such material, frequently refer to tall tales as lies, few Ozarkers label them in that way. In *We Always Lie to Strangers* (p. 3), Vance Randolph explains this seemingly curious circumstance:

> The pioneer hates a liar. In the early days there was little cash in the country, and there were few written contracts. People depended upon each other, and a man's word had to be good or the neighbors would have nothing to do with him. The hillfolk live close to the pioneer tradition, and liar is still a fightin' word in the Ozarks.

Whatever they are called, tall tales are popular in the Ozarks and elsewhere in the United States. Where or when this narrative form originated is unknown but it is of ancient vintage. The biographer and moralist Plutarch (A.D. 46–120) includes a version of type 1889F, "Frozen Words (Music) Thaw," in his *Lives,* but it seems likely that the form preceded Plutarch by many decades or even centuries. While not original to the Ozarks, this European genre is certainly characteristic of the region's oral narratives. In-

41

deed, they may be more popular here than in continental Europe, for even though the form developed in the Old World, tall tales have never been considered very numerous there.

Why did this narrative form become so popular in the Ozarks? One explanation must be the subject matter of most American tall tales. Hunting, fishing, the weather, fabulous animals, insects, and topography are some of their major themes—all topics of greater interest to residents of a rural area, such as the Ozarks, than to urbanites or suburbanites. Some other explanations for the popularity of tall tales in the Ozarks may be found in their general utility. For example, they may be used as a means of poking gentle fun at people from other sections of the country, explaining disabilities in a humorous way, or reinforcing certain community attitudes. Or possibly residents of a relatively recently settled area, such as the Ozarks, felt a need for a sort of reverse bragging. These few suggestions hardly deplete the many possible explanations for the popularity of the tall tale in the Ozarks; to discuss such matters in full, however, would make these comments something more than prefatory. Suffice it to say that accounting for the popularity of tall tales, or any kind of narrative, is exceedingly complex, and deserves extensive analysis based on various kinds of informant data that is missing from most texts available to date.

One point made clear by the texts in the following section is that Ozark narrators don't just tell tall tales about their own region. Often the yarns are set far afield in places like west Texas, Louisiana, southern Arkansas, or even the moon. Usually, though, the incidents described are set in the Ozarks and deal with such themes as giant watermelons, snakes, giant mosquitoes, remarkable fish, hunting escapades, extremely hot and cold weather, dense rain, unusually thick fog, extremely steep hills, and lying contests. Reported during the years from the 1930s to the 1980s, the following texts provide a sampling of the tall tale, Ozark style.

You Call That a Big Watermelon?

1. Out there in Arizona we would meet in a gang of us together, and we had a very close friend of ours. And this woman, when she laughed, she would laugh from the bottom of her feet to the top of her head. And she'd just shake all over. Well, every time we'd get together she'd want me to start telling some crazy story, you know. And then she would just die. And we had more fun than a little, you know what I mean. And I went in there this morning and they was three Texans there. I knew 'em, was acquainted with 'em, met 'em there for two or three years. And they was talking about watermelons. Well, I set there and never said nothing for a few minutes. And after a while I said, "Well, how big a watermelons are those down in Texas?"

"Oh," they said, "fella, they big watermelons." They said, "They weigh fifty or sixty pounds."

"Well," I said. "You call that a big watermelon?"

"Well sure, it's a big watermelon."

I said, "Fella, that's no watermelon at all." I said, "Where I come from in Arkansas there was a little town there by the name of Cave City." And I said, "There's a cave there and this cave runs right in under the highway." And I said, "Every July Fourth they had a picnic there." Which they did. And I said, "There was a man out west of Cave City by the name of Brat Crow, that raised watermelons and raised 'em for the picnic for the Fourth of July." And I said, "The third day of July he called for help to load his watermelons." And I said, "We didn't have no cars or trucks then, we had wagons." Well, I said, "We had to make two skids to roll these watermelons up in the wagon." And I said, "We got one in the wagon and didn't have no trouble. And the second one we got up to the edge of the wagon and we lost control of it." And I said, "That watermelon fell and busted and the juice of it drownded two men before they could get out of the way of it." And I said, "You Texans talking about a big watermelon." And I said, "Why don't you raise watermelons like that?"

Well, boy, they sold out. They took off and they never

said no more. Well, the manager of the lumber company, he commenced laughing and as they went out the door he said, "Now you Texans will blow about your state some more in front of this Arkansawyer, won't you."

His Trip to the Moon

2. My Uncle Will always walked with a wry neck: he walked with his head turned to the side. And on the night that I sat before the fireplace with him and he was telling me stories, he told me about his trip to the moon. Now, we think the astronauts have done a great job—and they have—but there's a lotta people don't realize that my Uncle Will had a trip to the moon back as early as before nineteen-and-three, because he told me about it that night.

He said that one day he went hunting. He had an old mare that was a little bit swaybacked that he took along with him to carry the game. Well, he went along, and old Betsy, his rifle, was loaded, and he saw a quail going across the road. He up with old Betsy and shot the quail. He picked up the quail, hung it on the saddle. Went on a little further, and he'd hit a rabbit. He put that on, until he finally came to where he had hit a deer. And he slung that on, and the old mare's back just couldn't carry the load, so it caved in on him.

Well, he didn't know what to do. So finally there was a slippery elm tree there, and he cut a good string switch from it, whittled it down to make a keystone-like shape. Slipped that down between the vertebrae that were caved in, and that enabled the old mare to carry the load. He got him home, unloaded his game, fed the mare, and dressed out his game.

The next morning he got up and looked over toward the barn. By golly, there was a tree growing right up through the roof of the barn—way up there—and he got to thinking about it. He wondered what he could see if he climbed that tree and looked over the hill. So he climbed up—this was early in the morning—he climbed up the tree, and as he got up as high as he could go, here came the moon along with

44

that horn just right, and he caught ahold of it, and slipped right over on the moon. With that the moon had moved on, and there he was up on the moon and no way down.

Well, there's some little animals up there. He found he could skin 'em out, eat the meat, and save the hides and tack one to the other—and he did till he thought he had enough to reach the ground. So he climbed down. When he got down to the end, he found he'd misjudged—he didn't have quite as many as he needed. But he said, "Well, I'm gonna jump." He jumped down, and he hit head-first, and he was right in up to his shoulders. Well, he twisted, and he squirmed. Finally, he pulled his head right off. He went up to the house, picked up a pickaxe, dug his head out, and he put it back on, and ever after that, why, he walked with a wry neck.

Pranksters

3a. Uncle Will had a running contest with Lyin' Frank Carlton. There'd always be something that they would be pulling on each other. So the boys around the square, and the post office, and the bank, decided that it'd be a nice thing, and be very interesting, to get those two men together and let 'em have a contest to see which could tell the biggest lie.

So they finally got them to agree to meet and have the contest. And they met on the north side of the square at the post office—which was on the north side then. They was a sheriff there, and the postmaster, and all the officers from the courthouse, and the bank—they all lined up there. Mr. Carlton was there and Uncle Will didn't show up.

So they began to get a little uneasy. And so finally they looked up the street, and there coming down by the bank was Uncle Will—and he was walking, swinging his arms, and stepping out like he was walking for wages. He came right down by where they were; walked right on by—didn't even look at 'em. And he got just by them. "Why! What in the—?! Hey—! Hey, Will, aren't you gonna stop?"

He turned around and looked at 'em. "Did you hear that

45

Bud Riggs fell in his saw and got cut all to pieces?"

Lying Frank Carlton, he said, "Oh my God, he's one of my best friends!"

He lit out running, and ran all the way down Springtown. Got down there, Bud Riggs was setting on the porch whittling. That ended the contest.

3b. One afternoon some men were working in a field near a road when they saw Colonel Blew coming, riding his old gray mule. Mr. Blew was noted for his ability to lie. One man suggested they stop Colonel and have him tell a good lie. They all went out to the road and one man said, "Hey, Colonel, stop and tell us a whopper."

Colonel said, "Can't, ain't got time. Jim Cole just fell outa the hayloft and broke his leg. I'm goin' for the doctor." Slapping his old mule with his hat, he took off down the road.

The men stood around and talked over this thought. Finally they decided to go over to Mr. Cole's, he might need help. So away they went.

When they arrived they found Mr. Cole plowing corn.

An Unconstitutional Fellow
4. Old Man Johnson is a modern Daniel Boone. He has lived a life that is absolutely unconstitutional. He is a "dental cripple" but don't limp, he has a bad case of "halitosis" but don't slobber or lisp. I guess he has gotten by with this because no one has told him about it. He says he has never had spots before his eyes in spite of the fact that he "overindulges" almost every Saturday. He has never stolen a horse, shot anyone, or burned his home to collect the insurance. I asked him if the Depression had bothered the folks in his neighborhood. For a moment he had a faraway look in his eyes, then he replied: "It didn't bother us right around here but it took a roof off of a barn two or three miles up the creek." He has never in his life had a shot of pep, energy, zip, or ginger from a soft drink, yet he can go coon hunting and walk all night. He eats hearty and sleeps well

when the racket from his breaking fruit trees does not disturb him. What are you going to do with a guy like that? He is bound to be unconstitutional.

A Curious Way to Lose Cattle

5. I think the best story is where years ago the Texans started into Arkansas in the cattle drive. They started with sixty-five head of cattle and they started to cross a river and the river was up. Well, they couldn't cross the river nowhere and they went up and down the river. And they finally found a big tree, a big hollow tree. It was tall enough to reach clear across this river. So they cut it down, then walked this log across the river and went out and cut the top out of it. And they run this sixty-five head of cattle through this hollow tree across the river. Well, when they got to the far side of it they was twenty-five head short. So they went back in this hollow tree. They found fifteen head still in the hollow tree and there was ten head had fell through the knotholes in this tree and drownded in the river. Now that is an actual fact of a river in Arkansas and the cattlemen that used to drive cattle.

A Bright Idea

6a. My dad used to tell this old story about this old lazy preacher lived over here . . . seem like that he had an old milk cow, best I remember—why, ever'body back then had a cow. This old preacher he's so lazy he didn't want to cut the ice in the wintertime when it got real cold and the ponds froze over. Why he'd have to go down ever' day and cut the ice.

Well, his old axe was dull and he was too lazy to do it, so we had a general store up here. Back in them days, you could buy dynamite in any store that had a lotta stuff in it like Mr. Osborne's did. So he got this bright idea to go get him a stick of dynamite one day. The bad mistake was that he'd trained this old dog that he had layin' around there—he'd fooled with him and raised him up—and he's about as lazy as the preacher. But one thing he's really good at was fetching a stick. He'd set there on the porch and whittle on this stick—that old preacher would—and directly he'd throw it just as far as he could and have the old dog go fetch it and brang it back to him and he'd set there and whittle some more. Well, he got so tired of cuttin' that ice he got up there to Mr. Osborne's and got the stick of dynamite—got him a foot of fuse and a cap, had 'em help rig it up. So he come home with this brilliant idea that he would just really make a hole in that pond 'thout havin' to go down there and cut ice with that old dull choppin' axe.

So, he goes down that morning to the edge of the pond, and he lights this foot of fuse he got on this dynamite, give it a slang out in the pond. He's going to blow him a hole the cow could get a drink out of nice and easy 'thout him havin' to work very hard. And the only thing about it, he'd forgot about the old lazy dog—he'd follered 'em down there and when he throwed that stick of dynamite out there, well the old dog thought, "Oh me, got a fetch job," so he took off out across the ice and he grabbed the stick of dynamite and I mean the fuse and ever'thing it 'as a-going strong! Well, the preacher turned around and he wudn't so lazy then. He took off just as hard as he could go. Well, the old dog was right after him—he run through one bob-wire fence trying to get away from the old dog and just as he got through the fence, well they—it was nailed to a great old big oak tree standin'. And the old hound dog just almost made it around the tree before the stick of dynamite went off in his jaws.

That sent the poor old lazy hound to heaven and blowed all the bark off the tree and scared the hell out of the preacher. So, that's supposed to be a true story.

6b. Me and my dad used to clear up ground. We'd go out and cut the trees down and get an acre or two cleared for new ground. We'd take these stumps and hitch a windlass to 'em and try to twist 'em out and dig around 'em and pull 'em out and hook the mules to 'em. Well, we seen that we wasn't a-getting nowhere. So Dad, he went and got a case of dynamite. And we was goin'-a blow them stumps out. So we set this dynamite out there at the barn and for three or four days why we was working at other things, wasn't a-doing that. So an old sow that we had broke into that case of dynamite and ate about half of it. Well, she went out through the hall of the barn and one of them mules kicked that old sow, that dynamite went off and for three months, gal, that was the sickest sow that we ever had around our place. I have never seen anything like it. And from then on we kept all the dynamite up where the hogs couldn't get ahold of it.

A Real Bad Snakebite

7a. We have a great variety of snakes up there in Carroll County, Arkansas.

There we have the copperhead; we have the rattlesnakes—different varieties; and the cottonmouth. They're all of the pit viper family. Then we have some— they's just old serpent types, like the chicken snake, the king snake.

And then we have a hoop snake, and when he gits after you, he gimmers—makes a hoop outa himself. Just—and starts rollin' after ya, and he's got a stinger in the end of his tail, and when he gets up close he'll sting you with that stinger—that's the way he poisons you.

Well, one old feller up there ran from him, had a hoe, turned around and struck at the hoop snake with the hoe, killed the snake, but the snake in the meantime hit the handle of the hoe. And that hoe swelled up so big, that evening he sawed it up and got four cords of wood out of it.

7b. My Uncle John went fishing a long time ago in the Buffalo River and there was this big water moccasin come up on him. He got scared and started to hit him with his oar and that water moccasin bit his oar and that oar started swelling till it stopped up the Buffalo River. It took twenty mules to pull it out of there. Uncle John took it to the sawmill and sawed it up and built him a huge house out of it. My Aunt Nattie she went to paint it one day and she mixed some turpentine up with the paint. That turpentine must have took the swelling out of it for now it ain't nothing but a birdhouse.

And He Didn't Care

8. The other night I was setting around the fire and I said, "Paul, let's go larping tarping scoonskin hunting." And he asked and he didn't care. So we called up all the old dogs except old Shorty and we called him up too. We went out in the valley on top of a mountain and treed a rabbit in a huckleberry log about three feet through at the little end. I said, "Paul, if you don't care I'll chop that rabbit out of there." And he asked and he didn't care so I took one lick with my axe, cut my dog's tail off. Cut my dog's tail off right behind his ears and just darn near ruined him.

We went on down in the valley and treed a possum up a sycamore sapling about a hundred feet off the ground and I said, "Paul, if you don't care I climb up there and shake that possum out." And he asked and he didn't care so I clumb up there and I shook and I shook, directly I heard something hit the ground and I looked all around and it was me and all those old dogs piled on top of me except old Shorty and he piled on me too and I said, "Paul, if you don't care you can pull those dogs off of me." And he asked and he didn't care so he pulled them all off except old Shorty and he pulled him off too. I told Paul seeing the next day was Sunday that I thought I'd go down to my gal Sal's house and see her and I remember riding and walking down the road there I went in and set down on the arm of the piano stool and Sal wanted to know if I wanted to go down to the plum orchard to get some peaches to make a blackberry pudding. She said she did, so we went down there and picked some of the prettiest red apricots off of a gooseberry vine and brought them back home and Mama made some onion jelly and it tasted just like peanut butter. That's about all that happened that day and I said, "Paul, time we get back home all them pigs will be out in the punkin patch." And I went out there and slammed one of them punkin's heads again—I don't remember.

I know the other night we went out and turned a rock over and there was ten under it and I killed nine of them and one of them got away and I went back that night and a wheel run off and had to jump out in a parachute and about that time a covey of bird dogs flew over.

Good Dog for Sale

9. An old boy was a-wanting him a coon dog. So he heard of one away off over in another place and he went over there. Man said, yeah, he had one. Old boy wanted to know if he'd sell him. Man said he would. Old boy says, "Well, can I try him?" Feller says, "Yeah, so any night just come over." Says, "Fact is," says, "moon's shining now fore part of the night. If you come over along about two or three o'clock in the morning, why," says, "it'd be better." Says, "We can get one." So he did and they'd taken off. And they was a lake around there and they went around that old lake. Directly the old dog struck and away he went. They followed him. Directly he started across a big old field laying out on the outside, no fences or anything. So they was a-following along watching. Daylight had come then. Every little bit, this old dog, he'd jump great high and over. And kept on doing that. And finally this feller said to him, he says, "What's that dog a-doing that for?" He says, "Oh well," he said, "when that coon went there there was a fence there."

Better'n a Dog Any Day

10. An old boy that always hunted together and they moved about thirty-five, forty miles apart. So one day the old one of these boys called the other one up. Told him, says, "How's your dogs?"

He says, "Oh, they pretty good."

And he says, "What about me a-bringing mine and coming over tonight and going hunting?"

"Be fine, just come over."

So he got there and they eat their supper and got out and just about ready to go. This feller got in the truck and had his dogs. Says, "Wait just a minute and let me run back

51

in the house." Come out and he had a monkey and his pistol.

And he said, "What are you going to do with that?"

He said, "Oh," he said, "I wouldn't go a-coon hunting without this monkey."

So they got over there and they turned the dogs out. And directly they struck and wasn't very long until they treed. He turned this monkey loose and handed him the pistol. And this monkey just beat her up that tree. He's gone and he's gone and he's gone. He says, "Don't understand it." He says, "He never is that long." Says, "Don't take him no time till he can find that coon and shoot it out." Here in a bit seen him come down. And he says, "There ain't no coon up there." When that monkey come down, he got down, he just turned around and he shot them dogs. "Doggone it," he says, "I forgot to tell you. That monkey hates a liar worse than anything."

A Good Job of Sewing

11. This guy, he was a-fox hunting. He was at a derby, fox derby. And everybody in different states brought their fox hounds out. Well, they take turn about running these fox. So this guy's dog, he was the fastest dog in the whole race, anywhere. And they ask him why and how fast, why that dog was so fast. "Well," he said, "years ago he was a-running a fox and," he said, "he got right behind that fox and he started to reach over and pick the fox up." And he said, "The fox turned right quick and that dog couldn't stop." And he said, "He hit a steel post and just split him half in two." And said, "I was there and I stuck him back together and sewed him up." And said, "I put two legs up and two legs down. And he'd run on two legs awhile and then he'd flop over on the other two legs and he'd outrun every dog in the whole pack."

The Old Hunter

12. You've probably heard the story 'bout the old man that liked to hunt so well and he finally got so old and crippled up with arthritis that he couldn't go on a hunt. And the young men in the family, they liked to hunt and they keep on making their hunts and coming in and telling Dad about them. What a good time they had and what they caught and so along. Finally, the old man was grieving so much about it that the young ones agreed to carry him alone on a stretcher. Just carry him along through the woods and give him one more hunt.

On one suitable night, the weather was nice for it. They put the old man on the stretcher and carried him on out into the woods with the dogs. It wasn't a great while till the hounds struck a trail. And directly they bayed—they had the varmint treed so the boys hurried along carrying the stretcher. Finally they arrived at the tree where the dogs were baying and directly they decided that one of 'em better climb the tree to see what it was and maybe make it jump out so dogs could get it. And so one climbed the tree and pretty promptly after he got up the tree it jumped out, an old bobcat. And just didn't miss the old man on the stretcher much. Hit the ground right close to him and terrified the dogs after he got a few slaps at them and lashing their hides. The dogs got away from there. And the boys—they were so scared, they headed for the bushes. And they happened to think about Dad. Dad, out there on that stretcher and the old bobcat dropped down to the ground right close to him. So they hurried back to the stretcher and the old man was gone. No trail of him. There lay the empty stretcher. Boy, how did they worry. So thoughtless of them, going off and leaving Dad there. The old bobcat dropping down so close to him and having to fight with the dogs. They were so scared—so scared they couldn't help it. Couldn't help it. But what's happened to Dad? So they decided they might after they couldn't get any answer calling to him, they might as well go on home and wait for daylight to hunt for him. So they went on home and when they got near the house through the dim light they saw the bulk of the old man sitting up on the porch.

"Oh, Dad, you home?"

"Well yes, I'm home all right."

"Well, when you get here—how'd you get here?"

"Well, I got here all right. I came in ahead of the dogs."

One Step Ahead

13. I heard of a dog in southern Arkansas that was so smart that any time his master got out his shotgun he started sniffing the ground in search of quail. But if his master grabbed a rifle he started searching the trees for squirrels. Once his master started fishing. The dog took a look at the rod and reel and tore out. Sure enough they found him digging worms.

No Ordinary Dog

14. My great-grandpappy used to have a coon dog. Now this dog just wasn't any ordinary coon dog. Great-grandpappy would simply put his tanning board out by the back door and the dog would look at it for a while and then head into the forest and return with a coon whose pelt would exactly fit that board. Well, things went along fine until Great-grandma forgot and set her ironing board by the back door. That old dog took one look at that board and let out a yelp and headed for the forest. He hasn't been seen to this very day.

Rabbit in Their Blood

15. Old Man Johnson, of Pole Cat Creek, says that he and his family have eaten so many rabbits this winter that every time a dog barks they all run under the house.

Sittin' on the Log

16. An old man, lived right up the holler up yonder, said he was back here in these hills squirrel hunting one day. Said he was a-slippin' along. Finally seen an old fox squirrel, but it seen him. It run up a tree and went in a hole. Well, he walked on up there and looked it over. Big old log laying off out there, an old black log been burnt. He just walked out there and thinks, "Well, I'll just sit down there on this log. And he'll come out of there directly and when he does, I'll shoot him." He walked up there and he sit down on that log. Every little bit he'd look up at that hole. And after a bit he looked up and the hole wadn't there. He get to looking and he couldn't find that hole at all. So he got to looking around and he'd sat down on a big black snake and it had crawled off with him.

Specialists

17a. Last week we were invited to go coon hunting. We accepted the invitation and last night we went after the coons. Henry Johnson, our host, had three wonderful coon dogs. One is a trailing dog, one he calls a tree dog, and the third one is a skinning dog. This is the way they work. The trailing dog smells the coon and trails him to a tree, the tree dog gets him out of the tree, and the skinning dog usually has the coon about skinned by the time you get there. All there is left for the hunters to do is pick up the hide and go after another coon. We got three large ones last night. Johnson is one of the best hunters I have ever seen. He never uses a gun, says the ammunition costs too much. He hunts with a bow and arrow all the time. He was telling me last night of one of the best shots he ever made with a bow and arrow. Said he went squirrel hunting one day and didn't have but one arrow. Arrows are hard to make and as a rule are more valuable than any game you can kill at one shot so he had to keep an eye on the arrow. He hadn't walked but a little ways until he saw a squirrel sitting in the forks of a tree. He cut down on him, the arrow went right through the squirrel, hit the creek, and ricocheted across and stuck in a big yellow oak tree. He kept his eye on the arrow, picked up the squirrel, and started wading across the creek to recover the arrow. When he was about the middle of the stream he noticed a large catfish, about four feet long, floating along with the current. He picked it up and discovered that when the arrow hit the water it had gone right through the catfish. When he pulled the arrow out of the tree a stream of honey started pouring out. It was a bee tree. He stuck his finger in the hole to stop the flow and reached behind him for a stick to plug the hole. He said he got hold of what he thought was a stick but it turned out to be the hind leg of a rabbit that had crouched there in the brush. He threw the rabbit down on a little pile of brush hard enough to kill it, plugged the hole, picked up the rabbit, and noticed that there was a covey of quail sitting under the little pile of brush. He had thrown the rabbit down with such force that he killed six of these quail. He gathered up the six quail, one rabbit, the twenty-pound catfish, and the squirrel and went back to the house to get some buckets and tubs to put the honey in. Then he returned to the tree and drew out nineteen gallons of honey. About the time he got all the honey out he heard some scratching on the inside of the hollow tree. Coons like honey, he said, so he built a fire at the roots of the tree to smoke them out. There were eight of them and he got them all. He says that this was one of the best shots he ever made with a bow and arrow, one squirrel, a twenty-pound catfish, six quail, one rabbit, nineteen gallons of honey, and eight coons—all in one shot, and he recovered his arrow.

Scared of His Gun

17b. Many years ago in Arkansas, a man was left a gun by his great-grandfather. It had a four-foot barrel and an undetermined gauge. Well, the man was a little scared of the gun, but he was determined to take it duck hunting. He was sitting in a boat when a bunch of ducks startled him. He had to shoot almost straight up. The force of the recoil drove him right through the boat. When he came out, he had twelve ducks and a string of trout that had been caught in his boots.

Like Dog, Like Dad

18. A man was prowling around his house and he got hungry. His wife was off somewhere—might have been a club meeting; she'd gone somewhere. He was hungry; looking around for something to eat and happened to find a biscuit lying on the radiator. Some kind of biscuit! He didn't know what kind it was; it was just a biscuit. He was hungry. He tried it and he liked it. He ate it and then after his wife got home he said to her, "What kind of biscuit was that on the radiator?"

"Why do you ask?" she replied. "What it was was one of the dog biscuits."

"Well now, I was hungry and I didn't know what kind of biscuit it was and I thought I'd try it and I did and it was good."

"It was a dog biscuit and you shouldn't have eaten it."

"Well, I was hungry and I didn't know what kind of biscuit it was and I thought I'd try it and I did and it was good."

"Oh now, you'd better not do that," she replied.

"Now, I want some more of them and when you do your shopping get some more dog biscuits."

"Well, then, if that is what you want."

So the next time she went marketing she bought just twice as many dog biscuits as she was in the habit of buying. And the clerk who had watched her in her buying for quite a while noted she was buying twice as many dog biscuits. She'd always bought the same amount every time.

"Buying twice as many?" the employee said. "I see you're buying twice as many dog biscuits. Have you got another dog?"

"No, I don't have another dog. It's just that my husband happened to get hold of a dog biscuit the other day and he didn't know what it was. He ate it and he was hungry and he ate it. I wasn't at home. He ate it; he was hungry so he ate it. And when I came home he asked me what kind it was and I told him. He said he wanted some more of them so that is why I'm buying twice as many."

"Now," the clerk said, "you better not encourage him to eat those dog biscuits, they might make him sick. They might not be good for him." But she went ahead and got them anyway.

She went ahead getting them regularly for quite a little spell. Then finally, she went in to do her shopping and just got her old original number that she'd got when she was just feeding the dog. The clerk again observed the different size order. "You're only getting the amount you used to get when you were only buying for your dog? What is the matter? Is your husband getting tired of dog biscuits and not wanting any more?"

"Oh, it's not that! My husband is dead. My husband is dead."

"I'm sorry to hear that, but I warned you. I told you they might make him sick. They might hurt him."

"Oh, no, no they didn't. He got killed!"

"Got killed? How?"

"Chasing cars," she replied.

Who Would Believe It?

19. And what a climate they have in these Ozarks. Last night on the higher hills was a sprinkle of snow and a very heavy frost this morning. Imagine such weather in June. Down in the valleys strawberries are ripening. They are as big as baseballs. You don't have bowls of strawberries over here, no sir, you have sliced strawberries; they look like sliced tomatoes and in eating them the only difference is that you put sugar on them instead of salt. One of the boys just returned from the boat landing. He has three more catfish. They jumped into the boat after we tied it up. Think of it. All the fish we can take care of and haven't wet a hook! Henry Johnson, the fellow that loaned us the boat, says that the best time to come fishing over here is during the fall when the acorns are falling. He says that catfish like acorns and will come out on the bank in droves to eat them. All you need is a sack and a good club and you can get all you can carry under one oak tree. I'm going to arrange to come back here this fall.

Coulda Caught It with a Magnet

20. Once there was this man who loved to fish. One time he started to fish in a pond where there was a catfish no one could ever catch. So he got his fishing pole and started over to it and when he got there the fish almost pulled him in. He got so mad because it hauled off his line but he went back and caught that old fish. But it had so many hooks in its mouth he sold it for scrap iron.

Losing Sleep

21. Just had a letter from Old Man Johnson who lives over on White River, Arkansas. He says that he hasn't been able to sleep nights since we were over there, that his fruit trees are so full of fruit they are all breaking down, and that the breaking limbs make so much racket at night he just can't sleep. Says the river overflowed all his crops and when the water went down he discovered that the catfish had eaten all the corn right off the stalk. He closes his letter by venturing to opine that there is a hard winter ahead.

A Big Catch

22. Arrived here yesterday, picked a dandy campsite near a big spring. No boat here so had to borrow one from a coon-hunting, hog-raising, rail-splitting, catfish-eating farmer down the river about a mile. He told us to take the boat and keep it as long as we wanted it and invited us to go a–coon hunting with him some night this week. We accepted the invitation. In rowing up the river to our camp sixteen fish jumped into the boat; nine channel catfish, three large bass, and four black perch. Spent the rest of the day cleaning fish; had fried fish, corn cakes, and coffee for supper.

He'd-a Known Him Anywhere

23. One day an old hillbilly went fishing. He really had hung one and was having a big battle getting it to the top. Just as he was about to get it in the boat the old catfish gave a heave and knocked the hillbilly's glasses off as it escaped. About a year later the old fellow was fishing in about the same place as before when he hooked a big one. When he landed the fish, it turned out to be the same one he had hooked last year. He knew because the fish was wearing his glasses.

Talented Fish

24. One time my uncle went fishing but all he could catch were dogfish. So he kept tossing them back behind him in the grass. Suddenly he heard a commotion. He looked around and he saw his pack of dogfish treeing a coon.

Working in Louisiana

25a. One time I went down in Louisiana and hired out to a farmer down there. I was there for about, oh I don't know, three or four days. And we come in from work one evening and he told me, "I want you to go to the back of the field and drive up my old milk cow." He said, "Now she's with a bunch of other cattle, but," said, "you'll know her, she's got a bell on." And said, "She'll probably be about a mile back there." And I said, "Well, okay." And I started back to the back of the field and I got about halfway, and I heard that bell a-jingling. So I went on over there and I got up where I thought the bell was. But I didn't see no cow with a bell on. And I said, "In a few minutes that bell started to ringing again." I looked over there and these mosquitoes had eat that cow up and was standing there ringing the bell for the calf.

25b. An old man one time said way back there before they went to dipping these cattle the ticks got real bad. And he said he had an old cow to come up missing. He said he got out looking for her and he could just hear the bell a-rattling, and a-rattling, and he kept a-looking and hunting. He said he got down there and it was one of these big old speck-backed ticks had eat the cow up and was up on the stump a-rattling the bell a-looking for the calf to come. He wanted to eat it up.

Undecided Mosquitoes

26. I come from Clover Bend and we do have large mosquitoes. As a matter of fact, I was hunting along Black River and two of them swooped down and grabbed me. The two of them were trying to decide what to do with me. One of them wanted to take me home but the other was afraid their big brother would take me away from them.

I've Heard of Big Mosquitoes Before

27. Once I was visiting some friends in the swamplands of Arkansas. Now I have heard of big mosquitoes before but the ones I found here could not be matched for all around mean temper. Just as I was about to fall asleep I heard the sounds of an angry mob of skeeters. So I got a torch and went around burning them. I just about had them all knocked off when I came across one that I couldn't kill. Every time I would get the torch close to his body he would blew out the flame. You know I had to get a jug of white lightning to put that skeeter out of his misery.

Suited-up Skeeters

28. We were camping out one night when a horde of mosquitoes descended on our tents. They stripped off all the canvas and rope. So we huddled together until the morning. When the sun rose we saw the mosquitoes that had attacked us. They were wearing slacks and suspenders made from our tent and rope.

The Importance of Tools

29. A group of fishermen were spending the night out. At dusk a band of mosquitoes descended on the camp and carried off a can of peas. About fifteen minutes later they came back for the can opener.

A Mosquito Fire

30. Mosquitoes are so thick around Clover Bend that once when some kids set fire to a mosquito's wings and turned him loose among his fellow skeeters, it set fire to all the others. The flame from all the burning wings attracted the fire trucks from the surrounding counties because they thought it was a great big grassfire.

The Makings of Hot Pepper

31. One night a traveler was riding across the prairies of west Texas when a "norther" came up. The man built a fire to keep warm by. It promptly froze. He ground it up and used it as red pepper all next summer—thus demonstrating how fast a "norther" can come up in west Texas.

Sparks Would Fly

32. My uncle heard of a case where it got so cold that the woodpeckers would find a piece of flint and start pecking so hard that sparks would fly. Then they would run and step on those sparks to warm their feet.

Throwing Out the Fire

33. One winter it got so cold that the flames froze in the fireplace. The only way we could get any room for a new fire was to chop cut all the frozen stuff and throw it out back. Unfortunately, the one old hen we had ate some of the frozen flames. The heat of her body must have thawed out the fire because she laid boiled eggs for the next two weeks.

He Thought Fast

34. One time a man was hunting on an extremely cold day. All of a sudden he was confronted by a huge bear. He didn't have any bullets left and was really in big trouble. In his fright he began to sweat great big drops of sweat. In the cold weather they froze before they could fall off so he grabbed some of them from his forehead and rammed them in his gun. He didn't have much hope but it was his only hope so he fired away. He got him right between the eyes. Now he has the hardest bear rug in town.

He Chopped It Up

35. My father tells of the time when my grandfather was out burning the trash and it was real cold. It got to be a big blaze when all of a sudden it froze because it was so cold out. He didn't know what to do so he just left it there. That night they couldn't sleep because the light from the frozen blaze was shining so bright in their room. He had to get up and chop it down before they could ever go to sleep.

No Shadow Till Spring

36. One winter a friend of mine was out walking on a clear but cold day when he looked down and noticed that he didn't have a shadow. This really puzzled him until he retraced his steps a few yards and found his shadow frozen to the ground. You know, he had to wait until spring before he could get his shadow loose.

An Acre of Air

37. One day a farmer was planting cotton when all of a sudden a thick fog rolled in. But since the farmer knew his ground real well he just went right on planting. About noon the sun broke through and lifted the fog. The farmer found he had planted about an acre of air.

Deep Mud

38. It had been raining for days and days in Lawrence County and the mud was getting pretty deep. One fellow was seen coming down the road almost waist-deep in the mud. When someone asked him if the mud was getting bad, he replied, "Yep, and it was a darn good thing I was riding a horse or I couldn't have made it to town."

They Froze at the Sight

39a. One summer it was really getting hot. In fact, some corn that I had been feeding the hens popped right on the ground. Well when the hens came out and saw that white popcorn lying all around, they thought it was snow and laid down and froze to death.

39b. One time there was a man driving a team beside a popcorn patch in west Texas. A real hot windstorm came up, the popcorn got so hot it began to pop and blow across the prairies. The mules took one look at it and froze to death.

Not Yet!

40a. One time I was in Arkansas and boy, it was hot. It was humidity about seventy-five or eighty percent, about a hundred degrees, and I was walking down the highway. I was just a-burning up. And there was a tree fell down alongside the highway. And I was kinda down in the valley and there's hills on both sides. I walked out and sat down on that tree. And after while I heard the blamedest racket a-coming down through them woods. Boy, it sounded like a cyclone. I's scared to death. I didn't know whether it was a bear or mountain lion. I jumped over behind that log and hid there and kept a-looking, looking, and looking. After while a woman come a-running off that hill. And she took down that road just for dear life. Never said a word, just kept a-running. I stood there and looked at her till she got out of sight. And I heard something coming down the hill again. And I wondered what in the Sam Hill was going on. In about five or ten minutes here a boy about twenty-two or -three years old come a-running out there. And he said, "Did you see anything of my mother going down this road?"

And I said, "Well, I don't know whether it was your mother or not but I seen a woman."

He said, "That was my mother." Said, "She thinks she's gonna wean me but she ain't about to."

40b. Not so long ago I was on a country road in Pole Cat Creek Valley. A woman came out of a cornfield in a dead run and disappeared over the next hill. In a short time an overgrown boy, about six feet tall, emerged from the same cornfield, loped over the fence, jumped into the road and stopped, looked all around, and asked, "Did you all see a woman pass here just now?" I said, "Yes, a woman just disappeared over the hill there, what's the matter, what's going on?" "Aw, that's just my ma," says he, "and she is trying to wean me."

Their Mouths Open

41. The keeper of the country general store, talking to the loafers around the potbellied stove in 1932, just after the Red Cross had started passing out free flour as a relief measure in his town: "Say I heard about a sure way to kill potato bugs. Yep, you take some of this Red Cross flour and sprinkle it on the potato plants, when the potato bugs get a taste of it, they set there with their mouths open waiting for more and starve to death."

The Biggest Fight I've Seen

42. I have seen wrestling matches, prize fights, and just plain old fistfights, but last night I saw the greatest fight I have ever seen. It was between two Hillside Moodies. These are wildcat-like animals a little larger than a coon. They live all their lives on hillsides and their left legs are shorter than their right ones. And how they can fight. The first one that gets turned around with his short legs downhill loses the fight. Their claws and teeth are as sharp as needles and are about one inch long. When two of them finish a fight they are usually both pretty well used up. It's a great show.

A Surprise

43. I was out squirrel hunting in the hills once. Hadn't even seen a squirrel or fired a gun, though, when a man fell out of a tree right in front of me.

I ran to him, bent over, rushed to a nearby stream, got some water and poured it on his face and he began to revive. I said, "Are you hurt, what hit you?"

"No," he replied, "I'm not hurt. But I'm getting awfully tired. I've fallen off my farm up there seven times today."

Self-Harvesting Potatoes

44. There once was a feller that had a tater patch on the side of a very, very steep hill. A city-slicker came through and asked him why he built the tater patch on the side of such a steep hill. The man replied, "Ground's so rich that all I have to do when it comes to be tater-harvesting time is to dig a hole at the bottom of the hill and all the taters come running out."

Fortunate Flatlanders

45. Well, that's something the Oklahoma farmers have to be thankful for. They may not have the misty mountain views, the purple splendor of the valleys, the pine forests—they may have only "flat, undulating waves" as William Cullen Bryant put it, but—coming down to earth a body can stay on their farms without much trouble—except on some of these windy days.

Local Characters

One of the most popular forms of American folk humor, and one of the least studied, deals with local characters. Traditional tales become attached to these familiar personalities, their local renown often being the reason such narratives are assigned to them. Just about every community in the United States has stories about the local character who is always looking for a handout from his friends, or who is distinctive for his ignorance, his miserliness, his drunkenness, his irascibility, his toughness, his wit, his eccentricity, or some other noteworthy feature. Yarns about these people are always told as true stories, and in some cases they may be about actual happenings, but in most instances widely traveled tales are merely localized by being connected with a specific person.

Local character yarns flourish in the Ozarks and are particularly long-lived there. Usually these narratives circulate both while their protagonists are living and long after they have died. Often, as in the case of Dr. Noe and his friend, these tales become the sole means by which these personalities are remembered. Many, but not all, local characters in Ozark humorous yarns are people of great naiveté or low intelligence. Sometimes, as in the tale about Walter Blyth, they are people who have become mentally unbalanced. Frequently the humor hinges on the protagonist's incompetence, demonstrated either through expressions of ignorance or someone taking advantage of him through pranks. Where ignorance or naiveté isn't involved, humor is provided by other types of eccentricity.

They Had Stories

46. The doctors were partners there in town. One of them, a Dr. Noe, was always slow in answering his calls. He repeatedly said: "I always wait awhile to give a man a chance for his life before I go." These two doctors were forever kidding each other and trying to get something on one another so they could spread it around town. Of course, being partners, this was a friendly feud and strictly for laughs.

One day the other doctor (I don't remember his name) got terribly sick at his stomach and sent for Dr. Noe. Dr. Noe, being as slow as usual, was quite some time in getting there. In the meantime, this doctor had begun to heave. He was weak and therefore laid across the bed and was heaving in the pot. The doctor's son was sitting in the room idly popping an old broken buggy whip, waiting to see if there was something he could do for his father.

A cat walked in the room and the son swatted it one on the rump with the whip. The cat jumped and went right between the doctor's face and the pot. It just so happened that Dr. Noe walked in just in time to see the cat light on four feet, barely out of the pot. "By God, you heaved a cat!" he said. "You sure oughta feel a lot better after heaving a cat." And Dr. Noe began to tell all over town that his colleague had heaved a cat.

Well, later on Dr. Noe got sick himself with a bad case of diarrhea, and his colleague began to circulate this tale on him in retaliation:

Dr. Noe had suffered all day with this diarrhea. Late that night another attack hit him. He crept slowly out the path to the outhouse in the dark. When he got there, it was so dark and he was in such misery that when he got the door open, he dropped his britches and started to back in. An old settin' hen that was setting in the paper box reached out and pecked him on the butt as he backed in. He immediately thought, *Snake!* It scared him so that he cut loose all over the place!

Just Like a Panther

47. Up here at Sidney, we had a guy by the name of John Brock; I went to school with him. And that guy could squall like a panther and yell. Oh, man, he could imitate one. Well, there was a bunch of old people a-hunting over there. So we decided, we were just boys, we decided we'd scare them people, see. So at that time the only victrolas that we had was that old-time Edison victrola with that little round cylinder record. You see a picture of them and that dog a-standing there. Well, we had one of 'em and there was a lot of them in this country. So he'd taken this horn off and he'd put it flat down on the ground. We'd clean off the ground and he'd put it flat down on the ground and we'd get up on a hillside and them guys'd be down in the flats and have a fire built up a-waiting for the dogs to tree a possum or a coon. So he'd lay that horn down on the ground and he'd squall through that and it'd sound like it was twenty miles off. Well, then we'd take a little stick, maybe not no bigger than your little finger, and he'd slip under that and put it down on that and he'd yell through it again, two or three times. Well, it sound like it's five or six miles closer, see. Well, he'd keep a-doing that and then them dogs could come in and they'd run up to us. Well, course half of them old hounds, they was friendly, you know. Well, we'd bunch them old dogs up to us and we'd twist their ears and make them old dogs holler. And boy, we run everything in that country out of there.

Driving Too Fast

48. Uncle Jim Rorie had been down to a farm on Flint Ridge down towards Spoon Flat. There wasn't no roads much in this country, then, just old trails like a log road that goes off down through the woods. George Crist and Old Man Phelps they had a T-Model and they was coming up the ridge and Uncle Jim was walking. He always wore a big long white beard, his hair was always pretty long. They stopped and picked him up and got him in the back seat. They said he was a-sitting up there a-looking over the seat, just a-holding on for dear life. They was going about ten or fifteen miles an hour. Old Man Phelps said he noticed he was scared and he punched George Crist to speed it up, you see. So George speeded up a little bit, I don't guess they got over fifteen miles an hour. They couldn't have gone very fast. He said Uncle Jim kept getting a little higher. He said directly he said, "Huh, Mr. Crist," he said, "if you don't care, stop this thing and I'll walk or drive it in slow."

Uncle Jim and His Money

49. Uncle Jim he sold his timber one time and he got four hundred dollars, I think it was, for it. Back then four hundred dollars was quite a bit of money. Boy, he just went to spending it, buying this and that, and Dad said, "Jim," he said, "you ought to lay a little of that back and not spend all of it."

He said, "I might die before I get it all spent."

Mr. Med's Hole

50. Mr. Med has this fellow digging a corner posthole in some particularly hard ground. After several tries to get Mr. Med to say the hole was deep enough, Mr. Med told the man, "You just dig till I get back."

He left and got involved in some pressing business. It was some time before he remembered that this fellow was still digging away. The man had tied extensions on the posthole-diggers and had the hole at least eight feet deep. Mr. Med looked down in the hole and slowly said, "Ah—gollies, sir. Just fill it up."

A Good Audience

51. Walter came to this country from Scotland as a small boy. He took a law degree in one of the Carolinas and later came to Arkansas to settle in Batesville. He fell madly in love with a girl and asked her to marry him. Since he was rather an odd character, he asked her in such a way so as to make her think that he was doing her a favor by asking her. The girl turned him down flat and he was so shaken up that he lost his mind. He was not violent and his family took care of him, putting him in a little two-room log cabin next to the family home about a mile from Pine Mountain.

Mr. Rutherford said that his daddy used to go up to see Blyth in his later years just to hear him talk, and sit back and laugh. It seems that the old man could plead an excellent case, even though he was crazy as a bedbug. The reason George's daddy got such a kick out of the old man was that Blyth always pleaded his cases for hours on end in front of, and to, an old red oak tree.

Edgar, the Nickel Man

52. At Aurora in Madison County there lived this old fellow called Edgar. Now, Edgar never wore any shoes; he always asked for nickels; he liked hot dogs; those were the outstanding things about Edgar. He was uptown every day, rain or shine, holding out his hand for nickels. It was said when he died people found a rain barrel of nickels in his shack. If anyone gave him a penny or a quarter he threw it away, he wanted nickels.

One fall day, after the nights were beginning to get cold, the men in Aurora took up a collection and bought Edgar a pair of new shoes. They put them on him and he started home, walking on the railroad tracks.

Pretty soon he was back in town barefooted. He had sold his shoes for fifty cents. He went into a little cafe there and bought ten hot dogs. Edgar came out, sat on a bench, and began to eat his hot dogs. One of the fellows slipped in the cafe, got a bottle of hot sauce. Edgar would take a bite, hold his hot dog on his shoulder, take another bite and repeat the process. Every time he'd bring his sandwich up to his shoulder this man would shake a little hot sauce on it. Poor old Edgar ate all of those hot dogs. When he finished he slapped both hands to his mouth and yelled, "Water! Water! I'm on fire inside."

Grateful

53. Did you hear about the time when Tom Winn's house blowed away? They had a tornado and it blowed it away, I've heard my dad talk about it. It blowed everything away but the floor and the people. It blowed old Tom off down towards the spring and it blowed up at him. And he come carrying the butter bowl back to the house and he said, "Lize, here's a bowl of butter we saved and there ain't a damn fly in it."

Warnings All Around

54. Uncle Bill Vickers had rode a big black horse there and tied it up in a log barn with a rope around its neck. And it blowed that horse off up on the hill and that rope still around the horse's neck and around the log and didn't hurt it. They said there was some preacher a-talking to Tom about that. He said, "Tom, you ought to get to doin' a little better, the Lord's a-warning you."

Said old Tom he stood around there a few minutes, punched that preacher. He said, "Preacher, I believe Uncle Bill ought to get to doin' a little better, too. He's a-warning him too."

The Rowdies

55. Ed Treat and Simp Curtis, every time they'd come to town, they'd fight. One time then Ed Treat said, "I'm just going to have it out with him. Either kill him or make him quit coming to town."

They had a fight and they just rolled all over the place. When they got up, now Ed was just a bullheaded thing—he thought nobody could whip him. Simp Curtis was a strong person too. He said, "Now, Ed, are you satisfied?"

He said, "Well, it'll do right now."

Not Too Hard Once You Know How

56. Jack Dover give Ed Treat a good beating. Some of 'em after they got up said, "Was it very hard to do?"

He said, "Oh, just about like playing marbles."

When Times Were Hard

57. An old guy lived back here in the mountains went over there and stayed all night with Miss Newton and them. They had a lot of molasses, that was back when times was kind of hard. Miss Newton took some hot biscuits and butter and had those molasses. The old man ate some and they'd pass some he'd take some more. Directly Floyd said he passed 'em to him and the old man said, "Well, I reckon you're going to have some of them in the morning, ain't you?"

He said, "We sure are."

He said, "Well, just set 'em back over there. I'll give 'em hell in the morning again."

Tell Us How

58. One time we was over here at Marshall, a bunch of us boys went in to eat breakfast. We got in there to eat breakfast and we ordered bacon and eggs. There was this old boy in there we used to have a lot of fun out of. Of course, they come around and asked this old boy, "How do you want your eggs cooked?"

He said, "Well, just put 'em in the pan with some grease and fry 'em."

Husbands, Wives, and Lovers

Love and the relationship between lovers has been a popular theme of international folklore for centuries. Not surprisingly, then, many Ozark jokes deal with these topics. Generally they convey a one-sided view of romance and marriage. Most of the yarns dealing with married couples involve some antagonism or competition between husbands and wives—hostility that may be explicitly stated or advanced more subtly. Or married and unmarried lovers may have other problems in this lore—unfaithfulness; the incredible stupidity of one partner; a woman who nags; a man who lacks sufficient interest in sex, or has too much interest in sex. Whatever the problem, Ozark jokes imply that, as the proverb says, the course of true love seldom runs smooth. Yet, perhaps because the road to romance is viewed as a rocky one, it is also persistently amusing to Ozarkers.

Heaven in Texas

59. There was this couple that had been married a long time and the husband died. His wife had heard that if she would go to a séance she might be able to talk with him, through the medium, in the spirit world. So she went to a séance and the medium went through the ritual and finally he contacted her husband and told her, "Lady, you can now talk to your husband."

So the wife she said, "Oh, darling, I miss you so much."

Says, "How are you? How are you getting along?"

"Oh," he said, "just fine, fine. Doing good."

She said, "Well, what do you do?"

"Oh," he says, "we get up in the morning, have breakfast. And," he says, "we have sex." He says, "Then we have our lunch, then we have more sex." Says, "Then we have dinner, then we have more sex. Then we go to bed and have more sex."

And his wife couldn't understand this and she said, "Darling, how can you have all this sex in heaven?"

He said, "Heaven? Help, I ain't in heaven. I'm a jackrabbit down in Texas."

Everybody Knows That Nose

60. Ben Malone lived on Frog Bayou down near Van Buren. He hauled timber to Delaney. Ben's wife was pregnant. When the midwife came Ben always left home and didn't come back until the event was over. This time when the midwife came Ben went over to the nearest neighbor's and spent the night. The next morning the midwife sent word for Ben to come home, that he had a son. Well, he hurried home and took a quick look at the little bundle in bed with his wife and said, "Well, it's got a Malone nose." Then the midwife unwrapped it. There was a baby pig. Ben never lived that down.

Their sow had pigs that night. Mrs. Malone and the midwife thought it would serve Ben right to play a joke on him. The Malones did have a peculiar nose, but the baby didn't look like a pig.

His and Her Accounting

61. There was an old hillbilly and his wife and one day the hillbilly got sick and was upon his deathbed. He called his wife in and told her that he had a confession to make. Then he proceeded to tell her that he hadn't been very faithful to her and for every time he wasn't he had put a tack under the bed and told her to look at them, then she would know how many times he had not been faithful. Then she said,

"Well, I might as well tell you that I haven't been very faithful, either, and every time I wasn't I placed a bean in the tub behind the stove." She told him he could go see them and he would then know how many times she had not been faithful, and that all the beans were there, "except the ones she had used to feed the Smith family when they were here last week."

Paying What's Due

62. The marriage ceremony had just been concluded and the groom thrust his hand into his pocket and inquired of the preacher how much he owed him. The preacher answered, "We don't charge for this service, but you may pay according to the beauty of your bride." The groom then handed the preacher a quarter. The minister raised the bride's veil, took a look, and dug into his own pocket. "Here's fifteen cents change," he said.

She Won't Quit

63. A group of men had a carpool for going to work on a WPA project. One fellow acted pretty grumpy several mornings, so finally the other men wanted to know what the trouble was. This man said, "Well, every morning that woman of mine wants two or three dollars." The other fellows said, "What in the world does she do with all that money?" The man answered, "I don't know, I haven't given her any yet."

Let Her Rest

64. There's a woman they thought she's dead and they started to the graveyard with her, they started into the gate with her, and the wagon wheel hit a post, and jarred the wagon, and she come to. She lived a long time after that and she died and they started back through the gate with her, and the old man said to be careful and don't hit the post again.

His Angel

65. A man, usually critical, one day made a point of addressing his wife as "an angel." She was pleased but puzzled over it all day. That evening she asked her husband why he had called her an angel. "Well," he said, "for one thing you are always flitting about; for another, you are forever harping on things; and finally, you keep insisting that you never have a thing to wear."

Expecting More

66. The honeymoon couple had just registered in the hotel and had been shown to their room. The new bride had been thrilled with everything, but when she saw the twin beds her face fell. "What's wrong, dear heart?" asked the groom. "Nothing much," she said sadly, "but I'd just hoped that we might get a room all to ourselves."

Ready to Eat

67. The bride and groom were having their first turkey dinner at home. "Just think," the new wife said proudly, "I fixed this turkey all by myself." "And what about the stuffing? Did you make it yourself?" asked the groom. "No, I didn't have to stuff this one. It wasn't hollow," answered the new bride.

He's Got Good Sense

68. A couple was celebrating their twentieth wedding anniversary and went to see one of those torrid and sexy films. When they returned home the wife turned to her spouse and said, "Darling, why is it that you never make love to me like they do in these movies?"

And the man says, "Are you crazy? Do you realize how much those fellas get paid for doing that?"

He Hadn't Realized

69. One time after the honeymoon a wife complained bitterly to her husband that he'd fooled her. She told him,

"You lied to me. Before we were married you told me you were well off."

He answered, and he said, "Well, I was, but I didn't know it."

The Obstacle

70. Not too many years ago people used to be very hospitable. If a stranger was traveling across the country, he could stop at a farmhouse, get supper, and spend the night. One night a young man came riding up to the farmhouse on his horse, and the farm family invited him in for supper and to spend the night. When they got ready for bed, it was found that the only place the stranger could sleep was with the farmer's daughter. The old farmer thought a minute and decided to put an ironing board between them and decided that would be all right. The next morning the family was out in the front yard seeing the young man off when the wind blew the girl's bonnet off and it landed across a barbwire fence. The young man jumped off his horse and started to go after it. The girl said, "Never mind, if you can't make it over an ironing board you sure can't make it over a barb-wire fence."

He Saw His Chance

71. One day in a diner there was a man at the counter drinking coffee. All of a sudden he heard the fire whistle. He told the woman behind the counter that he had to go, and she said that she didn't know he was a fireman. The man said that he wasn't, but his girlfriend's husband was.

72. Father had been winding the clock, dropping his shoes, and stomping about for some time without getting any results from daughter's boyfriend. Finally he shouted down the stairs, "Say there, it's two-thirty! Do you think you can stay all night?"

"Well, all right, thanks," replied the boy, "but I'll have to phone home first."

Father Got the Message

73. One time a father was talking to his daughter. The father told her, "While you were out someone called, his name was Albert and he asked to talk to Hot Lips. And it wadn't very long somebody else called. He said his name was Pete and he wanted to talk to Hot Lips." He said, "Another one called and his name was Lewis. And another one called and he said his name was Joe. And they all wanted to talk to Hot Lips." The father said, "I think it's time that you and I had a little serious talk."

So his daughter said, "Yes, Father, what do you want to talk about?"

The father said, "Have you been smoking?"

An Introduction

74. One time a young fella and his girl was going to get married and the justice of peace said, "I shouldn't marry you, this girl is only seventeen. You'll have to get her father's consent."

"Consent!" yelled the young man. "Who in the hell do you think this old guy is with the rifle?"

Foolish

Tales about fools are rife in international folklore and popular culture. Narrators often attribute stories about absurdly ignorant actions to specific cultural or ethnic groups. Thus, in Denmark such tales are told about the Fools of Molbo, in Germany about the citizens of Schilda, in England about the Men of Gotham, in the United States about Briers (a nickname for Kentuckians) or Aggies (students at Texas A&M University). In the Ozarks the most popular butt of "foolish" jokes is the hillbilly, a generic type whose ignorance of the modern world knows few bounds. Occasionally he is a person of great pretension who tries to "show off," but whose ignorance always gets him in trouble. Even when his intentions are good his stupidity prevents the achievement of desired goals. Thus, ignorance illustrated in various ways—absurd misunderstandings, forgotten words or instructions, exploitation of ignorance—is the element essential to the humor of the selections in this section.

Though they are less common than the hillbilly joke, generic types of ethnic humor, such as the Polack joke, do appear in Ozark jokelore. The reason for this is the region's cultural makeup. Conventional belief holds that the Ozarks consist essentially of white Anglo-Saxons who came here by way of southern Appalachia. There has been significant cultural traffic between the two mountain regions, but as Russel Gerlach points out in his book *Immigrants in the Ozarks* (1976), p. 1, the view of the Ozarks as Appalachia

West is erroneous, for "the Ozark Highland Region contains within its boundaries a wide variety of cultural elements that together have forged a complex cultural landscape." In other words, there is no such thing as Ozark culture in the sense of a uniform heritage of traditional values and beliefs maintained by everyone in the region. Instead, Ozark culture is a many-sided phenomenon that includes Negroes, the French, Germans, Italians, Poles, Belgians, Swiss, Swedes, Yugoslavians, Hungarians, Austrians, Bohemians, Dunkards, Amish, Mennonites, and other ethnic and religious groups that settled in the Ozarks.

Still, relatively few of the numerous cultures that exist in the Ozarks appear in the region's jokelore. By far the most frequently mentioned are the African-Americans, not surprisingly, since they are the largest non–Anglo-Saxon cultural group.[*] Moreover, they were among the earliest non-indigenous peoples in Arkansas, having come to the Bear State with De Soto in the 1540s. If one accepts the admittedly controversial assumption that the Spanish explorer traveled through the Ozarks, then Negroes were also among the first non-indigenous peoples in the hill country. At any rate, most other cultural groups do not figure strongly in traditional Ozark jokelore. Only the Irish, who once enjoyed greater prominence in humorous narratives than they do today, Scots, Germans, and Poles receive any significant mention. In recent years jokes about Poles have become more prominent with certain Ozarkers, but most of these seem to be derived mainly from printed sources and primarily circulate among college students in the region. Speculation about why the Swiss, Swedes, Italians, Mennonites, and other cultural groups are not more frequently represented in Ozark jokelore could prove endless and is probably better left to subsequent study.

---

[*] Jokes about blacks have been deleted from this edition at the publisher's request.

Most of the "foolish" jokes that appear below involve the hillbilly type. The ethnic jokes included at the end of the section are only a small sampling, not to be taken as fully representative.

He Wasn't Sure

75. There was an old pioneer who was living in the sticks, and they heard something coming around the road and it was making a racket, and he got his old rifle and he hid by the picket fence, sort of in the bushes, and so he saw it coming around the road and it was a man in a car. He had never seen a car, and he raised up and shot it, and he went back to his house, and his wife asked him if he killed whatever it was. He said he didn't know whether he did or not but he said he made it turn a man loose.

They Had Their Ways

76. There was a man that had twin boys, youngsters just getting up to about old enough to go to school. If they weren't identical twins just in physique and appearance, they were very much alike—but just as different as they could be when it came to personality and disposition and the way they conducted themselves.

One of them you couldn't please him no matter what you gave him. You couldn't please him with anything. You just couldn't. The other one, on the other hand, the cheapest or most inconsequential thing you'd do or give him just went over big with him. He was happy about it. Just anything at all made him happy. No matter what you did for him or what you gave him he was happy—easy to get along with and easy to please. Finally it went on that way long enough that the father got worried about his sons. He was awfully bothered. He believed it was his duty, if there could be anything done to correct it or change it that he ought to try it. Finally he decided to go to a psychiatrist.

He went to a psychiatrist and told him his story. He gave the psychiatrist a summary of how the boys acted. The psychiatrist said, "I want to work on this case but it will take a little time. You bring the boys back to see me. Set the date a few days ahead. I'll have to think this over and work it out and prepare for it. But you bring them back on the day I tell you I'm ready. I'll try to help you do something about this. Try to find out something."

So the man took his little boys home and the psychiatrist got busy and he prepared an area in a large building. One big room he just loaded to capacity with all sorts of interesting toys and playthings—electric trains, electric horses, all sorts of toys, musical instruments—to play with. Every toy imaginable—the great room was loaded.

The other room, a great big old rambling room, wasn't in the regular formation. You'd wind around over quite an area and couldn't see till you got around a corner where you were—just where you could go. Every bit of furniture, every picture, was taken out. It was just an empty room. The great big rambling room area had been stripped of every bit of furniture. The only thing in the room was a large pile of fresh horse manure. The psychiatrist put the little boy who couldn't be pleased with anything in that room with the wonderful toys in it. And the little boy who was pleased by anything you did, he put in the room with the pile of fresh horse manure.

The psychiatrist went about other things for a while and let nature take its course. Quite a little while later, he came back to listen to see what was going on in the rooms. He went to the room where the little boy was placed with all the toys that you can imagine and listened. The little fellow was fretting, fuming, and just as unhappy as he could be, according to what the psychiatrist heard from outside. He opened the door and began to talk to him. "What's the matter with you? With all these nice toys in here for you to play with and work with, why are you so unhappy, carrying on like you are? Why don't you climb on that mechanical horse?"

"I'm afraid I'll fall off and get hurt," the little boy cried.

"Well now, here's an electric train. Why don't you run that train?"

"I'm afraid, I'm afraid," he bawled. "I'm afraid, I'm a. . ."

And everything the psychiatrist asked about he'd find some reason for not taking to it and enjoying it. So the psychiatrist gave up on him and left.

He went to listen outside the other door. Pretty soon he heard the most cheerful sounds—laughter, giggles. He heard the little boy jabbering to himself—just as happy as a boy can be. So after he listened a little bit he opened the door to interview the little boy. "Well, how are you getting along in here?" he asked.

"Oh fine, just fine. I've been having a good time."

"Well, now I just wondered what could have given you so much joy? I've been listening outside the door and I heard the most joyful sounds I could imagine. Now, I'd like for you to explain how you can get so much joy and happiness out of a situation like this."

"It's like this," the little boy said. "I love horses better than anything else in the world. I've always wanted a horse. Never been able to own a horse and I've always wanted one. I've been a-hunting around and I'm going to hunt some more in this rambling house here. You told me I could keep whatever I found and I just figured that I ought to find a horse in here with that much fresh horse manure around."

A First Time for Everything

77. One time there was this guy had this dog named Shep. He was kinda like I was, he liked his dogs. That ole dog would follow him ever'where he went. Boy, he was just as fat as he could be and when it got hot weather he wouldn't go with him. He'd start to and then he'd go back to the shade. There's this grocery store down there and that old man loved baloney. Oh, he'd just eat baloney and he went down there and told that guy, said, "Say, would you buy a fat goat from me?" He said, "Yeah, yeah, I'll buy one." Well, he went back home and he killed old Shep and he dressed him and taken him down to that grocery store and sold him for a fat goat. Well, about three or four days that old man decided he'd go back down to the store. He went down

there, he wanted some baloney and he's a-eatin' that baloney and braggin' on how good it was and he said, "Say, would you tell me what that's made out of?" And the feller said, "Yeah, it was made outa that fat goat you brought down here." He said, "Shep, I've called you a many a time and you wouldn't come, this is one time you're comin'."

She Had It Figured

78. The five-year-old girl was sitting in her grandmother's lap. She was studying her face very closely. She traced the wrinkles on her grandmother's face with her fingers. "Grandma," she said seriously, "you must have left your face in the water too long."

A Big Disappointment

79. The farm had been mortgaged and their life savings had gone to give daughter a college education. Paw was driving the truck to the station to call for her after graduation. She climbed in beside him, slipped an arm through his, and whispered, "I ain't a virgin any more." Paw dropped his face in his hands and cried bitterly. "After all the sacrifices Maw an' me made for your education," he wailed, "you still say 'ain't.'"

As Good as His Word

80. When the first Ford cars came into this area, a salesman drove a car up to Mr. Sullivan's store and tried to sell it to him. Mr. Sullivan wasn't really interested in buying a car. Mr. Sullivan said that if the car could go up the steep hill next to the store building that he would buy the car.

The salesman laughed and said that the car could go up the hill backwards! The salesman got in the car and drove it up the hill backwards and Mr. Sullivan bought the car.

It was only later that he found out that the car wouldn't go up the hill forwards for anything.

For Certain

81. Two men were driving along a back road somewhere northwest of Calamine. They were stopped by a deputy sheriff for speeding. The deputy got out of his car and walked over to them and told them they were speeding.

The man that was driving the car told the deputy, "I'm going to walk over to your car, drop a twenty-dollar bill in the back seat, come back to my car, and drive away." He got out of his car, went over to the policeman's car, dropped a bill in the back seat, came back to his car and drove away.

After the two went down the road a ways he suddenly speeded up the car. His friend asked him why he was driving so fast. He said, "When he finds that one-dollar bill in his back seat he's going to come after us."

Good Enough for his Gal

82. This country boy took his girl to the Dairy Queen one night, and when they ordered she said she said she wanted a banana split. The country boy said, "Go ahead and give her the whole thing. I can afford it."

Once Too Many

83. One day there was a guy that was driving a truck, and he stopped in a truck stop. When he asked the lady behind the counter for some coffee there was a big jet flew over. When he heard it he told her to make it to go because he had to catch that plane, because it had already passed him once that day.

Stocky Kept Eating

84. My sister stayed with me when I had the store and she baked doughnuts and brought them over there. And she said, "Now, Stocky, you can have one of these doughnuts but you can't eat the hole."

And we watched him, he was eating all around that. Finally, he looked up at Marie and said, "How in hell can I keep from eating this hole?"

Cured Him for Good

85. This boy was always smoking, you know. I used to smoke and he was always bumming me for a smoke. I was coming up the road and I had my can nearly empty and I had another new one and I seen a little old snake going across the road so I just caught that little old snake and put it in that can. I went on up there and he said, "If you ain't got no Prince Albert I'll take Velvet." He said, "I'd take a ready-roll if you had it."

I said, "No, here's some in this can."

He said, "Let me have it." He opened it up and run his finger down in there and that snake run out of there. He throwed that down and I never heard such a jabbering.

I said, "Here, you want some of this?"

He said, "No, no."He never would bum from me no more.

He Thought He Oughta Tell

86. This here worker went up to this guy's house and he asked him if he had a drink. He said, "There's a spring out there in the back. There's a gourd hanging up there on a bush that you can use for a dipper."

He started out through there and he met this old turtle coming up. Then he ran back to the house and said, "Hey, mister, your spring's running dry. I seen your dipper walking home."

When in Kansas

87. Another old guy around here went to Kansas one time and they used to have tokens for sales tax there. They all eat breakfast and some of these boys he was with had to have some beer, but this old man was religious and he didn't, you know. And he got up there to pay for his meal. He asked that girl how much he owed her. She put it down there and she said, "Do you have a token, mister?"

He said, "No thanks, lady, I don't drink."

Strange Fruit

88. Back when Grandpa was a little boy they lived in the country and they'd never seen a banana before. They got to town and some of his friends got a job herding cattle. They got 'em up on this train and they seen this guy selling fruit. They said, "Let's try one of these funny-shaped fruit."

So they bought one and they didn't know how to get it open. They watched a man up front and then finally got it open and nobody would take the first bite. They said, "Well, since Grandpa's the oldest he'll take the first bite."

They was coming up on this tunnel where it got pitch black. Grandpa was just about to put his teeth into it and when he did they went in that tunnel. Grandpa said, "Lordy boys, don't take a bite out of her. It'll make you blind as a bat."

She Had Two

89. A well-developed young lady had a slight cold. As a precaution, upon going to a dinner party, she took along two handkerchiefs, placing the extra one in the bosom of her dress. As dinner progressed she found she needed her spare handkerchief, but feeling about her dress bosom she couldn't find it. She then began to search intently, from right to left, until suddenly she realized every eye at the table was on her. Reddening, she smiled and murmured, "I know I had two when I left home."

School Folks Still Searching

90. Little Sammy approached Papa in the evening with his schoolbooks. "Say, Pop," he asked, "will you help me with my 'rithmetic problems?"

"What are they about, son?" asked his father.

"Teacher says we gotta find the least common denominator," Sammy said.

"Good gosh!" his father yelled in disgust. "Ain't they found that yet? They was a-lookin' fer it when I was a boy."

One-Upmanship of Daddies

91. Two little kids one time were sitting out on the curb and they were bragging about their daddies. One of them said, "My father is a trustee at Penn State."

The second little boy said, "That ain't nothing. My father's a trusty in the State Pen."

A Little Gift, a Big Job

92. There was a country boy one time that wanted to take his girlfriend a present. He went into town to the drugstore to find one. Now he knew that good things come in small packages, so when he saw a box of Ex-Lax he thought this would be the ideal present. He wrapped it up and went to see his girl that night. The girl knew what it was, but didn't want to hurt his feelings, so while they were sitting on the front porch swing she pretended to eat it but was dropping it on the floor beside her. They didn't know that her old cat was on the porch eating the Ex-Lax as she was dropping it on the floor. After the whole package was gone, the couple moved on to sit in the front yard. In a little while they hear the old cat yowl and start running around the yard. The old cat then ran in the house to the back room where her kittens were and started dragging them into the back yard. After the cat had retrieved her kittens from the back room, things settled down. The couple got curious and went around to the back yard to see what she was doing. When they got there, they found that the old cat had two kittens digging holes and one covering.

Cheap Food

93. Two old mountaineers were talking about how they were feeding their families. The first said his family ate lots of oatmeal—it was cheap and filling. The second said his family didn't like oatmeal. The first said, "Oh, we think it's pretty good with lots of sugar and cream." Second: "Well, hell! Sugar and cream—I guess so!"

A Revelation

94. Back during the Depression, the Agricultural Department started a program of buying up and slaughtering nonproductive farm animals. On a certain day, usually Saturdays, the government agent would come to town and the farmers would bring their old cows, hogs, and sheep and have them bought. The government would take them, shoot them, and rend them down.

Many of the agents the government hired to go to the various towns were recent graduates from agriculture school. As a consequence the agents were pretty green. One day an old farmer brought in an old billygoat to be sold. The agent didn't know what to do because he'd never seen a billygoat before. He wired his boss in Washington, D.C.: "Tall, skinny, long, white whiskers; ragged behind; and has a terrible temper—What should I do with this animal?" The reply from his boss in Washington read as follows: "For God's sake don't shoot, that's the farmer."

He Had It Sized Up

95. At the beginning of World War II I got a job with Douglas Air Craft in Tulsa building bombers. The assembly line in Tulsa was in a huge building. It was five thousand feet long and three hundred feet wide. One day they hired an old cowboy from Claremore, Oklahoma, to build airplanes. When he arrived to start his job a personnel guard had to escort him from one end of the building to the other. The guard noticed that the old cowboy seemed rather awed by the size of the building. He finally asked him what he thought of the building. The old cowboy replied, "It sure would hold a hell of a lot of hay."

Getting the Right Question

96. A man went into a psychiatrist's office and they weren't acquainted, but the psychiatrist pretty soon wanted to know what the business was—what he had come for. And he told the psychiatrist, "Now, Doc, I'm bothered. That's what brought me here, I'm bothered!"

"Well now, my good man, lots of people in this old world are bothered nowadays. You'll have to give me some particulars—something definite to start working on your case. Isn't there something definite? Aren't there some particulars you can give?"

"Well, yes, Doc, there are some particulars, and here's—here's what it is, Doc. I came home from work the other night. I found my wife in another man's arms. Just right away he had me talked into going out and getting a cup of coffee. And Doc, the very same thing happened each night the next five nights."

"Oh, well, here here, my good fellow, you've made a mistake coming to me. It's not a doctor you want to see—it's a lawyer."

"Oh, no, Doc, I don't want a lawyer. I want a doctor all right. Now here, here, here's my question. You suppose it could be I'm drinking just a little too much coffee?"

Like No Chicken She'd Ever Seen

97. This story is about the little city girl that went to visit her grandmother out on her farm and grandmother had a lot of chickens and animals and things around the place and she had a couple of peacocks and one day the little girl went out to look at the chickens and it was the first time she had ever seen a peacock so when she saw it, it kindly startled her and she turned around and come running into the house hollering, "Grandma, Grandma, come quick—one of your chickens has bloomed."

A Helpful Suggestion

98. One day a city-slicker was walking down a country road and passed a farmer wrestling with one of his pigs out in a field. He stood and watched this for several minutes and as the farmer finally conquered the animal and came walking by, curiosity got the best of the city-slicker and he asked what the farmer was doing. The farmer replied that he was taking the hog down to the creek for a drink of water. The city-slicker then said, "Wouldn't it save time to bring the water up from the creek to the hogs?" The farmer answered, "Now what in the hell does time mean to hogs?"

The Perils of Conversation

99. This story comes from Bee Branch, Arkansas. It was there people gathered out in front of stores as they did in many rural sections of Arkansas to swap the time of day, fight the wars if one was going on, talk politics in general.

One fellow was always present when these talks were going on, these conversations. This fellow never said anything, he sat with his mouth wide open just looking and listening but never was he heard to speak. However, one day my father said this fellow spoke. He was listening intently as the conversation was becoming more heated and interesting and a tumble bug came by and flew into his wide open mouth and he said, "Who put, put, put, darn fool—hain't you got no eyes?"

How the Preacher Helped Out

100. Once there was a boy and his mother sent him after some soap, starch, and indigo. He said he told her he'd forget it before he got to town. She told him to go along saying soap, starch, and indigo. So he went along saying "Soap, starch, and indigo." He stumped his toe and fell down and forgot what he was going after so he got up and went around and around saying, "Here I fell and there I lost it, here I fell and there I lost it."

A preacher came along and asked him what was the matter and he would just say "Here I fell and there I lost it."

He said, "You little soap-headed fool."

He said, "Yes, that's it, soap, starch, and indigo, hellfire here I go."

Generous, But—

101. Fred told me the story of one old hillman who had been offered a lease on his land because they thought there was oil on it. They told the hillman they would give him every eighth barrel they took out, but the hillman had to turn down the offer because he didn't have no barrels to put the oil in.

Homestead

102. This old man went to homestead forty acres of land. Well, he went to the courthouse and got in there and, of course, they had to have the information about where it was at. This guy said to him, he said, "Well, sir, what township and section is that land in?"

The old man he looked at him and said, "They ain't no township and section to it." He said, "The range is fine. They's peavines and beggar lice waist-deep around the door."

They Told

103. One time there was two little boys talking. One said, "I have a brother who has a broken leg."

The other one said, "That's nothing. I have a sister who has a cedar chest."

All the Facts

104. One time there was a passenger in a plane setting relaxed at the window, drinking, looking out at the spectacle of the heavens. Suddenly a parachutist appeared and drifted by. As he went by he hollered, "Going to join me?"

This man said, "No, thank you very much. I'm happy just where I am."

The parachutist said, "Just as you like it. I'm the pilot."

Just a Little

105. A guy was in a hospital recuperating from an operation. Said he was hungry but all he got at mealtime was a teaspoon of custard. He said, "Is that all I get?"

The nurse said, "That's all for a while."

He swallowed it real quick and grumbled. The nurse took the dish away. In a few minutes this man called her back. He told her, "Nurse, would you mind bringing a postage stamp? I want to do a little reading."

A Lesson

106. Deciding that his son needed a education and to learn some culture, a mountaineer sent him to live with a relative that was an English professor. Some months later the father decided he would check on him and see how his son was doing. So he phoned the professor and said, "How's my son doing?"

The professor said, "That boy's doing fine. The fact is I'd say he's about the smartest dumb durn critter I ever seed in all my natural-born days."

There's One in Every Crowd

107. The politician was campaigning through the South and stopped at one cabin. "My, you have a fine family—eighteen boys!" he told the man in the cabin. "All good Democrats, I suppose?"

"Well," the man said, "I tried to bring 'em up right, and they're all good Christians, and all but Sam is Democrats—that ornery cuss, he got to readin'."

The Cat Woman

108. Mr. Starr tells me that one time there used to be a cat woman who used to live by them and she had many cats. He said she used to have several holes cut in the bottom of the back door and when he asked her what she had so many for, she said, "When I say 'scat,' I mean 'scat.'"

One day when the cat woman was walking by Fred's house they got into a discussion about cats. She said she had heard where some company in Chicago was giving fifty cents apiece for cat hides, so she thought she would get a lot of cats and let them eat the rats, which she had plenty of, and then when she skinned the cats she would feed the remains to the rats, this way there would be no expense. Next they got into an argument about whether a cat had nine lives or not. Fred argued that they didn't, but he couldn't convince the cat woman. After she had left Fred took his cat, which somebody had so graciously dropped off at his house, and knocked it in the head, then buried it. The next time the cat woman came by his house he took her over and showed her the dead cat and asked her why it was not still alive if they had nine lives. To this the cat woman answered, "Shame on you, Fred, for killing that poor little cat! Besides, you haven't proved a thing. How do you know that the cat hasn't already lived eight other lives?"

Those Mosquitoes Are Prepared

109. One time these two Irishmen lived up north. They came down to Arkansas. They never was out too much. They went down Black River bottom, spring of the year, fishin'. Lightnin' bugs just begin to come out. And they had their wagons and teams and got down there a half-hour before sundown, the mosquitoes got so bad they like to eat 'em up, now, they just like to eat 'em up. And they didn't know how in the world they'd git away from them mosquitoes. They decided they'd take the wagon bed off, turn it bottom side up, and git under there. About an hour or two later they wasn't no mosquitoes, and one of 'em decided they need to look out and see what happened. They looked out, one of 'em held the wagon bed up, the other stuck his head out from under there, and he said, "Say, we just as well get out from under this wagon bed—them mosquitoes got their lanterns lit a-lookin' for us!" It was lightnin' bugs: they thought they had their lanterns lit a-huntin' 'em!

The Scots and the Plane Ride

110. Did you hear the story about the Scots and the plane ride? A few years after World War I there were a number of light planes considered of no use to the army any longer. They were distributed around over the country. Folks that wanted to learn flying could do so for a very small price. And they were used to carrying passengers to learn flying and to carry passengers.

There was an old Scotsman and his wife present watching and they revealed that they would like to take a flight—they'd like to fly. The price was ten dollars a passenger, I believe. They wanted to fly but didn't like the idea of paying so much. In fact, I believe the old Scotsman finally said he didn't have but ten dollars. Well, the man flying the plane didn't care about bargaining with 'em at any special price until way up into the day. Kindly caught up with business and having some idle time and he took to talking to 'em to see what he could do with them. They didn't want to pay over ten dollars for both of them to ride.

"Well, my regular price is ten dollars a passenger."

"Nope," the Scotchwoman said. She was an awful talker. She's just a-jabbering and gabbing and talking all over the fellow all the time. And this young airplane fellow he'd been giving attention to her talking so much.

He finally said, "I'll tell you what I'll do. I'll make you a proposition. I'll take you up and if you go through the whole trip that I give you in the air, if you go the whole route without either one of you saying a word, don't either say a word from the time you leave the ground till the time you get back on the ground—the trip won't cost you a penny, won't cost you a thing! But if you talk, why, I'll have to have my pay."

The old Scotch couple agreed to it. He loaded them in and went up and up and directly he began to go through all the antics, you know—barrel rolling, the loop-de-loop, and everything. He thought that would bring something out. There'd be some squawking, some talking, but not a word. He just gave it everything in the book, you know. And finally, he decided to land. He thought he'd given them enough. He landed and then he looked back over his shoulder and asked, "Well, how—how in the world did you manage not to talk any, not to say a word when I was going through all of those loop-de-loops and barrel rolls? Everything I could think of. How in the world did you keep from saying something?"

"Well," the old man said, "I was pretty scared there for a

while, but after the old woman fell out, I had nothing more to worry about. I knew I had it made!"

Strange Way of Talking

111. Back when I used to live in Greenland we had some Pennsylvania Dutch neighbors who had a strange way of talking. The husband was named Alf, the two kids named Francis and Marvin, and the dog named Pood. One evening I went up to their house and asked the mother where everyone was. The reply went like this: "Alf is out at the barn milking the cow and Marvin, and Francis is out in the backyard crawling under the fence and Pood."

Studyin'

112. There was three Polacks hunting one day when they came onto some tracks. The first one said that they were bear tracks, and the second one said that he was wrong, because they were moose tracks. Then the third one said that they were both wrong, but he didn't know what kind they were. And while they stood there a train ran over them.

Wise

While jokes about fools are common in Ozark folklore, they are scarcely more popular than those about wise or clever persons. This situation is not unique to the Ozarks; the folktale scholar Stith Thompson notes that "in one way or another a large proportion of the most popular anecdotes and jests are concerned with cleverness" (*The Folktale*, pp. 188–89). Moreover, for centuries they have been an important part of the folk narrative tradition of many countries throughout the world, but they have not been kept alive solely by oral tradition. During the Renaissance large numbers of such stories appeared in jestbooks and collections of *exempla*, often being borrowed from Oriental literary works. So for at least five centuries jokes about wise or clever persons have figured prominently in folk and popular culture, and there is no indication of a decline in their appeal. If anything, they are more popular now than ever before.

Some of the following selections are set during the Civil War, the late nineteenth century, or the Great Depression, but most are tied to no specific time period, making them much more adaptable than time-bound yarns. Wisdom, as revealed in these stories, is manifested in a variety of ways. Sometimes it is demonstrated by an act of deception, such as in the story about Captain George Rutherford. At other times the display of cleverness is in verbal retorts or puns. On still other occasions it is revealed by the pains the protagonist takes to remain tactful. Sometimes there is an innocence connected with wit, particularly when the wise one is a child, as in text 117. Often the distinction between the clever man and the fool is not sharply drawn and characters, such as the farmer in text 120, might be construed by some as a fool. Most, however, would likely find him witty, albeit tactless.

Short on Weapons, Long on Brains

113. At one time, during the Yankee advance from the south side of the White River, the Yankees camped on the bank of the river at one of its crossings. Captain George was on the opposite bank. He commanded a group of volunteers from Batesville and surrounding territory. The Rebs were short of men, weapons, and ammunition. Late in the evening, in face of what was sure to be a massacre the next morning just through superior numbers, Captain George got an idea how to turn back the Yankees and save his own men from the fight which was sure to come. As it grew dark, he started his men cutting logs. He had them line the logs up along the riverbank to look like cannons. When dawn came, the Yankees saw the line of cannons on the opposite bank and decided to retreat. Captain George had tricked the Yankees.

Barking

114. Here's one about that great evangelist, Sam Jones, and that popular political leader from Tennessee, Bob Taylor. Bob Taylor became governor of the state of Tennessee and possibly senator too. I know he was governor. He was quite an orator, political orator, and Sam Jones was a great theological speaker, church worker, you know. They were having a big debate. I don't know the subject of the debate. And Bob Taylor spoke first and it looked like when Bob Taylor finished up his major address that he had Sam Jones badly worsted. Oh, how the crowd did roar with applause. But it didn't seem to bother the old preacher very much. Sam got up, made a few remarks: "You know, my friend here, Bob, reminds me of a little dog I used to have down in Atlanta, Georgia. Till one day the little dog was always going out and barking at streetcars when they passed by. Ran out and as usual barked at the car and he went just a little too far this time and the car sucked him under. Ran over him and of course, I thought my little dog was gone. But after the car went on and the dust cleared out, my little dog trotted out. The only difference in him was that it just made a little 'bobtailer' out of him. Just made a little 'bobtailer' out of him."

He's For Sure

115. A Republican canvasser was trying to persuade a voter to support his party. "I'm sorry," the voter said, "but my father was a Democrat and his father before him, so I won't vote anything but the Democratic ticket."

"That's a poor argument," said the canvasser. "Suppose your father and grandfather had been horse thieves— would that make you a horse thief?"

"No," the voter replied, "that would make me a Republican."

The Right Reply

116. A gentleman who made a point of politeness under all circumstances one day made the remark that he had never seen an ugly woman. A nearby woman with a very flat nose overheard him and put him to the test. "Look at me, sir, and admit that I am ugly," she said. "No, madam," he said, "like all of your sex you are an angel fallen from heaven, and it is not your fault that you landed on your nose."

Moving to St. Louis

117. The little girl was moving with her family from a small town in Illinois to St. Louis. Saying her prayers the last night in her old house, she ended with "God bless Mommy, Daddy, Freddie, and Susy, and this is goodbye, God, we're moving to St. Louis."

Known in the End

118. A man was paying a visit to his native village after having been away for many years, and he paid a call at his boyhood school. The old schoolmaster failed to recognize his former pupil, saying "You seem to know me quite well, but I don't remember ever having seen your face before." The former pupil replied, "That's not to be wondered at, for you were much better acquainted with my other end."

Revelation

119. A foreigner who had become quite friendly with a Kentucky colonel living in New York decided to spend the winter in the South. After a week there he wrote his friend a letter in which he declared: "You never told me the South was like this. Why, man, it's God's country!" The Colonel wired back: "Of course it is. You didn't think God was a damned Yankee, did you?"

In Business for Himself

120. There was a farmer in the Depression who got very discouraged by the fact that it always seemed to cost more to grow things than you made on them. So he decided to go into business for himself—he decided to sell axe handles. He went into the hardware store and bought one dozen and went out and peddled them. He came back for another dozen axe handles and went out and peddled them. When he showed up for the third dozen the hardware store owner asked what he was doing with them. The man replied that he was out peddling them. The dealer asked how much he was getting for them. He replied, "Twenty-five cents apiece." The hardware man said, "You can't make a profit that way. You pay me thirty cents; you're losing a nickel on each one." The man replied, "But it sure beats the hell out of farming."

The Hog Started It All

121. A man over in the Newport, Arkansas, area lost a hog on the Iron Mountain Railroad track down below Newport a little ways about forty-odd years ago. He decided to send in a written claim before the time for making the claims expired. He wrote in verse.

To the Claim Agent for the Railroad

My razorback strolled down your track
Just a month ago today,
Your twenty-nine came down the line
And snuffed his life away.

You can't blame me—the hog, you see,
Slipped through the gate,
So kindly pen a check for ten,
The debt to liquidate.

The claim agent mulled over that letter when he received it. He thought, "Well, why not reply to him in kind?" So he got his pencil and paper and directly he had the reply in verse.

To the Man with the Razorback

Our twenty-nine came down the line
And killed your hog, we know,
But razorbacks on railroad tracks
Quite often meet with woe.

Therefore, my friend, we cannot pen
The check for which you pine,
Just bury the dead and place o'er his head
"Here Lies a Foolish Swine."

She Meant To Hitch a Ride

122. A girl hitchhiker stood beside the road for some time thumbing every car that passed. Finally one pulled up, the driver opened the door and said, "What's the matter, you want to ride?" The girl replied, "Certainly I want to ride—what do you think I was doing with my thumb, standing there goosing a ghost?"

Explanation Required

123. They say that George Washington did not drink. Well, maybe not, but any fisherman knows that there is bound to be something wrong with a man who stands up in the front end of a rowboat on a dark night.

The Widow Jones

124. One time there was a farmer went up to a farmhouse and knocked on the door. A lady come and the farmer said, "Are you the Widow Jones?"

The lady said, "Well, my name's Jones, but I'm no widow."

This farmer said, "Yeah, well, wait till you see what they're bringing up out of the holler."

A Job Well Done

125. We people down here in the hills aren't accustomed to using modern means of transportation. We ride in log wagons and hacks and whatnot. And it came time when I was going to be leaving here, and I had never ridden a train. So I got on the train, and was riding along. The porter come through, and he was brushing the people down, and polishing their shoes. And I got to thinking about it, and I wondered how much of a tip I was gonna give that fella.

So when he came by I said, "Say, Sam, what's the average tip you git?"

"Mmmhhhh, I don't know—'bout a dollar."

"'Bout a dollar, huh?"

"Yes, about a dollar."

Well, went on, and came to the place where I was gonna git off, and he came by, and he brushed me down, took my luggage out, set it down with the other. And I went out and picked up my bag. I put a dollar in his hand, and turned to go away.

He says, "Hey, boss, you know you're the first one that come up to the average."

He Would Finish the Job

126. Years ago when the town of Strawberry was called Cathytown this area was a great deal like the Old West. One day a young man came into the barber shop wearing a six-gun. He sat down in the barber chair and told the barber to give him a shave. The young man looked like a bandit or some sort of troublemaker. He very plainly told the barber that if he so much as nicked him while he was giving him his shave that he would kill him.

The barber didn't say anything, he just went ahead and shaved him. He shaved him without nicking him and it was a good clean shave.

When he finished shaving him, the young man paid the barber for the shave and told him that if he had nicked him he would have shot him, just like that. The barber smiled and said, "If I had nicked you, I would have just gone ahead and slit your throat."

False Teeth

127. There were these two men fishing on a boat one day. One of the men had false teeth which always clanked together. The man's false teeth clanked so much, he pulled them out, threw the upper teeth down the river, threw the lower teeth up the river, and said, "Now let's see you dang things get together."

Working in Kansas

128. Now this actually happened, when I was hoboing. I stopped off in Kansas and was working. And Arkansas has always had the backwoods name of the forty-eight states. It has. I know that. And everywhere I went they made fun of me and laughed at me about Arkansas. And about this and about that. There's a little town in Kansas and I got off and got a job there. And I worked a week or two there. And the guy found out I was from Arkansas, and he went to asking me questions about Arkansas and this and that. And finally, he kinda slurred it in a way, you know. And finally, he said, "Well, what do you do with the fools down in Arkansas?"

"Well," I said, "I don't know what they doing now, I've been gone a little over a year. But," I said, "last account we set 'em up in Kansas to teach school." And that, now that's the way I'd answer them people because I've always been witty. Any time you got anything on me I'd come back.

The Editor's Regrets

129. The country editor was confronted by a fierce-looking man who was very angry. "That report of my death in your paper was a lie, sir, and I'll horsewhip you in public if you don't apologize in your next issue," he shouted. When the next edition appeared it contained the following item: "We regret very much that the notice of Colonel Burly's death that appeared in our last issue was not true."

Well Practiced

130. Soon after a convict arrived at prison, he was getting acquainted with his fellow convicts. He was sitting around talking with them and noticed that one prisoner would say "35" and everybody there but him would laugh. Next the same convict said "27" and everybody laughed. This continued through several numbers and then the discussion broke up. The new convict went up to the storyteller and asked him what everyone was laughing at the numbers for. The storyteller replied, "Well, we've told the same old stories so long that we have numbered them instead of going to the trouble of telling the whole story."

The next time a group of convicts got together the newcomer said "35," and nobody laughed. Next he said "27," and once again nobody laughed—so he shut up. After the discussion broke up, he asked another convict why nobody laughed at his numbers. The other convict replied, "I guess you just aren't a natural-born storyteller."

Who's Ignorant Here?

131. Two city fellows were lost in the woods one day and they came upon an old hillbilly and asked him where they were, but the hillbilly said, "I don't know." Then they asked him how to get back to town, but the hillbilly said, "I don't know." Everything they asked the hillbilly he would always say he didn't know. Finally, one of the city boys said, "Say, mister, you just don't know anything, do you?" And the old hillbilly answered, "Maybe not, but I ain't lost."

Those Texans Reminded Me . . .

132. One day, when Mr. Starr was out in his yard, an old hillman, who had been having trouble with new neighbors from Texas, stopped to remark that all this country really needed was some good people to move in and plenty of water. "Come to think of it," Mr. Starr told him, "that's about all hell needs."

No Good Time To Move

133. Since the Starrs were moving around from one place to the other so often, they had many warnings about what and when to move, such things as "Never move a cat or a broom." They were also warned not to move on Friday, and to wait until the right time of the moon. No two seemed to agree on whether the book of rules said move in the dark or light of the moon, so they moved on Monday and let the moon do its damnedest.

A Quick Look

134. One of the favorite places to loaf was around the blacksmith shop. One day the handyman was beating out a horseshoe, he would throw the hot shoe over on the ground to cool. About the time he threw one on the ground another loafer came up, saw the shoe, picked it up, and naturally dropped it quickly.

One of the loafers asked the question, "Hot, wasn't it?"

"No," was the reply. "It just don't take me long to look at a horseshoe."

Negotiating

135. There is a man by the name of West who lives south of Calamine. It was a well-known fact that West would steal anything that wasn't tied down. I heard that once West and his sons caught a snake, cooked it, and ate it.

One day Mr. Sullivan was sweeping off his front porch when he saw West coming down the hill. He knew that West was planning on buying a pair of shoes that he had been looking at. Mr. Sullivan went inside and changed the price of the shoes from two dollars to four dollars. West came in the store and offered him a dollar for the shoes. Sullivan said he wanted three dollars and wouldn't take any less. West offered him a dollar and a quarter. Mr. Sullivan got angry and jumped the price back to four dollars. West gave in and paid him three for the shoes. Roscoe threw in a pair of socks.

At Least They're Scarce Somewhere

136. I left home when I was a kid. And I began to travel; and I begin to go here, and I begin to go there, and in different states. That's when I first left home, when I was fifteen years old. And I was in Kansas, working, and boy I taken a beating. Arkansas at that time was a backwoods place in the forty-eight states; and ever'body razzed ever-'body 'bout being from Arkansas. And man, they poured it on me.

And one day a guy asked me, he said, "You from Arkansas?"

I said, "Yeah, I'm from Arkansas."

He said, "Do you have any fools back there?"

I said, "Yeah, yeah, we got quite a few of 'em. But," I said, "They's one thing I found out about it: they don't go in droves like they do up here."

The Math Problem

137. The teacher was giving the class a little problem in arithmetic. And she said, "If I cut a beef steak in half and then cut the halves in two what do I get?"

One little boy hollered, "Quarters."

The teacher said, "That's good. Now if I cut the quarters in half what do I get?"

The little boy hollered, "Eighths."

The teacher said, "Good. Now if I cut the eighths in half what do I get?"

"Sixteenths."

"If I cut the sixteenths in half what do I get?"

"Thirty-seconds."

"If I cut the thirty-seconds in half what do I get?"

"Hamburger."

Fast on His Feet

138. One time there was a guy went up to a cigar counter and said, "How much are these cigars?"

The clerk said, "They're two for a quarter."

The man said, "I'll take one."

The clerk said, "That'll be fifteen cents."

Well, there was another fellow standing by the side a-listening. So, when this first man had left he told the clerk, "Here's a dime, give me the second one."

Don't Believe a Word I Say

139. An old boy back over here had been hunting and he was a-walking down the road. He had his old shotgun and he had his old hound. He was walking down the road and the game warden came along and picked him up. He didn't know him and he didn't know the game warden, see. He asked him if he wanted a ride and he said, "Yeah." So he just throwed his old hound up in the back of the pickup and got in with the game warden.

Going down the road he told the game warden about all the hunting he had done that day. Directly the game warden asked him his name and he told him. So he asked the game warden and he told him. They went on down the road a little bit. Directly he said to this fellow, "You didn't know I was the game warden of this county, did you?"

He said, "No, I thought you said you were So-and-so."

He said, "No, I'm the game warden from over here at Mountain Home."

This old boy said, "Well, you don't know who you're a-talking to either, do you?"

He said, "Well, you told me So-and-so was your name."

He said, "You're talking to the biggest damn liar in this country." He said, "That dog back there won't run a thing in the world."

A Railroad Dog

140. This man was on a train and he seen a little bitty dog there. And he was about six inches tall. And this guy said, "I have never seen a dog like that." He said, "What kind of a dog is that?"

"Well," he said, "that's a railroad dog."

"Well," he said, "that dog ain't big enough for anything." He said, "He's not even big enough to eat a biscuit." He said, "That dog is too little for anything." He said, "That's the shortest-legged dog that I ever seen."

This guy said, "Yeah, mister, his legs's short but there's one thing about it: they all four reach the ground."

Modified

141. I heard one about this guy, he had a little bitty bandy-legged feist and he advertised him for a coon dog. This guy went and answered the ad. He said, "I come here to see that coon dog."

He said, "All right, we'll go out here." So went out there. There laid that little old bandy-legged feist out there. And he said, "There he is right there."

"Aw, that's a coon dog?"

"Yeah," he said, "that's a coon dog."

"Oh, no, feller," he said, "I know better than that." He said, "A coon dog is a great big hound that stands like that." He said, "I know that ain't."

"Yeah," he said, "That's a coon dog."

"No," he said, "Feller, you ain't putting that dog off on me as a coon dog."

And this guy said, "Well, feller, you don't understand." He said, "He was a big coon dog but," said, "now we've got him screwed down to a rabbit dog now."

Look Out for Some Nut with a Shotgun

142. Once old man Jones was driving home from work when he saw a deer with his horns hung in a apple tree on his farm. Jones, who loved deer meat, drove his truck to the house and loaded his old double-barreled shotgun and walked back to the tree to get him some winter meat. As he walked up to the deer it started jumping, trying to get free from the tree, but Jones was fast and shot him dead. He then went and cut the horns out of the tree and started back to the house with his deer. He got a quarter-mile or so away when he saw his friend the game warden coming at a run trying to catch up with him. Well, old man Jones didn't want to give up his deer and get a fine too, so he started to try to go faster with the deer, but it was no use, 'cause the deer was too big. Well, Jones was a mean bastard, and he just raised his gun up and shot it about four feet above the game warden's head. The warden turned around and hauled ass in the other direction after that and Jones had him some real good meat.

Jones went to town a few weeks later to get a haircut and he was in the barber's chair when the game warden came in and sat down and started to read magazines. Jones was scared at first that the warden had recognized him, but he was really relieved when the warden warned him about some crazy deer hunter on his farm who had took a few shots at him.

He Made a Sale

143. There is the story of the man who came down to the Ozarks to buy some land. When he reached the Ozarks he acquired the services of a local real estate agent. When the agent discovered that the man was from Chicago, he figured this would be a good time to get rid of some of the old bottomland. Upon reaching the bottomland, the Chicago man noticed a white line along the top of the trees where the creek had been. However, he did not know this is what caused the line and he asked the agent what exactly did cause this mark. The agent then told him that the line was made by razorbacks that had come along and rubbed their backs up against the tree. The Chicago man didn't say much after that and left town that same day. The agent called him up a few days later and asked him if he had decided to buy the land or not, and the Chicago man answered, "Well, I'll tell you, I don't want to buy the land but I would sure be interested in a truckload of those hogs."

Fertilizer Rocks

144. There is the story of the foreigner who came from France to the Ozarks to buy some land. When he got there he found a real estate agent who took him around to different farms trying to sell him some of the land that he couldn't get rid of. Upon reaching one farm the foreigner noticed a bunch of rocks all over the fields and asked the agent what they were. The agent then answered, "Why, that is good fertilizer." Later on they approached another farm and the foreigner noticed a farmer out in the fields hauling off a wagon load of these rocks and said to the agent, "If those are so valuable as fertilizer, why is he hauling them off?" Then the agent answered, "Well, he is stealing them for his own farm."

A Big Trade

145. Years and years ago rough land was almost worthless. One day a foreigner came riding into an Ozark town on a horse. He rode up to the local real estate agent and said he had noticed a forty-acre farm close by that he wanted to trade his horse for, so the agent gave him a deed for the land and took the horse. When the foreigner went to the land office to register this deed he noticed that the real estate agent had slipped in an extra forty acres of the same type of land.

She's Willing

146. Mr. Starr said one day they decided to buy a cow and went over to their neighbor's house to buy the one they had for sale. After looking over the cow, they asked the owner how much milk the cow would give. The owner then remarked, "Well, I really couldn't say, but I'll tell you this: she is a very nice and friendly cow and will be glad to give you as much milk as she can."

Religion

Religion as viewed in Ozark jokelore is a far different matter from that phenomenon discussed by proselytizing churchmen. It is a subject that at best is not taken seriously by most of the people in the narratives, and at worst concerns mainly hypocrites who don't even try to practice what they preach. In the world of the jokes ministers are unethical, even to the point of having no qualms about plagiarizing a sermon. They are frequently depicted as lustful, deceitful, having a great craving for strong drink, quick to use profanity, selfish, and, perhaps worst of all, both foolish and boring. Some of these tales are of ancient vintage, originally surfacing in Europe as anecdotes about priests; here the priests have usually been replaced by Methodist ministers, Baptist preachers, or some members of the Protestant fundamentalist clergy.

But Ozark joketellers have not completely dispensed with Catholics, although nuns figure more frequently than priests in their yarns. Some people may be surprised by the inclusion of jokes about Roman Catholics in these pages, perhaps assuming that they would be rare in the Ozarks and jokes about them would be equally difficult to find. Yet while the Ozarks can hardly be considered a hotbed of Catholicism, it has been hospitable to that denomination. Indeed, most of the first whites who moved into the Ozarks in the eighteenth century were Catholics, and today, two centuries later, there are several communities in the region that are wholly Catholic. Yet, despite their long history in the Ozarks, the Roman clergy don't receive any better treatment from area joketellers than their Protestant counterparts. Priests are presented as greedy and nuns are said to have an inordinate interest in sex.

Do Ozarkers who tell jokes really find all clergymen so undesirable? Some perhaps do, but it seems unlikely that most of those who keep these narratives alive regard men of the cloth in such light. Most of the jokes do not seem meanspirited; instead they merely offer an acceptable means of making fun of a group that otherwise the narrators can rarely openly criticize. Possibly these jokes are the means by which Ozarkers imply that even so serious a matter as religion shouldn't be taken too seriously. As one hillman put it, "There's nothing wrong with telling jokes about preachers and churches. Even Jesus Christ liked to laugh once in a while."

The Lord Works in Mysterious Ways

147. There is an open-air meeting place in Calamine where religious services are held. Years ago the services were multidenominational and often lasted several days. People came from as far away as Lynn to the services.

When the babies fell asleep in the evening, the mothers would take the babies and put them in the wagon and then come back to the meeting. One night after the women had put the babies in the wagons and it was dark, two boys went out to the wagons and switched the babies.

Later that night after everyone got home after the services were over, the parents were able to get a good look at their baby in the lamplight. They discovered that they had someone else's baby.

Wagon wheels rolled all night.

City Religion

148. The old man lived way back in the backwoods. He was a great churchman through the years. He'd grown up in a little backwoods church—just a little old shack of a crude structure, but he was a very loyal church member through the years. He began to take a more active interest and go to the little corner they called "the amen corner." That was the regular place for him for years and when things were going to please him—the preacher said something that went over big with him—he'd come out with an *amen!*

He'd never been to church anywhere except out there in the backwoods—never been to a city until he became quite old. But finally he got an opportunity to go to the city. Looking around over the city, he came along by one of these huge monstrosities, a jet-age, streamlined job they usually call a sanctuary. Finally the old man found what it was and he was curious to know how services were carried on. So he learned when the next services would be and he got around to the church a little before service time. Went in and took a seat way back yonder. He didn't want to be so forward as to try to crowd into "the amen corner." After a while the services were opened and not long afterwards the preacher began his discourse. Then the preacher came out with something that really sounded good. It went over big with the old man and he said, *"Amen."* That stopped the preacher and the members of the audience all around the sanctuary looked about to see if they could tell where the noise had come from. Well, finally the preacher tried it again and pretty soon he made a mistake of coming out with something extra good. The old man exclaimed, "AMEN!" And that really stopped the works. The church official hopped up and hurried back to the row of seats to the old man, bent over him, and said, "What's the matter with you? Are you sick?"

"No, I'm not sick! There's nothing the matter with me. I just love the Lord, that's it. I just love the Lord."

"Well, you can't love Him *here.*"

Willie Was Enlightened

149. The Sunday School teacher had just finished a detailed account of Jonah and the whale. "And now, Willie, can you tell us what lesson this story teaches?" she asked.

"Yes'm," replied Willie, "it teaches that you can't keep a good man down."

She Knew Her Bible

150. The minister was circulating among the various Sunday school classes and he paused to ask one small girl if she came to Sunday school regularly.

"Oh, yes, sir," she answered.

"Then I guess you can tell me some of the things in your Bible," he said.

"I can tell you everything that is in it. There's mom's recipe for ketchup, Sis's snapshots of the boyfriend, one of my baby curls, and the hock ticket for Pop's watch."

Acquitted

151. A minister approached one of the members of his congregation in anger. "I am told that you are saying that I stole the sermon I gave last Sunday," he exclaimed. "I demand an apology."

The church member said with a slight smile, "I suppose I do owe you an apology, sir. I said you'd stolen the sermon, but when I got home," he went on, "I found it still in the book from which I'd thought you'd taken it."

Giving God Some Help

152. The preacher was visiting a farmer, and they was looking over the place. "Well," said the preacher, "you and the Lord have sure raised some fine corn here." When he seen the hogs he said, "With God's help, you have a lot of fine-looking hogs." Finally, they was looking at the garden next to the barn, and the preacher said, "You and God sure have growed a fine garden." The farmer said, "Preacher, you ought to have seen this place when God was running it Hisself."

Methodist Drink

153. A prospector came into a saloon and ordered milk punch. "And make it strong with forty-rod liquor," he said; "And when I say strong I don't mean weak." He then went to the bathroom while his drink was being fixed. Before he came back a man came in wearing a black threadbare coat. He came up to the bartender and timidly said, "Sir, I'm a poor traveling preacher of the Methodist faith. For a week I've traveled across the desert, often suffering for water and sometimes for food. I have no earthly money save one dime. Would you sell me that glass of foamy milk for a dime?"

"Take the milk," said the bartender, "and keep your dime. I ain't so hard up that I got to charge a poor old parson for a glass of milk. Take it and drink it."

The preacher drank awful slow, and he acted like he liked it a lot. When he had drained the glass dry, he wipes his mouth and looks up and says, "Lord, what a cow!"

A Houseful of Preachers

154. One cold winter day a small boy came into the house from his chores to find it full of preachers. Either a quarterly conference or a fifth-Sunday meeting was about to start. The preachers didn't pay any attention to the shivering boy, and they completely encircled the fireplace. Finally, one preacher noticed the boy and asked, "Is it cold outside?" "Yes," said the boy, "cold as hell." Somewhat shocked, the minister replied, "Why, my boy, my Bible tells me that it's hot in hell, not cold." "Oh," said the boy, "it's just like in here. There's so many preachers a feller can't get close to the fire."

An Oath Is an Oath

155. This little boy came home from church and told his mama that the preacher cussed in church. "No, son," said the mama, "I think you're wrong." But the boy insisted that he was right. Finally the mama said, "Okay, son, I'll go to church with you next time, and if the preacher cusses I'll bake you a cherry pie all for yourself." The next Sunday in church the preacher was getting down on sin, and raised his arms and shouted, "By God we live, and by God we will die." The little boy jumped up in back and hollered, "Yeah, and by God I win me a cherry pie."

He Sure Does!

156. One Sunday morning this preacher was preaching, and some of the boys in the church saw that he always looked up at the stovepipe, and said, "I see the Lord, I see the Lord." They took down the stove that week, and put a possum in the stovepipe so the preacher would see it in church.

The next Sunday the preacher got all wound up, and looked up, and said, "I see the Lord, I see the Lord." And just as he turned around he looked back, and said, "You know, by God, I *do* see something."

The Lord's Ways

157. A preacher calls upon a sick man whose crop has washed away and whose cows have all been drowned. "Whom the Lord loveth he chasteneth," quotes the preacher. To which the sick man replies, "Well, I'll be god-damned if he didn't overdo it this time."

Just Checkin'

158. A preacher wanted to find out if a well-known deacon said grace at mealtime. "What does your father say when he sits down to dinner?" he asked the deacon's small son. The boy thought a minute and then replied, "He usually says, 'Goddamn these biscuits; they're heavy as lead.'"

Saved by a Metaphor

159. Two preachers were arguing about the Baptists and Methodists. The Baptist was getting in some good licks. He said, "You can take a piece of white cloth and roll it around and get it dirty, and when you bury it in water and wash it, it will come forth and will glitter all beautiful and white."

"Yes," replied the Methodist, "but you gotta sprinkle it before you iron it or it won't iron worth a damn."

Failed the Corn Test

160. A preacher from some other town come and preached one Sunday in our church. He wanted to be the regular pastor there, but they didn't give him the job. Talking about it later, he said everybody seemed to like his preaching, and he couldn't make out why they wouldn't hire him. "There's just one thing I did," he said. "I had supper with one of the deacons. When the deacon said, 'Preacher, have some more corn,' I passed my cup instead of my plate."

Riddlemania

161. People used to be plumb crazy about riddles. Back in the 1880s, strangers would stop each other right on the street in Mountain View to tell a new riddle. A big old wagon was stuck clear to the hubs just outside town. The teamster was a-whipping all four mules, and cussing as loud as he could. Just then a jackleg preacher come along. "My friend," says he, "do you know the name of Him who died for our sins?" The driver spit out a chaw of tobacco. "I got no time for riddles now," he says. "Can't you see I got this goddamn wagon stuck in the son-of-a-bitching mud?"

"Do As I Say . . ."

162. A little boy was riding his tricycle across the neighbor's yard. One of the wheels fell off the tricycle and the little boy said, "Well, I'll be goddamn!" The neighbor, who was a preacher, heard the boy cuss and ran out and scolded him. "Don't say that, child," said the preacher, "Say, 'Lord, help us.'" The next day the boy was in the yard again and this time two wheels fell off. "Well, I'll be goddamn!" said the boy. The preacher heard him and warned him to say, "Lord, help us." The next day the boy was in the yard when all three wheels fell off. This time the boy says, "Lord, help us." Them wheels just jumped right up off the ground and hopped right back on the tricycle. "Well, I'll be goddamn!" said the preacher.

The Blessing

163. These two men were out hunting when they noticed it was time to attend the revival meeting in a nearby church. Rather than to go home and change, they went directly to the church. They got here before anyone else, and since they just had one old possum, they threw it up in the church rafters so the dogs wouldn't get it during services. During the meeting the preacher was asking God's blessing on the church. "God bless these people," said the preacher. "And God bless this floor," he asked, pointing to the floor. "And God bless these walls," he said, pointing to the walls. As he looked up and pointed to the roof to ask for it to be blessed, he saw the old possum, and he said, "And God . . . damn, what a rat!"

Prayer Meetings and Bear Meetings

164. One day this old preacher was making his rounds. He had to cross a creek on a log. When he was right in the middle of the log a bear stepped up on the end of the log. The scared preacher turned around to go off the other end, but he saw another bear step up on that end. The bears started walking toward the preacher and the preacher started praying, "Lord, I have just one request to make. Help me if you will, but whatever you do, don't help them bears." But the bears kept coming closer. Then he dove in the creek and got away. The preacher went on to church and told the faithful about his experience. When he finished, one of the sisters told him that he should have kept praying. "Prayer, sister," said the preacher, "is all right at prayer meeting, but it ain't worth a damn at bear-meeting."

Faithful at Mealtime

165. The preacher asked the little boy if his family said prayers before meals. "No, we don't have to," said the little boy. "Mom is a good cook."

It's Fair to Ask

166. A boy went out with a girl and he started getting a little fresh with her. She said, "I can't—it's Lent." He said, "When are you going to get it back?"

Looking for the Real Thing

167. In the town of my boyhood the village drunkard one night started his wobbly way home. There was a religious tent meeting going on out in the edge of town and it was necessary that Wyley (this was the drunkard's name) pass the meeting on his way home. When he arrived at this point he was pretty well under the weather so sat down on one of the back benches to kinda get his bearings. The minister was just finishing his sermon and was announcing that all who wanted to go to heaven should stand up. The whole congregation stood up except Wyley. Soon the minister spied him and approaching asked, "My man, do you mean to say that you don't want to go to heaven?" Wyley replied, "Yes, I would like to go to heaven but I don't want to go on an excursion like this. When I go I want to stay."

In His Condition

168. A preacher and a friend were standing on the street visiting when a drunk man came staggering along. He staggered over to a car and got in behind the steering wheel. The preacher said, "My word, do you suppose he is going to try to drive in that condition?" His friend said, "It looks like he is." Sure enough, he zoomed off down the street. The man said to the preacher, "Maybe you ought to follow him. He's likely to get into trouble and need your help." So the preacher got into his car and followed. A little way down the highway the drunk happened to look into his rear-view mirror and noticed the car following him. As he looked in the mirror he saw the preacher's car leave the road and crash into a tree. The drunk stopped and went to see if he could help the preacher. When he got to the wrecked car he said, "Are you hurt?" The preacher answered, "No, I have the Lord riding with me." The drunk said, "Well, you better let him come and ride with me. You'll kill him the way you drive."

Crying in the Wilderness

169. The revival meeting had reached the time for baptism and the elders were standing in the water performing the ceremony on one after the other. One old gent, a recent convert, was brought out and the usual question was asked, whether there was any reason baptism should not be done. One guy in the crowd spoke up, "I don't want to butt in, elder, but one dip ain't a-gonna do that old sinner much good—you'll have to anchor him out in deep water overnight."

The Stand-In

170. A clergyman was suddenly called out of town and he asked his new assistant to conduct services on Sunday. When he returned, he asked his wife how the assistant had done. "Not so well," she reported. "It was the poorest sermon I'd ever heard—nothing to it at all." Meeting his assistant later, the preacher asked him how he'd done. "Very well, sir," he replied. "Since I didn't have time to prepare anything myself, I just used one of your sermons."

Restless

171. The sermon dragged on and on and little Johnny was getting restless. "Say, Mom," he whispered, "if we give him the money now will he let us go?"

Bee Calm

172. The preacher was telling his Sunday school class: "You must strive always to keep calm and never lose your tempers. You should never swear or get angry or excited. And it isn't hard. For example, see that fly on my nose? Well, most wicked men would be excited and swear, but I just say, 'Go away, fly,' and I—good God! It's a bee, damn it to hell!'"

Candidating

173. This was a candidate that was out candidating the country, and he swore it was true.

And he stopped to candidate a man plowing a mule with a double-shovel plow, and a boy about sixteen years of age.

And while he was candidating him he sent him to the house after a can of water. The kid come back without any water; says, "Pa, there's a preacher at the house."

The ole man says, "What kind was he?"

He says, "I didn't find out."

"Why didn't you?"

"Thought I'd better come tell you."

Now they used to treat these preachers there with all the charm in the world—they got the best of everything.

"You get back to the house: if he's a Holy Roller, you git that money outa the top drawer; if he's a Methodist, you run everything that's got feathers on it clear back the other side of the farm; but, if he's an old hard-shelled Primitive Baptist you get on your mammy's lap, sit there till I git there, and don't you dare get off."

The Comparison

174. These two preachers, a rabbi and a priest, they were having a glass of wine, so they got to confiding in each other. The priest asked the rabbi if he ever ate any pork. The rabbi confessed he had tried it one time. Then the rabbi asked the priest if he ever screwed a woman. The priest said that he had one time. The rabbi said, "I bet it was better than the pig I had."

They Surprised the Methodist

175. These three preachers—a Methodist, a priest, and a rabbi—were out fishing one day. The rabbi and the priest would go walking out across the water ever so often to pick up beer at the bank. So the Methodist was amazed and wondered if he could walk on water like that. Next time he offered to go get the beer, but when he stepped out of the boat, he went under. The priest and rabbi began laughing and decided to tell the Methodist where the rocks were they had been stepping on, just under the water.

Even a Peaceful Man

176. One night a Quaker was out milking his cow. It was a cold night and the cow had a tail full of cockleburrs. The cow kept swatting him with her tail. About the tenth time, the old Quaker lost his temper and said, "Old cow, I believe thou knowest my religion will not permit me to curse, revile, or physically abuse thee. But what thou dost not know, old cow, is that I can sell you to a Baptist who can beat the hell out of you."

In Favor of Salvation

177. A fellow called the Salvation Army and said, "Do you save young girls?"

And the Salvation Army said, "We sure do."

And he said, "Well, save me one for tonight. I'll be over."

Ready to Forgive

178. A colored nun and a white nun were walking down the street and some men dragged them in an alley and raped them.

The white nun said, "Forgive them, for they know not what they do."

The colored nun said, "Mine sho' does."

The Concerned Nun

179. A nun was working in a hospital and she was assigned to the maternity ward. She was walking around to all the beds. She said, "Mrs. Jones, how many children does this make for you?" Mrs. Jones said, "Eight." The nun said, "My, what a nice Catholic family."

The nun went on to the next bed and said, "Mrs. Smith, how many does this make for you?" Mrs. Smith said, "Nine." And the nun said, "My, what a nice Catholic family."

She went on to the next bed and said, "Mrs. Brown, how many does this make for you?" Mrs. Brown said, "Six." The nun said, "Don't you Baptists know when to stop?"

The Road Well Traveled

180. Two nuns were walking to another parish out in the country. Two mountaineers dragged them into the woods and raped them. When they got back on the road one said, "What are we going to tell the Mother Superior?"

The other one said, "We'll tell her we were raped twice."

The first one said, "Why tell her we were raped twice?"

The other one said, "Well, we're going back the same way, aren't we?"

Confessions and Lemons

181. There was a two-story convent and a sex maniac broke into the upper story and raped a young nun. She went down and told the Mother Superior what had happened. The Mother Superior said, "Go to the refrigerator, cut a lemon in half, and suck on it." The young nun said, "What good will that do?" The Mother Superior said, "It will take that silly grin off your face."

Repose with Dignity

182. One time a woman came in and asked a priest to have a funeral for her cat. "That's ridiculous! Who ever heard of having a funeral for a cat?" the priest asked.

She said, "Father, you've got to. I've been everywhere, to the Baptist church, the Methodist church, and no one will take my money for holding the service."

The priest asked, "How much were you willing to pay?"

She said, "Oh, five hundred dollars, I guess."

"Hm," said the priest, "that was a Catholic cat, wasn't it?"

Beatnik Religion

183. Two beatniks were walking down the street and they saw a priest with his arm in a cast. One of the beatniks said, "Hey, man, what happened to you?"

The priest said, "I slipped and fell in the bathtub."

One beatnik said, "What's a bathtub?"

"Don't ask me," said the other. "I don't know anything about this Catholic religion."

Heaven and Hell

Throughout the history of Christianity believers have envisioned heaven as a place where the faithful spend eternity in solitude with God alone or as a paradisiacal site where they will be reunited with friends, spouses, or families. Heaven as depicted in jokes told in the Ozarks, however, bears only a faint similarity to the idyllic locale of Christian belief. It is a desirable place to inhabit but very difficult to enter. Space is, understandably, limited, and one must undergo very exacting tests to gain admission from saintly gatekeepers whose actions and attitudes are often anything but saintly. Moreover, their language frequently sounds slangy rather than heavenly. Those who do get into heaven often arrive there by means of trickery.

While in Christian belief hell is the exact opposite of heaven, in Ozark jokelore the places are very similar. There are only three significant differences in the way the two eternal depositories of souls are depicted: Satan presides over hell, an undesirable place to spend eternity, and is much more in evidence in his dwelling place than God is in his home. While applicants for entry to hell never have problems getting in, they are often tormented by requirements of making choices about how to spend the rest of eternity. It is only at joke's end that the protagonist discovers just how devilish is his Satanic majesty. But in every instance the Devil's language sounds very contemporary, not at all like that of a citizen of the other world.

St. Peter's Accounting

184. Once there was a real stingy man and when he died he was brought up in front of St. Peter and Gabriel. Gabe was setting there checking off good and bad deeds people had done. So St. Peter asked one man what was some of the good things he had done in his life. He says, "Well, one time I bought a paper from an old woman and gave her a penny." St. Peter looked over at Gabriel and said, "Is that recorded there, Gabe?"

Gabe said, "Yep, here it is."

And St. Peter said, "What else have you done good?"

The stingy man said, "One time there was a little girl out walking the streets and she didn't needed some money for something and I gave her a penny."

St. Peter said, "Is that right, Gabe?"

Gabe said, "Yep, here it is."

And St. Peter asked the old boy if there was anything else he had done good. He said he couldn't think of any more things he had done good. He said he would ask Gabe to look and see. So they checked all through the records and there wasn't another good deed that was done. So it kindly had St. Peter buffaloed and he says, "Gabe I—I—I don't know hardly what to do with this fellow. Here, what do you think we ought to do?"

Gabe said, "You know, you are the one that checks them, but if it was me I'd give him back his two cents and tell him to go to hell!"

The Lord's Work

185. There was this preacher and a tour driver who died on the same day. The preacher had been preaching for almost twenty years and the tour driver had been driving for ten years.

But it seems when they got there they found out there was only room enough for only one more person in heaven and St. Peter was looking over their life history on earth to see who would get admitted.

Well, after several hours had passed, St. Peter announced that the driver would be admitted. That preacher got all upset and was asking why in the world he wasn't accepted to go in. He just couldn't understand why a man who drove tours, gambled, drank, and fooled around with loose women would be admitted before a man who preached the word of God for twenty years. After arguing with St. Peter about it, St. Peter said, "Well, we did some checking up on both of you and it looks as though the bus driver scared the hell out of a lot more people than you did."

At Heaven's Back Door
186. St. Peter was walking around in heaven and he saw all these shady characters walking around. He told one of the saints that he didn't know how these people were getting in but he sure didn't let them in. On a hunch he went to the back door of heaven and there was the Virgin Mary, pulling them through the door with her rosary.

Acting Proprietary
187. A quiet-looking little man arrived in hell. As soon as he got there, he began asserting himself with some authority. "Hey, you!" hollered Satan. "You act like you own the dump." The little man replied, "I sort of figure I do. My wife, my boss, and my neighbor gave it to me often enough."

The Devil's Choices
188. This man died, he went down below and met up with the Devil, and the Devil told him that he had three choices of how to spend the rest of his time till eternity. So the Devil opened up this big door and just as far as you could see, there were people standing on their heads on spikes that were driven in the ground—nails, spikes just as thick as they could be. And so the man said, "Let's go on see what the next one is." The Devil opened up another door and behind it was these red-hot coals and there was people standing on their heads just as far as you could see on red-hot coals. So he showed him the last one and it was people

standing up to their waist in manure. So he looks up and said, "That don't look so bad. I believe I'll take this one here." So the Devil told him to get his clothes off and get in line in there and get ready for it. Just about the time he was getting lined up in there the Devil come by and said, "Okay, coffee break is over, back on your heads again."

Drinking, Gambling,
and Other Vices

In most communities, especially smaller ones where most people are likely to know all or most of the other residents, stories about humorous incidents that occurred while someone was drunk are legion. Possibly such stories are popular because, in addition to being funny, one can tell about someone's absurd actions while he was drunk with less risk of making him angry. Of course humorous narratives about drunkenness are found in both fictitious yarns and those told as true stories. Such tales seem to have been popular almost as long as people have been telling stories. Among the oldest known accounts of humor based on drunkenness are those contained in Icelandic and Irish myths. Humor about gambling is much less common in Ozark folklore than that about drinking; often, as is the case with the tale about gambling given in the following section, a yarn originally about drinking has been reworked and is now about gambling. Jokes and anecdotes about laziness are another matter altogether, having been popular internationally for centuries. Stith Thompson notes in *The Folktale*, p. 211, that "a thorough exploration of these tales of laziness would take one through most of the literary collections of tales, both in Europe and the Orient, for many of them have considerable antiquity and have been repeated by nearly everyone who has issued a book of anecdotes."

The various jokes in the following section deal mostly with generic figures rather than specific local characters, and they deal with the three major vices—drinking, gambling, and laziness—that turn up in Ozark jokelore. By casting them in humorous light they are made to appear relatively harmless. Certainly in the real world drinking, gambling, and even sloth often lead to results that are anything but funny. Realism, however, is not the purpose of jokes, even though they may unintentionally illuminate the reality behind the laughter.

Down the Hatch

189. Had you rather have a morning after than never have a night before? That's the question, boys and girls, that's the question. I was very happy to get an invitation to a party the other day. The invitation said that we were just going to have a big time—no speeches, no bridge, just do as you liked. The invitation further said that you wouldn't need an appetizer to enjoy the food, that it was going to be delicious, and it was just that. My wife and I made big plans to attend the party but right at the last minute some folks came and she couldn't get away. She let me go alone with a solemn promise that I wouldn't disgrace myself by trying to drink all the beer, talk loud, or sing or make any speeches and I promised that I would not do these things. When I arrived at the party I saw so many of my old friends and fine folks and I became a little excited. About this time someone patted me on the back and insisted that I take just a "little" snort. I thought the thing over and decided that just a "little" under such circumstances would not violate my promise, and just as I was smacking my lips over this first "little" I turned and what do you think? There stood my old friend Rosa, who had just arrived. He called my attention to the fact that we had not had a drink together for over twenty years, so I figured that such an unusual occasion would justify one more. We both said a toast that ended in "Down the hatch." Just as Rosa and I finished I turned around and there stood a beer salesman that I had not seen in years. After a warm greeting, he explained that the beer he was selling, or really giving away, was not intoxicating but exhilarating and insisted that I sample the same. I tried to renege by explaining that I was already "exhilled" but it wouldn't work. Next I met three friends just exactly alike. You couldn't tell one from the other. They were triplets, quadruplets, maybe a sextet or something like that. Anyway, they insisted that we celebrate the meeting by having a drink of my other friend's beer. So I said, "Down the hatch." That was all I could remember of my toast. About this time I became conscious that everyone was calling on me for a speech so the next time the room came around I walked in. The applause was deafening (or maybe it was some other kind of a roar). As I spoke I have a faint recollection of everyone laughing so hard that they had to leave the room. About this time the tables turned, I accidentally broke a glass so began to sing tenor. Someone poured the hatch down my back, or backed up the hatch or something like that. Anyway I was sleepy and decided to take a short nap. I left the room through what I thought was a door, but turned out to be a window. I awoke the next morning sitting on the curb weeping bitterly because my friend Rosa had lost his hat. Did you ever make an ass out of yourself? Try it sometime and see just how bad you can feel without being sick. NO, a night before is not worth a morning after. At least, I will feel that way a week or two anyway.

The Drunk Can't Help

190. One time a drunk needed to go to the bathroom real bad and he stumbled into a church. He happened to get into the confessional. The priest was hearing the confession on the other side. When he got through he closed that window and opened the one on the drunk's side. He wanted to attract the drunk's attention so he knocked on the window.

The drunk said, "No need to knock, there isn't any paper over here either."

He Made It Look Easy

191. A drunk was doing his best to spear an olive with a toothpick in a bar one time. Time after time he kept trying and the olive would scoot away from his toothpick. Finally, a man that was sitting next to him became annoyed with him and he took the toothpick. He said, "This is the way to do it," and he speared the olive on the first try.

The old drunk said, "I'd already gotten him so tired, though, he couldn't get away."

A Parrot's Education

192. There was a man who had a pet parrot. He thought a great deal of that parrot. He tried to take good care of him, but he had business to tend, trips to make. And when he went away, there was nobody to look after his parrot. He'd put the parrot in the cage. When he'd be around with it, he liked to let him fly about, take exercise. On one occasion he was wanting to get off on a trip and it was nearly night. The parrot had had quite a bit of exercise and he got ready to put the parrot up and the parrot wasn't ready. Just sat up in that tree and kind of saucy when he'd tell the parrot to come on down. He was in a hurry to get off on his trip. But now to bring you up on something I might have told you earlier. The man that owned the parrot liked liquor pretty well, used liquor pretty freely. And finally after he got the parrot pretty well-trained, it would be funny he decided to see what the parrot would do if he let him have a little bit of that liquor. And the parrot took to it just like a boy, you know. He liked it. He wanted more liquor and more liquor and the man put liquor on the sunflower seed—that's the way he got him started.

The parrot got to calling for more and more liquor. Well, when the man was trying to coax the parrot down out of the tree so he could put him up. The parrot wouldn't come and finally he said to his owner, "No sunflower seed, no sunflower seed, want sunflower seed."

"Oh, well then I'm in a hurry, if you have to have sunflower seed I'll be willing to get you some sunflower seed." He went and brought out the sunflower seed, put it down. Still the parrot wouldn't come down.

"Well, now I got the sunflower seed for you. Come on down."

"No liquor, want liquor, no liquor, I want liquor."

"Oh, now you don't have to have liquor every time you have sunflower seed. Come on down. I'm in a hurry."

"Liquor, I want liquor."

"Oh, well then, if you have to have liquor, I'll go and get the liquor."

So he went and brought out a bottle of liquor and began to sprinkle the sunflower seed with liquor. And the parrot still kept his perch in the tree.

"Now, you're going to come down and get the liquor I put on the sunflower seed. You're going to come on down. Come on, I'm in a hurry."

"Not enough liquor, more liquor, more liquor."

"Oh, well then, if you have to have more liquor."

He gave the sunflower seed a pretty good dousing with liquor. And the parrot just ate and ate that sunflower seed soaked in liquor until he just dropped over on his side. The man picked him up and carried him in and put him in the cage and went off on his trip. And he didn't see anything more of the parrot until the next morning. He got up and went around to see how his parrot was and asked, "Well, how, how, how are you this morning?"

"I don't want to see another sunflower seed as long as I live," exclaimed the parrot.

He Took His Medicine

193. The very proper little old lady had been sipping the first glass of beer she had ever had. After tasting it for a minute or two, she looked up with a puzzled frown and said, "How very strange! It tastes just like the medicine my husband has been taking every night for the past thirty years."

His Wife Was Predictable

194. A fellow got drunk one time way back yonder. I ain't going to call his name. He got drunk and I reckon he got so drunk he didn't know where he was at. And he went home and he come to the door and he knocked on the door and his wife come to the door and called him by name and said, "Come on in."

"Well," he said, "well, I'd just as well, my wife will run me off when I get home anyway."

Developing a Taste for Moonshine

195. The GI was walking down the street of an Ozark town when he met a hillbilly carrying a gun and a jug. The hillbilly stepped up to the GI and said, "Howdy, stranger, have a drink." The GI said, "No, thank you. I don't care for any." The hillbilly raised his gun and stuck it in the GI's ribs and repeated, "Have a drink." Naturally, the GI took a drink. He shuddered and handed the jug back. The hillbilly said, "Rough, ain't it! Now hold the gun on me while I take a swig."

Never Ask

196. The temperance lecturer was loudly condemning human stupidity in putting vile alcohol in the stomach. "Suppose," he explained, "I set a pail of water and a pail of beer before a donkey; which would he drink?" "The water," yelled a man from the audience. "Exactly," agreed the lecturer, "and why would the creature drink the water?" "Because he's an ass," replied the man from the audience.

Either a Winner or a Loser

197. Years ago there was a regular Sunday afternoon dice game near Big Flat. One of the stories coming from this meeting is the one about one of the regular members who was walking home from the game late one Sunday afternoon carrying a bridle on his shoulder.

A passing motorist stopped to give him a ride. Knowing where his rider had been the driver asked how his luck had been that day.

The gambler picked up the bridle and told the driver he wasn't sure. Said that he'd been walking along trying to remember whether he'd won a bridle or lost a horse.

He Was a Patient Man

198. The Arkansas hillbilly was at his favorite occupation—lying in the sun. The flies buzzed around and settled thickly on his face, but he was too lazy to shoo them away. Finally, a hornet lit amongst the flies and stung his nose. He slowly wiped his hand across his face and muttered to the insects, "As long as *some* o' ye won't behave ye'll jist *all* have to git off."

Seeing Is Believing

199. And this guy was named Snow. He lived right back up here. And he wouldn't work. His wife and the kids made the crop. And he just absolutely wouldn't work. Well, he got on relief, so he went up here. He'd been on relief for a year or two and he went up here to Evening Shade to the relief office. And Whit Wasson was the kind of a guy like I am. He kidded a lot, you know. So he seen Snow a-coming and he just thought, "Well, I'm gonna have some fun out of him." So Snow come in and he said, "Uh, uh, Mr. Wasson," he talked long, you know, and he said, "Mr. Wasson, have you got my order ready?" "Yeah," he said, "Mr. Snow, we've got it ready." And said, "In fact it's doubled this month." He said, "The government is taking a survey of all the people that's like you, that's not able to work and make a living for the family." And said, "They're gonna feed 'em for ninety days and double their orders and then they're gonna kill 'em." And said, "They've got Coley Evans down here making the caskets now." Well, Coley was a-making caskets for PWA people, see. Well Snow said, "You just set my order back there and I'll be in to get it." Well Whit knew where he was a-going so he watched him. And he went in the shop where Coley was making the caskets and there set three or four caskets. He said, "Mr. Evans, who is them caskets for?" Well Coley didn't know what was going on, see, and he said, "Well they for PWA people." Boy, Snow jumped up and he want back up there and he said, "You tell the government they can go to hell with that order and they can have it. I don't want no more of it." And he took out home. And Whit

Wasson had to hire a car and take his order down to him. Like to scared him to death.

He Wouldn't Accept Just Any Offer

200. This guy was too lazy to work and support his family. So the neighbors had give him stuff and give him stuff and, and kept him up for three or four years and he wouldn't work. So finally they went and told him, and said, "Now John, now we've kept you up for three or four years. We've supported your family and you won't work. Now you either going to work or we're going to bury you alive."

Well, he said, "I'm not going to work."

So it went on for about three or four days and they went over and got him and started to the cemetery with him. And they met a guy and they said, "Who's dead?"

Well, said, "Ain't nobody dead." Said, "Mr. Jones over here, you know won't support his family." And said, "We're gonna bury him alive." Said, "He don't have nothing in the house to eat."

"Oh," he said, "I wouldn't bury him alive." He said, "I'll give him some corn. And he can take it to the mill and have it ground and have some cornbread."

Mr. Jones raised up in the casket and he said, "Is it shelled?"

He said, "No."

He said, "Drive on."

Eerie Humor

Some Ozark jokelore deals with the supernatural in one form or another. Admittedly this body of material is not large, but it is very persistent, much of it consisting of tales with an ancient international lineage. Often these stories get attached to racial or ethnic groups, but such association is purely incidental to the narratives. Sometimes they are presented in essentially the same manner as a ghost story; in fact some narrators refer to them as ghost stories, even though ghosts usually do not appear in the yarns. Typically, most of these jokes deal with death or the dead or fears concerning such matters. A corpse raising up in a casket for what are, to the cast in these tales, inexplicable reasons, or voices heard in a cemetery at night, or people who fall in open graves, would not seem the most likely topics for humor, but they are motifs from some of the most popular jokes told in the Ozarks.

Why does such material appeal to the hillfolk? Why do they find it funny? As with all such questions there are no easy answers, the matter being too complex to be adequately resolved by a single solution. Perhaps, as has been suggested by Ray B. Browne for Alabama (in *A Night With the Hants*), the comic treatment is a means of balancing an interest in death that is seen as unhealthy. Possibly it is just a means of making death and the dead less fearsome. Probably those who tell these tales couldn't fully answer such questions, but that doesn't mean they are not worth contemplating.

Selections in the Cemetery

201. These two boys were out gathering walnuts and they had gathered this sack full of walnuts. And course they was another tree they liked and it was on the inside of the cemetery. And so they had to go in there and so as they were going in they happened to drop two walnuts. But they didn't fool with picking them up. They just went on in to gather them up under the tree. Well, these two guys, they were out walking, too, you know. And it was after night. And they had to pass the cemetery going home. And so they, those kids were out there and they'd say, "You take this one and I'll take that one. You take this one, and I'll take that one." They were dividing them up you know. And so they got down to the last ones and he said, "Well you take this one and I'll take that one." And this other little boy said, "Oh you forgot about those two on the outside of the gate." And those two men were a-resting and they were on the outside of the gate. So they'd stopped there to rest and he said, "You take that one and I'll take this one." Those two men take off down that road just running just as hard as they could. Says, "Oh Moses, that's Jesus and Satan out there counting out."

A Surprise at the Funeral

202a. One time some black people were having a funeral when all of a sudden the body raised up in the casket. All the people started running out of the church. After all the people came back and settled down a bit two of the men were talking, and one of them said that the preacher was not worthy of doing the services. The other asked why. Then the first said that when all the people were running out that he heard the preacher say something dirty. He went on to say that the preacher said, "Damn them churches with locked doors anyway."

202b. A bunch of them boys—and they was pretty rough and tough, you see. An old man, an old German, an old bachelor, lived back in there and he got sick and he died.

They set up with them until they buried 'em back then. These two guys was setting up with this old man. They was in an old log cabin. And this old German he raised a whole bunch of sweet potatoes. He had a whole bunch of 'em there, see. They got hungry and there was an old fireplace, they had a fire in there. They was roasting them potatoes in that fireplace. They got 'em roasted and they was setting there eating 'em. Directly one of 'em said, "That damned ol' devil, if he knowed we was eating his sweet potatoes he'd come alive."

Directly one of 'em looked around and he rared up. And they say, boy, they hit the door and one of 'em run into the face of the door, a little ol' low door. Knocked him out and that one grabbed him up across the shoulder and they run off and went off, finally found somebody to go back with 'em and said they told him that old man come alive up there. Said he was sitting up in the bed. When they got back up there and started checking and when they laid him out his toes had got under that metal rail across the foot of the bed and his leaders had drawed and pulled him up there. They wouldn't go back until they got somebody to go back with 'em. They was supposed to be rough and tough.

Not Easily Spooked

203. They said this guy claimed that he wasn't scary. Said there would nothing scare him. And there was a house that was haunted and nobody would go in that house of a night. He said, well, he'd go in there and stay all night. So he went in and he cooked his supper. He got through eating his supper, went in the living room and he set down there. And he was setting there writing by a table and all at once he heard something and he looked up. And there was a little lady hanging to the ceiling. And she just dropped down on the floor right beside of him. And she said, "Well, mister, this is a nice day, isn't it?"

"Yeah, but," he said, "if you'll just follow me, I'll take you to where it's a lot nicer day than this." So he took out at the door and he run for about a half a mile until he give out and he went out and he set down on a log. And she just run out by the side of him and set down on a log and looked up at him and said, "Mister, we had a nice race, didn't we?"

And he said, "Yeah, but lady, if you'll just keep up with me, we're gonna have a lot better one, the next time."

Motivation in the Grave

204a. Some kind of job that several were working on and I don't know how long it had been going on, but this particular day they were trying to complete the job and they worked on till just practically night. Well, in fact it was getting dusky and one of the workers said, "I've got to be going home, I can't stay any longer. I've got to be going home." So he was making his way out through the cemetery and happened there was an unusually deep grave been prepared and hadn't been used—going to be open overnight. They don't usually have them that way, but this boy, this man, going through the dusk and in a hurry too, happened to walk right into that open grave. Shocked. Surprised. He began scrambling doing everything he had the power to do in the way of getting out of there. He try this way and that and failed and finally just wore himself out. He wouldn't quit to rest he was so intent to getting out of there. He just collapsed, fell down flat into the bottom of the grave.

Well, after a little while, another fellow decided he had to go home. It was darker. He didn't stay for the job to be finished. He undertook to get out of the cemetery 'bout as quickly as he could. He had the same misfortune. He just happened to go the route the other fellow did. Then he walked right into that open grave. And the man was already in there—he had already exhausted himself. He was out for a while. He didn't know what was going on and this second man all he could think about was trying to get out of there. Finally, after he was getting pretty weary, but not going on until he exhausted himself completely like the other—he got himself on one knee. He didn't know what was under his knee. And just to himself at first thinking, "I've gotta get out of here. I've done everything and tried as hard as I can, but oh there must be a way." And then out loud, "I've gotta get out of here. I've just got to get out of here." And finally he got to talking out loud and just about that moment the man that was under him began to come to. He heard what the second man was saying.

The second man, "I've just got to get out, I've just got to get out of here. I can't stay. I've got to get out of here."

The man under him reviving said, "Just as well forget about it, brother, you'll never get out of here."

But he did!

204b. One night as a man was crossing through a grave-yard he fell into an open grave. For several hours he jumped and climbed and tried everything he could, but couldn't get out, so he just sat down at one side and gave up. A few minutes later another man came walking by and also fell into the same grave. He immediately started trying to jump out. The other man watched him for a while and then said, "It's no use, buddy, I've already tried it and you can't get out." However, the other man did get out and quick.

Notes

These notes give as much detail on informants as is available; for most texts this includes name, age, place of residence, date of collection, and other relevant biographical material. In many cases remarks about how, when, and where the texts are used are given. Where any of these details are missing it is because they were not supplied by the collectors. Some fieldworkers provide copious accompanying information with their texts, while others provide nothing more than the informant's name. For various reasons many collectors fail to include the detailed accompanying data with jokes that they do for most other types of folklore. Jokes are relatively simple and seemingly ubiquitous, so some fieldworkers make the mistaken assumptions that their meaning is obvious and is always the same. Happily, most of the collectors whose work is utilized here were aware of the necessity for providing more than just a text.

For most texts motif numbers are supplied at the end of the notes; in a few cases they are given in the body of the notes. These refer to the systems employed in Ernest W. Baughman, *Type and Motif-Index of the Folktales of England and North America;* Antti Aarne and Stith Thompson, *The Types of the Folktale;* Stith Thompson, *Motif-Index of Folk Literature;* and Frank Hoffman, *Analytical Survey of Anglo-American Traditional Erotica*—the standard indices of narrative elements found in American folk tradition. Baughman's numbers are cited first because he is more directly concerned with the type of material presented here, but in some cases, he does not list parallel material. In these instances Thompson's or Hoffman's numbers are given. Type and motif numbers are a kind of shorthand used by folklorists to demonstrate that a narrative is in folk tradition, and to indicate how popular it is, how widely distributed it may be, and what the relationship is between versions and variants found in places geographically distant from each other.

Tall Tales

1. Collected May 4, 1978, by Kathy Nicol from Jessie Hubert Wilkes, Cave City, Arkansas. Wilkes was born one of seven children of Lafayette and Martha Rush Wilkes in Sidney, Arkansas, a tiny village about twenty-five miles from the area's largest town, Batesville, on December 12, 1905. His grandparents moved into this area from Tennessee shortly after the Civil War, and Hubert lived near Sidney until 1927 when he joined the army. After five years in military service, he returned to Arkansas for a few months, then in 1934 moved to Phoenix, Arizona, where he remained for a number of years. During this time Hubert earned his living primarily as a carpenter and painter, but he also worked as a baker, cook, and factory hand. Always interested in seeing new places, Wilkes spent much time traveling throughout the United States and was very proud of his far-ranging visits. In 1971 Hubert moved back to Arkansas and spent the last thirteen years of his life in a home about five miles north of Cave City, Arkansas.

Although Wilkes was well-known in his community as a teller of tall tales who would come forth with a yarn upon request, he generally told them only in certain situations. One was a setting such as a music party where he served as unofficial entertainment. At one such party, on a June night in 1977, I first met Hubert. I later recorded several of his tales for an LP titled *Not Far From Here*. During his working years another favorite time for telling his tall tales was just before work. He once described one of these occasions for me: "I was in Phoenix, Arizona, working. I was a carpenter. And every morning I'd go to the—not every morning but every morning that I did go to the lumber yard, why they didn't open the lumber yard till eight o'clock. Well, I'd get there about seven-thirty where I could shoot the breeze and go with all of the guys you know, and kid and joke." Sometimes, as in the text given here, the tales were occasioned by a gathering of friends.

Besides functioning as a popular form of entertainment, Wilkes's tale repertoire provided him with a special place in the community around Cave City—that of storyteller par excellence. After my first encounter with Hubert, several of his acquaintances remarked, "He can go on all night like that." One man added, "Nobody can tell them big stories (tall tales) like Mr. Wilkes." Hubert also recognized his abilities and told me on several occasions, not boastingly but in a matter-of-fact style, that he was a good talker who could go on all day and night if necessary. His specialty was the tall tale, although he said he once knew a lot of fairy tales (by which he meant the sort of story that folklorists call *Märchen*), but by the time I knew him he had forgotten most of those narratives.

Wilkes's presentation was an important part of the success of his tales. He related his narratives in a rapid-fire, almost breathless, manner of speaking. His face was virtually stoic, even when he was telling some hilarious, totally outlandish tale. To judge from his expression one might think he was listening to a eulogy or attending some formal event rather than recounting a humorous narrative. In several instances it was only when Hubert got to the punchline that one realized he was recounting a tall tale, for the totally deadpan delivery was purposely designed to imply that the story being told was true. This "put-on" gave added force to the humorous ending.

This text was recorded by Kathy Nicol, who at the time was doing fieldwork for a movie later released as *They Tell It For the Truth*. Wilkes was specifically asked for tall tales that might be suitable for inclusion in that film. Because tall tales were specifically requested it is hardly surprising that most of the material he gave Nicol was of that type, but he also related for her a few "true" incidents and at least one story of the type that he called fairy tales.

This tale is based on a series of motifs common in the Anglo-

American tradition. The most common of these is cited by Baughman as X1411.1.1, "Lie: large watermelon." Related motifs include X1411.1.1(b), "Watermelon is so big that when it collapses it kills several people" and X1411.1.1(c), "Watermelon is so large that farmer has to saw it off the vine. When released, the melon rolls down the hill, bursts, drowns eight people in the juice." Arkansans have long been noted for tales about big watermelons, and a number of these are recounted in Vance Randolph's *We Always Lie to Strangers*, pp. 86–90. Although it seems unlikely that tales like this one are not known in other watermelon-producing areas, to date it has only been reported from Arkansas.

2. Collected in 1979 by W.K. McNeil and George West from Dr. William Hudson, Jasper, Arkansas. Dr. Hudson was born in Jasper, February 23, 1891, the grandson of one of the first white settlers to venture into the Little Buffalo River country in what has since been named Newton County, Arkansas. He left the community in 1915, and pioneered in his own right as a research scientist and medical doctor. His research on blood iodine in 1921–22 resulted in the industrial manufacture of iodized salt. At the Ford Hospital in Detroit, Michigan, he developed the first motion-picture X-ray of the lung, and went on to become president of the American College of Lung Surgeons.

In 1961 Dr. Hudson returned to Jasper and built a retirement home on the Hudson family homestead. More precisely, he built his house around the 1828 cabin of his grandfather, to protect and preserve the original structure. The porch of the original cabin serves as the vestibule of the Hudson home, and the bedroom of the original home is still used as a bedroom. Since his return Dr. Hudson has been locally renowned as an excellent storyteller, known primarily for his "Uncle Will" stories, mostly tall tales related to him around the turn of the century by his uncle. The one given here was recorded at a public meeting of the Newton County Historical Society in Jasper. Hudson was invited to give a history of his medical career as well as to exhibit pioneer farming implements used by the Hudson men who first settled the valley. At the request of the audience, Doc Hudson (as he is known locally) also began to tell some of the favorite stories by and about his two uncles, Will and Sammy, who were familiar figures in the community in previous generations.

Doc Hudson sets the stage for this adventure by describing in detail the circumstances under which Uncle Will first told him the story. The beginning of the story is quite imaginable, especially because Doc Hudson held, as he talked, the actual dulcimer that his Uncle Will played to him that night. Thereafter, however, one absurdity is stacked on another until Uncle Will finds himself stranded on the moon. The wry neck refers to a neck that is slightly askew or twisted to one side.

A similar tale about a trip to the moon is related by Davy Crockett (or rather, by those who published an almanac in his name) about an unidentified backwoodsman on Whangdoodle Knob. The Crockett yarn is less complex and lacks the explanation about why the man has a wry neck.

Thompson's F16, "Visit to land of moon," and Baughman's F900, "Extraordinary occurrences," and X910, "Lie: the remarkable man," are applicable.

3a. Collected in 1979 by George West from Dr. William Hudson, Jasper, Arkansas. For information on Hudson see the notes to text 2. This widely known tale is type 1920, "Contest in lying," which probably originated in Europe. Certainly it has been collected in many places on the continent including Finland, Sweden, France, Germany, Austria, and Slovenia. It has also been reported from Ireland, the West Indies, Canada, and, of course, from several of the United States. In *The Folktale*, p. 215, Stith Thompson suggests that tales of lying possibly have the most diverse origins and histories of all folk narratives. In many American versions the champion liar says that he doesn't have time to tell a lie, an action that is implied here but not explicitly stated. The phrase "walkin' for wages" means striding purposefully.

3b. Collected in 1961 by Beulah Faye Tucker Davis from her father-in-law, Fayetteville, Arkansas. Davis, the collector, says "Papa Davis said this happened. He was one of the men who went to see about Mr. Cole." For a discussion of this tale see the notes to text 3a.

4. This yarn appeared in the column "Jimmy (or Jimmie; it is spelled both ways) Wilson Opines," July 13, 1935. These columns, which appeared in a Tulsa radio entertainment publication, *Radio Wave,* were very popular in eastern Oklahoma during the early 1930s. Wilson, a humorist with the folksy style of Will Rogers, was born H.L. Wilson in Manchester, Tennessee, April 29, 1890. In 1910 he moved to Sapulpa, Oklahoma, where he spent the remainder of his life. During the years 1931 to 1933 he was a state representative and later ran, more or less as a joke, unsuccessfully for a variety of offices. Basically, he ran when his friends wanted to spread or split the vote. So frequently did he run that he often listed his occupation as "perpetual candidate for congressman-at-large."

As well known as he was for his various campaigns, Wilson's greatest fame was as the leader of his Cat Fish String Band, a very popular country music group that was together for approximately eighteen years before finally disbanding in 1938. The Cat Fish Band was a group of businessmen who made music for fun, not for profit. They were often billed as the "first country band to ever broadcast over radio." The claim is dubious but they certainly were one of the first such bands on radio, performing on Bristow station KFRU in 1924 before it was officially licensed. All the members of the Cat Fish String Band belonged to the Sapulpa Rotary Club, and they originally got together to put on a program for a meeting of the club. Eventually they recorded six sides for RCA Victor and even appeared in a 1930 movie for Pathe News. That same year they toured the Southwest with Will Rogers. Throughout their career they were in constant demand as entertainers for national conventions. Their popularity was aided not only by their abilities as entertainers but by their unusual instrumentation; familiar instruments such as violin, banjo, mandolin, guitar, and bass were used by group members, but they also played such unusual instruments as gas pipes, bones, and various types of whistles. Wilson died September 2, 1946, eight years after his group disbanded.

The general motif J1730, "Absurd ignorance," applies here.

5. Collected May 4, 1978, by Kathy Nicol from Jessie Hubert Wilkes, Cave City, Arkansas. For information about Wilkes see the notes for text 1. Although this yarn sounds familiar I have been unable to locate parallels in any of the standard folklore reference works.

6a. Collected November 27, 1986, by Vaughn Ward from his father, Fred Ward, Cord, Arkansas. Fred Ward is a restaurant owner who frequently shares stories with his customers and, like most such people, has a small stock of standby material that he brings out periodically. This particular yarn he learned as a boy from his father and now tells it whenever he "wants a laugh outa somebody up at the coffee shop." For various reasons he finds the story more useful in the winter "when the ponds all freeze over and ever'thing's cold." His cafe is frequented mainly by farmers for whom the weather is often the main topic of conversation. Also during this coldest time of year "life in Cord is very slow." In order to "compensate for this terribly boring time when we experience harsh weather, and farmers must indeed chop the ice and do various other chores in the freezing weather," Ward tells this tale for a laugh. Fred Ward's father also told it mainly in the winter, primarily because, according to his son, that was when people had "time to 'set around' and talk and 'tell stories.'"

Although Vaughn Ward fails to mention it in his comments on this text, it seems likely that one reason Fred tells this yarn is in order to reinforce community attitudes about industriousness. The preacher who, by being lazy, violated local standards got his comeuppance. Most likely the narrative is also remembered and passed on because it was learned from a parent and, thus, is considered as part of local and family history and lore. Obviously, though, the story's humor is the main reason why it is recalled and passed on. There can be little doubt that Fred Ward finds this story very funny, for he began to laugh on four occasions while telling this tale, a yarn that would be distasteful to some people—Humane Society personnel, for example. Obviously, the farmers who can relate to the story also find it amusing; otherwise Ward wouldn't keep telling this item.

This joke, or variants and versions of it, were told by Bob Burns and other radio comedians. Apparently, though, Fred Ward was not influenced by their versions. In fact he always tells the story as a true event, although he now has some doubt that it actually happened, because he has never been able to find anyone who could provide the name of the lazy preacher. Most forms of the yarn involve a hog who often merely gets sick for several days rather than dies. A tale similar to this in which a man deliberately rids himself of a pesky dog by seeing to it that the canine gets blown up is given in David Rattlehead's *The Life and Adventures of an Arkansaw Doctor* (1851); see chapter titled "Blowing Up a Dog." Widely known in the United States, versions of this narrative have been reported from traditional taletellers in Arkansas, Indiana, New Jersey, Tennessee, and Texas. Apparently the tale is unknown in Europe, for Stith Thompson in his *Motif-Index* cites only Baughman's references.

X1233.2.1, "Hog finds dynamite supply, eats it, walks behind mule; the mule kicks the hog. The explosion kills the mule, blows down the barn, breaks windows out of house, etc. The hog is ill for several days."

6b. Collected May 4, 1978, by Kathy Nicol from Jessie Hubert Wilkes, Cave City, Arkansas. For more information about Wilkes see the notes for the first text in this section. For more information on this tale see the notes for the immediately preceding text. Wilkes's version of this old story is less violent than most for in his telling no one gets killed, although the hog is usually sick for only a few days rather than the three months cited here.

7. Collected in 1979 by W.K. McNeil from Melvin Anglin, Berryville, Arkansas. Born February 10, 1906, to George Anglin and Lovey May Hammond, both of whom were born and reared in Williamson County, Tennessee, Melvin moved with his mother and siblings to Berryville in 1912. Anglin spent several summers in middle Tennessee with grandparents, from whom he heard numerous stories of the Civil War period and among whom he observed many a character that later appeared in his own repertoire of hillbilly stories. Later, after spending time in the Navy, Melvin returned to Berryville, where he entered private law practice and occasionally printed pamphlets featuring portions of his many stories. He made several television appearances, most notably twice on "What's My Line?" as an impersonator and once on "You Bet Your Life," the show of the formidable comedian Groucho Marx (against whom Melvin proudly claimed that he more than held his own.)

Anglin's index of snakes in Carroll County, Arkansas, has no basis in scientific fact but does have a long history in folk tradition. The lore of the hoop snake, for example, dates back to colonial America, where it was originally known as the horn snake. In *A New Voyage to Carolina* (1709) John Lawson vividly described such a serpent as "hissing exactly like a goose when anything approaches them" and striking at their enemy with their tail "which is armed at the end with a horny substance, like a cock's spur" (quoted in Richard M. Dorson, *Man and Beast,* p. 55). At some point this tradition merged with that of the hoop snake to make a truly formidable reptile. Now, the hoop snake is generally regarded as just another fictitious creature that tellers of tall tales describe, but it was not always viewed in that light. Vance Randolph, *Ozark Magic and Folklore,* p. 254, noted that even into the mid-twentieth century "the old story of the hoop snake which puts its tail in its mouth and rolls downhill is believed by many."

Relevant to Anglin's account are the several following tale types and motifs: type 1889M, "Snakebite causes object to swell"; motif B765.1, "Hoop snake. Snake takes tail in mouth and rolls like wheel"; motif B765.1(a), "Method of attack by hoop snake"; and motif B765.1(ab), "Snake rolls at person or object, strikes it with poisonous stinger at end of tail." Some printed references relevant to the present text include Harden E. Taliaferro, *Fisher's River,* pp. 55–58; Mary Alicia Owen, *Voodoo Tales,* pp. 246–53; Clifton Johnson, *What They Say in New England,* pp. 64–65; Newbell Niles Puckett, *Folk Beliefs of the Southern Negro,* 42–43; John B. Sale, *A Tree Named John,* p. 94; Vance Randolph, *We Always Lie to Strangers,* pp. 132–36, which contains an extended discussion of the hoop snake tradition in the Ozarks; Richard M. Dorson, *America Begins,* pp. 93–94; *American Folklore*, p. 13, and *Man and Beast*, pp. 55–62, which gives a capsule history of the hoop snake tradition in America; *North Carolina Folklore*, vol. 1, p. 637; Ronald L. Baker, *Jokelore*, pp. 13–14, and *Hoosier Folk Legends*, p. 123; Wayland D. Hand and Jeannine E. Talley, *Popular Beliefs and Superstitions from Utah*, pp. 389, 404–5; Lowell Thomas, *Tall Stories*, p. 127; Ray B. Browne, "A Night with the Hants," pp. 120–21; Bill Ring, *Tall Tales*, p. 19; and Loyal Jones and Billy Edd Wheeler, *Laughter in Appalachia*, p. 131.

7b. Collected November 1982 by W.K. McNeil and George West from Toby Treat, Big Flat, Arkansas. Treat was at the time a twelve-year-old student in the sixth grade at the Big Flat School and was, perhaps, the best of the many youngsters asked to tell "stories" for the video camera. Most of the kids had only one or two narratives they were willing to share but Toby had several, all of which he told very well. Even though the collectors did not specify what type of material they wanted (beyond stipulating that they be stories) all of the youngsters offered tall tales.

This text bears strong similarity to Melvin Anglin's index of snakes given in the preceding text but differs in some important respects. Most notable of these is that Treat gives more of a narrative, at least a more detailed one. In most versions of this tale the wooden object is a hoe handle (as in Anglin's version), a toothpick, a fork handle, a wagon tongue, or a peavy handle. The oar is relatively rare and the end of the story in which turpentine reduces the size of the house is less common than Anglin's ending.

X1205.1(g), "Small wooden object struck by snake swells so that man cuts great quantity of lumber from it."

8. Collected December 1962 by Bill Knowles from Darrell Knowles, Mountain Home, Arkansas. The two men were brothers. According to the collector, "Darrell said while he was going to school there was a boy that used to come down to his room every night and take some recordings on his old disc type recorder. One he especially like to record was "Larping Tarping Scoonskin Hunting." The Knowles text differs from most reported versions of this yarn in its length and the conclusion. Knowles also gives the various events in different order from most reported narrators. In most versions the dog is named Shorty and the girlfriend Sal, but the name of the person who accompanies the narrator changes frequently. In some versions he is "Bud," in others "Paw" (the most frequent name). "Paul," however, is rarely used and leads one to suspect that whoever told Darrell Knowles the yarn used "Paw," which Knowles misunderstood to be "Paul."

This story, according to Joseph Jacobs in *More English Fairy Tales*, p. 245, is derived from an old English story and play. Jacobs includes a version as number 51 in his collection. Other texts are found in Joel Chandler Harris, *Uncle Remus*, number 27; Elsie Clews Parsons, *Folk-Lore of the Sea Islands, South Carolina*, number 80; Annie Weston Whitney and Caroline Caulfield Bullock, *Folk-Lore from Maryland*, pp. 179–80; Richard Chase, *Grandfather Tales*, number 15; Benjamin A.

Botkin, *A Treasury of Southern Folklore,* p. 525–26; Leonard Roberts, *South from Hell-for-Sartin,* pp. 158–60 (three versions); John M. Ramsay, *Dog Tales,* pp. 71–72. In *South from Hell-for-Sartin,* Roberts remarks that early recordings may account for the wide distribution of this and similar yarns in the United States (p. 266). One of his three informants heard the tale on a "talking machine" record when he was a boy. While commercial recordings may have helped spread the tale, its frequent appearance in print would seem to be an even more important factor in its widespread distribution in this country.

Roberts, p. 266, lists this as type 2225, "Scrambled tale," and gives the motif number X954, "Topsy-turvy talk." These both make sense but the problem is that neither types nor motifs with those numbers appear in any type or motif indexes available to me.

9. Collected March 16, 1978, by Kathy Nicol from T.H. "Peck" Weaver, Charlotte, Arkansas. Nicol was interviewing various traditional narrators in the Arkansas Ozarks for a movie on tall tale tellers, eventually issued in 1979 as *They Tell It For the Truth.* Weaver was one of several people chosen to be in the film, which was aired several times on the Arkansas Educational Television Network during the 1980s. Weaver told his tales at a slower pace than Hubert Wilkes but with the same kind of deadpan delivery intended to lead listeners to believe they are hearing a serious story until the punch line indicates otherwise. Born in 1902, Weaver learned most of his humorous stories in 1915–16, as he did the present yarn, from various people in Charlotte, Arkansas. He can not remember who told him this specific tale. For another version of this yarn see John M. Ramsay, *Dog Tales,* pp. 13–14.

X1215, "Lies about dogs," and X1215.8(a), "Intelligent hunting dog," are both applicable.

10. Collected March 16, 1978, by Kathy Nicol from T.H. "Peck" Weaver, Charlotte, Arkansas. For more about Weaver see the notes to text 9. Versions of the present tale appear in Bill Ring, *Tall Tales,* p. 37, and in Loyal Jones and Billy Edd Wheeler, *Laughter in Appalachia,* pp. 129–31.

X1200, "Lie: remarkable animals," and X1232, "Lies about monkeys."

11. Collected May 11, 1978, by Kathy Nicol from Jessie Hubert Wilkes, Cave City, Arkansas. For more information about Wilkes see the notes to text 1. This well-known lie is type 1889L, "Lie: the split dog," and probably originated in Europe. It is one of the tales attributed to Baron Munchausen and has also been reported from England, from several sections of Canada, and from Illinois, Indiana, Iowa, Kentucky, New Jersey, New York, North Carolina, Oregon, Texas, Vermont, and Wisconsin, among other places. In *Jonathan Draws the Long Bow,* pp. 102–3, Richard M. Dorson prints an early New England version of the tale in which the animal that is patched up is a fox. For some representative texts see Harden E. Taliaferro, *Fisher's River,* pp. 149–51; Leonard Roberts, *South from Hell-fer-Sartin,* p. 145; B.A. Botkin, *A Treasury of American Folk-*

lore, pp. 593–94; Richard Chase, *American Folk Tales and Songs,* pp. 97–98; Ronald L. Baker, *Jokelore,* p. 19; and John M. Ramsay, *Dog Tales,* pp. 76–77. Baughman also assigns the yarn motif number X1215.11(c).

12. Collected in 1964 by Robin Jordan from Lee Parker, Goshen, Arkansas. Jordan says, "Mr. Parker is a delightful old gentleman with sparkling blue eyes and a crop of white hair. As he relates his tale, his eyes glow as he projects his entire self into his story." Jordan also provides an unusually detailed amount of biographical data on Parker and on his family background. Parker was born November 21, 1891, in a machine shed shack by a red oak tree right outside Goshen. His father, Addison Jackson Parker, was born in Whitley County, Kentucky, on February 25, 1853. He moved to Arkansas in 1879 to teach school but on January 18, 1883, he bought a farm and retired from teaching. He died suddenly of a stroke in 1929. Parker's mother, Mary Elizabeth Kelley Parker, was born in Georgia on January 21, 1859, and moved to Arkansas with her family when she was one year old. They resided near Hindsville and moved to Goshen in 1877. The following year she attended the University of Arkansas. She died of a heart attack in 1947.

Parker entered the University of Arkansas in September 1908, but after two years he decided on a commercial course not offered there. He graduated from commercial college in bookkeeping, banking, commercial law, shorthand, and typewriting. Immediately following his graduation he took a job with corporation lawyers in Newport, Arkansas. After nine years working in Newport he returned to Goshen, where he started farming on the old homestead. At the time Jordan interviewed him his wife, Beulah, was an invalid and Parker spent most of his time caring for her. Jordan noted, "They now lead a very simple existence since he is unable to do much of anything besides care for her. He has a small garden and sells produce in town occasionally."

This is an interesting variant of the widely known and ancient type 1791, "The Sexton Carries the Parson," an example of which is given in the section titled "Eerie Humor." In most versions the action takes place in, or near, a cemetery, the humor deriving from the mistaken assumption that the Lord and the Devil are dividing up souls. Actually, it is two boys dividing nuts or some other articles in the graveyard or sheep thieves, or some other type of thieves, dividing their spoils. That form of the tale dates back at least to 1526 when it was printed in the first jokebook published in English, *A C Mery Talys* (A Hundred Merry Tales). See W. Carew Hazlitt, *Shakespeare Jest-Books,* vol. 1, pp. 31–36. The racial identity Parker gave this narrative has been edited from this version at the publisher's request; it is frequently associated with this yarn. For a very similar text see Irvin S. Cobb, *A Laugh a Day,* pp. 14–15.

13. Collected December 26, 1968, by Mike and Judy Cate from Francis Marion Cate, Walnut Ridge, Arkansas. The informant is Mike Cate's father, who at the time of collection had been superintendent of the Clover Bend, Arkansas, public schools. Born April 27, 1925, at Tiperary, Arkansas, Francis Cate earned an undergraduate degree from the University of Arkansas, Fayetteville, in 1951 and at the time of the interview was working on a doctorate at Arkansas State University, Jonesboro. Although it is not clear from the data supplied by the collectors it seems likely that Francis Cate told this, and other jokes and tall tales in his repertoire, infrequently. Versions of this widely known tale are found in the following books: Lowell Thomas, *Tall Stories*, pp. 96–98, includes versions, or references to them, from Indiana, Pennsylvania, Minnesota, and West Virginia; John M. Ramsay, *Dog Tales*, pp. 3–4, includes a version from Brasstown, North Carolina, and in his notes, p. 97, Ramsay says he has not otherwise heard this story; Bill Ring, *Tall Tales*, p. 16.

X1215.8(ab), "Dog hunts various game according to equipment master carries: if master takes shotgun, dog hunts rabbits; if he takes rifle, the dog hunts deer; if he takes fishing rod, dog digs worms."

14. Collected December 26, 1968, by Mike and Judy Cate from Francis Marion Cate in Clover Bend, Arkansas. According to the collectors the informant heard this yarn "from one of his buddies in the army when they were stationed in the Philippine Islands during the war." It is surprising that Cate did not hear this story earlier, for it is very popular in American folk tradition and has been printed several times. Some representative texts are found in the following publications: Vance Randolph, *We Always Lie to Strangers*, pp. 126–27; Warren Stanley Walker, "Dan'l Stamps," p. 155; Ronald L. Baker, *Jokelore*, p. 18; Bill Ring, *Tall Tales*, pp. 86–87; and John M. Ramsay, *Dog Tales*, pp. 1–2.

X1215.8(aa), "Master shows dog a skin stretching–board; the dog brings in a raccoon just the size of the board. Master's mother puts ironing board outside one day. The dog never returns."

15. From the column "Jimmy Wilson Opines," February 9, 1935. For information about Wilson see the notes to text 4. A2270, "Animal characteristics from miscellaneous causes."

16. Collected March 16, 1978, by Kathy Nicol from T.H. "Peck" Weaver, Charlotte, Arkansas. For information on Weaver see the notes to text 9. A very similar tale is given in Ronald L. Baker, *Jokelore*, p. 28.

J1760, "Animal or person mistaken for something else," and X1321.1.2.1, "Men sit on log in woods; the log moves and the men discover that it is really a snake."

17a. From the column "Jimmy Wilson Opines," undated but probably 1934. For information on Wilson see the notes to text 4. The present narrative, and text 17b, are versions of type 1890, "The Lucky Shot," a tale that has been popular in both England and America for centuries. According to an anonymous correspondent in the English magazine *Choice Notes*, p. 134, it can be traced back to the twelfth century. The feature of not using a gun because of the cost of ammunition is rare; usually the arrow is used simply because nothing else is immediately available. Also uncommon is the motif of the three dogs, each with a different skill. As Ernest Baughman notes (*Type and Motif-Index*, p. 54), the weapon is generally used deliberately with very lucky results for the hunter. In the most lengthy versions seven major subdivisions are used; most American texts, however, include only the shooting of the animal(s) on a tree limb, the fish in boots, and the honey tree. For some representative texts see Joseph Jacobs, *More English*, pp. 43–45; Herbert Halpert, "John Darling," pp. 102–103; Lowell Thomas, *Tall Stories*, pp. 79–81; Arthur Huff Fauset, "Negro Folk Tales from the South," p. 250; B.A. Botkin, *A Treasury of American Folklore*, p. 604; Roger L. Welsch, *A Treasury of Nebraska Pioneer Folklore*, p. 160, and *Shingling the Fog*, pp. 82–83; Ronald L. Baker, *Jokelore*, pp. 10–11; Bill Ring, *Tall Tales*, pp. 81, 88; and J. Russell Reaver, *Florida Folktales*, pp. 21, 80.

17b. Collected December 23, 1968, by Mike Cate from his uncle, David Johnson, Hardy, Arkansas. Johnson, a part-time carpenter and a full-time farmer, was forty-five years old at the time of collection. His very abbreviated version of what is usually a much longer tale suggests that Johnson was either not a skillful narrator or someone who did not tell the story often. For a discussion of this tale see the notes to text 17a.

18. Collected in 1964 by Robin Jordan from Lee Parker, Goshen, Arkansas. For information on Parker see the notes to text 12. This is a modern adaptation of type 660, "The Three Doctors," a tale that appears in the 1812 collection of the Grimm Brothers as number 118. In the fullest versions of that tale three doctors make a trial of their skill. One removes one of his eyes, one his heart, and the other a hand. They are to replace the body parts without injury the next morning but, during the night, they are eaten and others substituted. By this means one doctor acquires a cat's eye that sees best at night, one a thief's hand that wants to steal, and one a hog's heart that makes him want to root in the ground. In most American renderings of this tale the three doctors have been replaced by a single protagonist, as in this case. Other versions are found in Marie Campbell, *Tales from the Cloud-Walking Country*, pp. 187–88, and Jan H. Brunvand, *Study of American Folklore*, p. 121.

19. From the column "Jimmy Wilson Opines," June 15, 1934. For information about Wilson see the notes to text 4. The several relevant motifs are X1305, "Fish lives on dry land"; X1307, "Fish which are eager to be caught"; and X1410(d), "Large strawberries."

20. Collected November 1982 by W.K. McNeil and George West from Trisha Haffner, Big Flat, Arkansas. Haffner was also among the sixth-grade students who volunteered to tell a "story" for our video camera (see the notes for text 7b). She was shy about talking to the camera but managed to get through the ordeal. A version of this tale appears in Ben Kitchens, *Tomatoes in the Tree Tops*, p. 4, a collection of tall tales associated with Harry Rhine (1883–1962), a man known as the "Biggest Liar in Tishomingo County, Mississippi." Otherwise it seems to be previously unreported, although it may well be more widely known than printed reports indicate. It seems like the sort of material that might be found in ephemeral jokebooks.

X1154.1, "Fisherman catches fish with amazing contents."

21. From the column "Jimmie Wilson Opines," July 13, 1935. For information about Wilson see the notes to text 4. The several motifs here include F971, "Miraculous blossoming and bearing of fruit"; X1300, "Lies about fish"; X1303, "Remarkable actions of big fish"; X1313, "Hungry fish"; and X1400, "Plants, fruits, and trees."

22. From the column "Jimmy Wilson Opines," June 15, 1934. For information on Wilson see the notes to text 4. This narrative is a version of type 1960C, "The Great Catch of Fish," a tale known throughout Scandinavia and Yugoslavia and, of course, not uncommon in the United States. The relevant motifs are X1150.1, "Lie: the great catch of fish," and X1307, "Fish which are eager to be caught."

23. Collected December 26, 1968, by Mike and Judy Cate from Francis Marion Cate, Walnut Ridge, Arkansas. For information about Francis Cate see the notes to text 14. Another version of this tale is given in Lowell Thomas, *Tall Stories*, p. 49.

X1154.1(b), "Fisherman loses spectacles trying unsuccessfully to land a fish. The next year he catches the fish which is wearing the spectacles."

24. Collected December 27, 1968, by Mike and Judy Cate from Willis Jones, Alicia, Arkansas. Jones, an uncle of Judy Cate, was a farmer but several years earlier had been a semi-pro baseball player, a career that was interrupted by World War II. He was also well-known locally as a bird hunter and, according to the collectors, "he really enjoyed hearing some of the tales we collected from other people." See Lowell Thomas, *Tall Stories*, p. 46, for a version of the tale given here. X1316, "Dogfish act like dogs."

25a. Collected May 11, 1978, by Kathy Nicol from Jessie Hubert Wilkes, Cave City, Arkansas. For more about Wilkes see the notes to the first text in this section. This old windy is assigned motif X1286.2.1.1, "Mosquitoes eat cow, ring bell to call calf"; it is widespread in American tradition. Vance Randolph prints a version in *Ozark Mountain Folks*, pp. 158–59, and states that it is a tale of the lumber-camps, but it seems to be well known by people who have never set foot in a lumber-camp. Although this particular yarn has been collected in New Jersey and Illinois, a majority of the printed texts have been from collections made in Arkansas. This item is also relatively common in African-American tradition. For some representative texts see Lowell Thomas, *Tall Tales*, p. 110; Benjamin A. Botkin, *A Treasury of American Folklore*, pp. 607–8; Vance Randolph, *We Always Lie to Strangers*, pp. 149–50; Warren Stanley Walker, "Dan'l Stamps," pp. 155–56.

For some other large mosquito stories see Richard Walser, *Tar Heel Laughter*, p. 121 (a reprint from an 1855 issue of the *Spirit of the Times*) and pp. 273–74 (a reprint of O. Henry's story "The Confession of a Murderer").

25b. Collected March 1983 by W.K. McNeil from George Vickers, Big Flat, Arkansas. Vickers, born in 1919, returned to Big Flat, a tiny community in Baxter County but closer to the seats of three counties other than its own, after retirement. At the time of collection he lived in an old two-story building that in earlier times had been a hotel. Very interested in his community, he was active with a group of other locals in working to bring greater publicity to Big Flat. The town is popular as a watering spot for residents of adjoining Stone County, which is legally "dry."

For a discussion of the history of this tale see the notes for text 25a. Vickers's text is unusual in that it contains a tick, rather than the mosquito that is usually described.

26. Collected December 27, 1968, by Mike and Judy Cate from Kenneth Jones, Alicia, Arkansas. Jones was born August 12, 1914, in Jackson County, Arkansas, and earns his living as an independent trucker. The collectors say, "When he is not on the road, he spends a lot of time at LeMays Store. Alicia is a very small town and this is where all the men gather under the sycamore tree in the summer and the coal stove in the winter to shoot the bull." Jones, apparently, gained most of his experience in telling tall tales at the store. This particular story Jones heard from a friend at nearby Clover Bend, a community whose greatest claim to fame is that it was for many years home to Alice French (1850–1934), who under the pseudonym Octave Thanet was one of the most popular American short story writers of the late nineteenth century.

This is type 1960M2, "Large mosquitoes carry off men or animals," a yarn popular in America for well over a hundred years. It is among the yarns printed in Fred H. Hart's *The Sazerac Lying Club*, p. 93, a book made up of material printed in the Austin, Nevada, newspaper *The Reese River Reveille* during the 1870s. The Jones text is unusual in that it doesn't say whether the man was carried away or not. Most versions have the man either being eaten right where he is found or taken to a hiding place so that the large mosquitoes can't take their prey away and eat it themselves. For other versions see Lowell Thomas, *Tall Stories*, p. 121; *North Carolina Folklore*, vol. 1, p. 372; Vance Randolph, *We Always Lie to Strangers*, pp. 146, 149; Ray B. Browne, "A Night with the Hants," p. 43; and J. Russell Reaver, *Florida Folktales*, p. 79.

27. Collected December 26, 1968, by Mike and Judy Cate from Kenneth Jones, Alicia, Arkansas. For information on Jones see the notes to text 26. Another version of the same tale is given in Lowell Thomas, *Tall Stories*, p. 120. Also compare the stories about large mosquitoes in Richard Walser, *Tar Heel Laughter*, pp. 120–121, 273, 274, the latter being a reprinting of O. Henry's posthumously published "The Confession of a Murderer," in which the killing of an enormous mosquito is detailed.

X1286.1, "Lie: the large mosquito"; X1286.5, "Ferocious mosquitoes: miscellaneous"; and X1286.5(e), "Man holds candle under mosquitoes to kill them. One large mosquito blows the candle out."

28. Collected December 25, 1968, by Mike and Judy Cate from Mrs. Willie Massey, Smithville, Arkansas. According to the collectors, "Mrs. Willie Massey is an elderly lady who now lives at Smithville, Arkansas, but used to live at Clover Bend when Mike went to school there. She and her late husband had a farm there and Mike and his brother spent most of their spare time with them." Mrs. Massey seems typical of most of the several people that the Cates collected tall tales from in that she apparently does not tell the material often and is not a particularly skilled narrator. She is in other words what might be called a passive informant, i.e., a person knowledgeable about tall tales current in her community but not one who ordinarily relates them.

X1286.5(c), "Mosquitoes steal canvas, make canvas trousers."

29. Collected December 24, 1968, by Mike and Judy Cate from Francis Marion Cate in Hardy, Arkansas. For information about the informant see the notes to text 13. He heard this particular yarn at one of the schools where he taught for fifteen years prior to the collection. A version of the same tale is given in Lowell Thomas, *Tall Stories*, p. 113. X1286.1.6(na), "Mosquitoes steal can of peas, return later for can opener."

30. Told to Mike Cate in 1960 by Mrs. Willie Massey, at the time a resident of Clover Bend, Arkansas. For more information about Mrs. Massey see the notes for text 28. A North Carolina version of this story appears in Lowell Thomas, *Tall Stories*, p. 118.

X1286.4(f), "Man sets fire to wings of a mosquito; this mosquito fires a whole cloud of mosquitoes; the conflagration spreads over seven counties."

31. Collected in 1971 by Joe Lindsey from H.R. "Rip" Lindsey, Fayetteville, Arkansas. H.R. Lindsey was born June 28, 1918, in Greenland, Arkansas, but during his childhood his family alternated living on a farm south of Greenland and in the tiny western Texas town of Dodsonville. Just before World War II "Rip" married Bernice Johnston and the two spent the war years working for Douglas Aircraft in Tulsa, Oklahoma. After the war he moved to Fayetteville, Arkansas, where he briefly operated an electronics store. Then, in 1946, "armed with some knowledge of radio and electronics picked up during World War II, I started working as an engineer at Fayetteville's brand new only radio station KGRH 1450 on your radio dial. As the low man on the engineering staff, I was nominated to open up the station every morning at 5:30 (A.M., that is). The announcers assigned to the early shift had a way of oversleeping, and I soon found myself stuck with a radio station on the air but sans announcer. So very accidentally I became not only the engineer but also the early morning announcer or disk jockey. I sold chicken feed, guaranteed genuine simulated diamond rings, burial insurance, song books, baby chickens, the services of the local Graces, filling stations, garages, just about everything anyone had to offer—we pushed it. In between I played the country records and began to tell a few of the stories that kept me in business for the next fourteen years. Some of my stories were true, some were good stories that just should have been true. Most of the true stories happened to the poor folks I knew growing up in the thirties."

The extensive quote is from an autobiographical statement "Rip" Lindsey gave the collector, who is his son. The program he mentions lasted from 1946 to 1961, KGRH later becoming KHOG to fit with the nickname of the University of Arkansas sports teams. Lindsey became quite well known for his stories, which apparently were as much of the entertainment as the music he played. Several relevant motifs here include X1600, "Lies about weather and climate"; X1606, "Lies about changes in weather"; X1620, "Lies about cold weather"; X1623.3, "Lie: flame freezes; startling results"; and X1623.3.3.2, "Man eats or sells frozen flames for strawberries."

32. Collected December 24, 1968, by Mike and Judy Cate from David Johnson, Hardy, Arkansas. For information about Johnson see the notes for text 17b. Another version of this yarn is given in Lowell Thomas, *Tall Stories,* pp. 143–44. X1622.2.2, "Woodpecker taps its feet on granite or pecks at granite; sparks which fly warm his feet."

33. Mike Cate recalled hearing this from his younger brother, Ronnie Cate, while he was in high school at Walnut Ridge, Arkansas. Ronnie Cate was born in Jonesboro, Arkansas, November 27, 1952, and at the time his brother Mike made this report in 1968, was planning to attend Southern Baptist College at Walnut Ridge where he intended to major in psychology. Another version of this yarn appears in Lowell Thomas, *Tall Stories,* p. 148.

X1623.3.3.1, "Man feeds frozen flames to hens; they lay hard-boiled eggs."

34. Collected December 26, 1968, by Mike and Judy Cate from Kenneth Jones. For information about Jones see the notes to text 26. The Cates said they collected another version of this tale from Syd Stevens, a traveling salesman from Little Rock. According to them, the Stevens version had the hunter using his frozen tears to bag the saddest bear in town. Compare the versions in Lowell Thomas, *Tall Stories,* pp. 83–85, 157. X1121.3, "Lie: remarkable ammunition used by great hunter," and X1122.4.2(b), "Hunter meets bear, perspires; drops of sweat freeze; he shoots the frozen drops."

35. Collected December 25, 1968, by Mike and Judy Cate from Kenneth Jones, Alicia, Arkansas. For information about Jones see the notes to text 26. This was a tall tale that Jones had forgotten but remembered when he heard some of the other yarns that the Cates collected. For other versions see Lowell Thomas, *Tall Stories,* pp. 148–50, and Roger L. Welsch, *Shingling the Fog,* p. 28.

X1623.3.1, "Flames freeze with unusual results."

36. Collected December 27, 1968, by Mike Cate from Ronnie Tolson, Clover Bend, Arkansas. Tolson was one of several friends that Cate asked for tall tales, so he recalled this item. This suggests that Tolson rarely told the story, but the fact he remembered it implies that it was one he liked. Other versions of this yarn are given in Lowell Thomas, *Tall Stories*, pp. 154–56.

X1623.1 "Shadow freezes."

37. Collected December 26, 1968, by Mike and Judy Cate from Francis Marion Cate, Walnut Ridge, Arkansas. For information about Francis Cate see the notes for text 13. Although there are numerous tall tales about thick fog, this one seems previously unreported.

X1651, "Fog," and X1651.1, "Man, shingling building during thick fog, shingles several feet of fog when he gets beyond the fog line."

38. Recalled by Mike Cate as a story he heard in 1962 when he was a student at the Clover Bend Junior High School, Clover Bend, Arkansas. A version of this yarn is given in Roger L. Welsch, *Shingling the Fog*, p. 50.

X1654.3, "Hard rain"; X1655, "Extraordinary mud"; X1655.1, "The man under the hat, which is the only thing seen above the mud"; and X1655.2, "Deep mud."

39a. Recalled by Mike Cate as a story he heard in 1962 when he was a student at the Clover Bend Junior High School, Clover Bend, Arkansas. This, and text 39b, are versions of motif X1633.1, "Heat causes corn to pop in crib or in field. Animals (cows, horses, mules) think the popping corn is snow, freeze to death," a motif that is very widespread in American folk tradition. The Cate text is unusual in that it is a hen, rather than a cow, horse, or mule who freezes to death. It is, however, typical in that it is relatively short. Most printed versions indicate that there is usually variation in some minor details. For example, a New York version given in Harold W. Thompson, *Body, Boots and Britches,* p. 149, has the corn harvested and in a barn when it pops on a hot July day. A Kansas variant in Roger L. Welsch, *Shingling the Fog,* p. 31, has the cane melting and running into the popped corn to form one huge "sticky mess of popcorn balls, which the farmer sold for fifty cents each." Welsch further comments that this is the most widely known summer heat story and the one most frequently encountered by collectors. In his notes, p. 141, he provides the following useful comments: "It is worth noting that this tale was one of the most frequently received by the Nebraska Farmer during its 1924–1925 contest. On one occasion—December 20, 1924—the editors complained that they had received ten versions of this story in one week. On February 14, 1925, the editors said that they were receiving the story at least once a day and sometimes two or three times a day."

Representative versions of this item appear in Richard M. Dorson, "Maine Master Narrators," *Southern Folklore Quarterly* 8 (1944): 283; Lowell Thomas, *Tall Stories,* pp. 162–65; Vance Randolph, *We Always Lie to Strangers,* pp. 184; Grace Partridge Smith, "Tall Tales from Southern Illinois," *Southern Folklore Quarterly* 6 (1943): 146; Warren Stanley Walker, "Dan'l Stamps," *Midwest Folklore* 4 (1954): 158; B.A. Botkin, *A Treasury of American Folklore,* p. 628; Richard Walser, *Tar Heel Laughter,* p. 212; and J. Russell Reaver, *Florida Folktales,* p. 77.

39b. Collected in 1971 by Joe Lindsey from H.R. "Rip" Lindsey, Fayetteville, Arkansas. For information about H.R. Lindsey see the notes to text 31. For information about the present tale see the notes to text 39a. To the list of printed versions cited there add Bennett Cerf, *Sound of Laughter*, p. 13.

40a. Collected May 11, 1978, by Kathy Nicol from Jessie Hubert Wilkes, Cave City, Arkansas. For information about Wilkes see the notes to text 1. Vance Randolph prints a related tale in *Hot Springs and Hell*, p. 5, which he had from a man in Eureka Springs, Arkansas, who first heard it about 1954 in Texas. In the Randolph text the man throws rocks at his mother every time she attempts to wean him. That particular narrative has a long history in Britain as well as in the United States. Randolph supplies, p. 171, a number of printed references to the yarn. I have been unable to find any other published text exactly like Wilkes's or Jimmy Wilson's version, which is text 40b. Compare the tale titled "The Way of the Neighborhood" in Irvin S. Cobb, *A Laugh a Day*, p. 26.

X912(fa), "Young giant, wanting to nurse, throws stones at mother."

40b. From the column "Jimmy Wilson Opines," May 11, 1935. For information about Wilson see the notes to text 4. For a discussion of this tale see the notes to text 40a.

41. Collected in 1971 by Joe Lindsey from H.R. "Rip" Lindsey, Fayetteville, Arkansas. For information about H.R. Lindsey see the notes to text 31.

X1280, "Lies about insects," and X1283, "Lies about potato bugs."

42. From the column "Jimmy Wilson Opines," June 15, 1934. For information about Wilson see the notes to text 4. This is type 1913, "The Side-Hill Beast," a figure of American comic lore that was first discussed in print in an 1856 article in the *New York Spirit of the Times* titled "A Marvellous Hunting Story." He was called the "haggletopelter," a name that is not used in any subsequent reports. In numerous publications the creature is called the sidehill dodger, sidehill hoofer, sidehill wowser, sidehill winder, gwinter, prock, guyiscutus, yamhill lunkus, wampus cat, and rackabore, among other names. The name hillside moodies is previously unreported. Some other versions of this tale appear in Vance Randolph, *We Always Lie to Strangers*, pp. 23, 61–63; Harold W. Thompson, *Body, Boots and Britches*, p. 273; Henry H. Tryon, *Fearsome Critters*, pp. 39–40; Roger L. Welsch, *Shingling the Fog*, pp. 88–89; and Richard M. Dorson, *Man and Beast*, pp. 29–35, which gives a succinct history of this creature. Baughman also gives this tale motif X1381.

43. From the column "Jimmie (the way it is spelled in this specific issue) Wilson Opines," March 1930. For information about Wilson see the notes to text 4. Jokes about steep hills and farms located on them are plentiful in the Ozarks, as is indicated by the chapter "Steep Hills and Razorbacks" in Vance Randolph, *We Always Lie to Strangers*, pp. 14–40. The joke given here appears in, among other places, George Milburn, *Best Yankee Jokes,* p. 20.

X1523, "Lies about steep slopes of mountains or hills," and X1523.2, "Lies: farming on steep mountain."

44. Collected in 1971 by Joe Lindsey from H.R. "Rip" Lindsey, Fayetteville, Arkansas. For information about H.R. Lindsey see the notes to text 31. According to Vance Randolph, *We Always Lie to Strangers,* pp. 15–16, a farmer near Fayetteville, Arkansas, once told this line about potato farming to a newspaper reporter. Other versions are in George Milburn, *Best Yankee Jokes,* p. 20, and Roger L. Welsch, *Shingling the Fog,* p. 49.

X1523.2.3(c), "Man opens bottom end of potato row; potatoes roll into sack."

45. From the column "Jimmie Wilson Opines," March 1930. For information about Wilson see the notes to text 4. Other versions of the present yarn appear in Welsch, *Shingling the Fog,* pp. 16–22, and in James R. Masterson, *Arkansas Folklore,* p. 392.

X1523, "Lies about steep slopes of mountains or hills"; X1524, "Remarkable high hills or mountains"; X1611, "Lies about the wind"; X1611.1, "Remarkably strong wind (including tornado, cyclone)"; and X1611.1.5, "Remarkable wind blows objects and living things about."

Local Characters

46. Collected in 1958 by James McClain Stalker from Clarence Vaughn, Sulphur Rock, Arkansas. Stalker notes that "Mr. Vaughn is one of the gentry of Sulphur Rock, Arkansas. He has lived in the area all his life and has a fabulous collection of tales." Apparently, Vaughn considered the yarn given here a part of local history because he told it primarily to those, such as Stalker, who were seeking information about area history. The two doctors of the story were once prominent, now long deceased former residents of Sulphur Rock. Although told for a true story, this is a variant of a traditional tale that is widely known in the Southwest. Often, as in the text published in Vance Randolph, *Sticks in the Knapsack,* p. 95, the man who thinks he has been snakebit is drunk. In the earliest known printing, however, in an 1836 issue of the *New York Spirit of the Times* there is no mention of drunkenness. The protagonist is just "a big, fat fellow" who "had occasion to go to the woods." (Reprinted in James R. Masterson, *Arkansas Folklore,* p. 37.) The friendly competition between two men is missing from all other printed versions, as is the "settin' hen"; most versions have the person being "attacked" by his own spurs. The Vaughn text is also unusual in that the protagonist doesn't immediately discover the cause of his "bite."

J1760, "Animal or person mistaken for something else."

47. Collected May 11, 1978, by Kathy Nicol from Jessie Hubert Wilkes, Cave City, Arkansas. For information about Wilkes see the notes to text 1. Although "victrola" was once used by people as a generic name for a phonograph, it was actually a brand name. The Victrola was a product of the Victor Talking Machine Company and, of course, was never used by Thomas A. Edison, who headed a rival company. Nipper, the dog that listened to his master's voice, was an advertising symbol used by the Victor Talking Machine Company beginning about 1903.

48. Collected March 1983 by W.K. McNeil from George Vickers, Big Flat, Arkansas. For information about Vickers see the notes to text 25b. Stories about the hillman's ignorance of modern means of transportation are fairly common in the Ozarks and in other parts of the United States. Vance Randolph prints a number of stories about the mountaineer's ignorance of trains in *Hot Springs and Hell* (see numbers 61, 186, 437) and includes another example in *Sticks in the Knapsack,* p. 69. Also see the section titled "Humorous Stories" in my article "Folklore from Big Flat, Arkansas. Part II: Folk Narratives," *Mid-America Folklore* 11 (1983): 11–14. In a sense the motifs X0, "Humor of discomfiture"; J1730, "Absurd ignorance"; and J1742, "The countryman in the great world" all apply here.

49. Collected March 1983 by W.K. McNeil from George Vickers, Big Flat, Arkansas. For information about Vickers see the notes to text 25b. The relevant motif here is J2050, "Absurd short-sightedness."

50. Collected in 1958 by James McClain Stalker from Frank Rounds, Batesville, Arkansas. According to Stalker, Rounds "knows everybody and all that has gone on in the area in years past. He works as a sawmill operator and farm laborer." The story given here concerns a man named Medford M. Rutherford who was locally known as Mr. Med. Stalker describes him as "the picture of an old southern gentleman who stood straight as an arrow until the day he died in the summer of 1957 at the age of eighty-four. He didn't quit riding horse-back over his place until he was eighty." Rutherford was, apparently, a big, strong man who "was known to be able to shake a freshly set fencepost when no one else could." He was also well-known for being extremely hard to satisfy "when it came to fence-building. All of the posts that anyone set for Mr. Med had to be set deep and solid. If he could shake a post, it was a poor job of setting. Most of the hands working for him could get along better with him if they followed his orders blindly."

51. Collected in 1958 by James McClain Stalker from George Rutherford, Newark, Arkansas. According to Stalker, the informant does not tell many narratives, "but when he does tell one, it is accurate and well worth hearing." At the time of the collection he was living on a plantation that originally belonged to his grandfather. The text given here concerns one of Rutherford's ancestors named Walter Blyth.

J1730, "Absurd ignorance," and Thompson's T243, "Madness from love," are relevant.

52. Collected June 26, 1961, by Beulah Faye Tucker Davis from Mary Fritz, Fayetteville, Arkansas. Fritz heard about Edgar when she was a little girl from a man who gave milk to her family.

J1700, "Fools."

53. Collected March 1983 by W.K. McNeil from George Vickers, Big Flat, Arkansas. For information on Vickers see the notes to text 25b. Motif X800, "Humor based on drunkenness," applies here, although the hero's love of the bottle is not explicitly stated. Presumably those familiar with him, or accounts about him, will be able to make the deduction without much difficulty.

54. Collected March 1983 by W.K. McNeil from George Vickers, Big Flat, Arkansas. For information about Vickers see the notes to text 25b. The Tom is Tom Winn, the protagonist of text 53. A number of traditional motifs are found in the present narrative, of which the most obvious is X800, "Humor based on drunkenness." Others included are J1730, "Absurd ignorance"; J1738, "Absurd ignorance of religious matters"; and Q552.14, "Storm as punishment," an ancient narrative element found in Jewish and Indian folklore, among other places. Finally, in a sense this belongs to the class of stories that consist of jokes on preachers, a category that is extremely popular throughout the United States and western Europe.

55. Collected March 1983 by W.K. McNeil from Julie Kelley, Big Flat, Arkansas. Kelley, born in 1902, is well regarded in her community for her knowledge of local history. Like her neighbor, George Vickers, she is interested in seeing Big Flat promoted as something more than just a watering hole for those with a taste for alcohol. A woman with an easygoing personality, Kelley related several tales with an enthusiasm that belied her then eighty-one years. Never rushing the story, she told it clearly, and understandably, but with vigor.

Two traditions seem to be represented here, that of fighting and that of the remarkably strong man. In frontier America a large body of humor revolved around the fights in which local toughs and strong men engaged. Anyone seeking more information on this subject should read Joseph J. Arpad, "The Fight Story: Quotation and Originality in Native American Humor," *Journal of the Folklore Institute* 10 (1973): 141–72. In *Tar Heel Laughter,* p. 207, Richard Walser reprints a yarn similar to Kelley's from *Humor and Humanity* (1945), a book by Hickory, North Carolina, industrialist George Franks Ivey (1870–1952). In that tale a Negro shows up at a doctor's office after very obviously being in a fight. When asked to explain what happened, he details the fight and concludes by saying, "I was never so sick of a nigger in all my life."

Generally, stories about strong men are categorized as tall tales but often, as is the case here, they are told as "true" accounts of actual events.

56. Collected March 1983 by W.K. McNeil from Julie Kelley, Big Flat, Arkansas. For information about Kelley see the notes to text 55. Both this story, and the one immediately preceding it, are helped by knowing that Ed Treat was a man who, according to local tradition, dearly loved a good scrap. Generally he got the best of his opponents but, as in text 55 and the present one, he sometimes was licked.

Thompson F610, "Remarkably strong man."

57. Collected March 1983 by W.K. McNeil from George Vickers, Big Flat, Arkansas. For information about Vickers see the notes to text 25b. The motif Thompson lists as F632, "Mighty eater," crops up numerous times in fictional tales, being found in Irish, Icelandic, Jewish, Indian, and Hawaiian myths, among other places. Its appearance in "true stories" is less common but, as the present text reveals, is not unknown.

58. Collected March 1983 by W.K. McNeil from George Vickers, Big Flat, Arkansas. For information about Vickers see the notes to text 25b. This is another example of the motif J1730, "Absurd ignorance." In this case the main character fails to comprehend the true meaning of the waitress's question, which of course was designed to find out if he wanted his eggs over easy, sunny side up, etc. Hence the totally inappropriate reply. Essentially the same story is given in *Jim Owen's Hillbilly Humor*, p. 68, but Owen's version has a different ending line. A waitress in a city restaurant asks a country boy how he likes his eggs, to which he replies, "Just fine." Seeing that he has misunderstood her, she then asks, "How do you like them cooked?" to which he responds, "Hell, I'm crazy about 'em that way." Owen says he told this on Don McNeill's "Breakfast Club" show and it proved to be one of the host's favorite stories.

Husbands, Wives, and Lovers
59. Collected August 19, 1972, by Max Hunter from his wife, Virginia, Springfield, Missouri. She had heard the story at a sorority meeting a few days earlier. This story has been printed in a number of popular joke collections such as Shelli Sonstein, *Thoroughly Tasteful Dirty Joke Book*, p. 85.

E610, "Reincarnation as animal."

60. Collected June 29, 1961, by Beulah Faye Tucker Davis from John D. Anderson, Fayetteville, Arkansas. Similar stories have been popular for centuries, as is made clear by two eighteenth-century tales, the first from *The Town and Country Almanac* for 1799 (reprinted in Robert K. Dodge, *Early American Almanac Humor*, p. 97):

> A Gentleman riding out one morning early in a place where he happened not to be acquainted; coming up by the side of a young woman who was carrying a pig in her arms, and hearing it scream violently, addressed her thus, "Why my dear. Your child cries amazingly." The young woman readily turning round and looking him in the face, said, with a smile upon her countenance, "I know it, sir, it always does when it sees its daddy."

The second story is from *The Farmer's, Merchant's and Mechanic's Almanack: or, The Register of Maine* for 1799 (reprinted in Robert K. Dodge, *Early American Almanac Humor*, p. 146):

> People who are resolved to please always at all events, frequently overshoot themselves, and render themselves ridiculous by being too good—A lady going to eat plumb cake and candie at a

friend's house one morning, ran to the cradle to see the fine boy, as soon as she came in. Unfortunately the cat had taken up the baby's place; but before she could give herself time to see her mistake, she exclaimed with uplifted eyes and hands, "Oh! What a sweet child! the very Picture of its father."

There is no exact parallel to the Anderson story in any of the type and motif indexes, but the general category of absurd misunderstandings (J1750–1849) and motif J2301, "Gullible husbands," are implied.

61. Collected in 1959 by Gene H. Brooks from Fred Starr, Fayetteville, Arkansas. Fred Starr was born in 1896 in Waco, Georgia, one of a family of seven boys and one girl. His father was a cotton farmer and Fred helped him with the farm just as soon as he was able to work in the fields. When Fred was ten years old the family moved to Oklahoma. For several years they moved back and forth from Oklahoma to Georgia so much that Fred said "they could borrow meal at one place and be back soon enough to pay it back before they would miss it." After several years of travel the family wound up in southern Arkansas, where Fred started teaching when he was twenty-one years old. At the time he had not finished high school, but he continued his education while he was teaching. After fighting in World War I Fred taught eleven years in western Oklahoma; then he moved to the Arkansas Ozarks, where he spent the remainder of his teaching career of thirty-plus years. Starr served from 1955 to 1959 in the Arkansas General Assembly, but his greatest acclaim came from several books of essays, observations, and reminiscences about the Ozarks that he authored and from weekly columns he wrote for the *Tulsa World* and the *Northwest Arkansas Times*. Fred was one of the early members of the Arkansas Folklore Society, which was founded in 1950 by John Gould Fletcher, Vance Randolph, and others. He died in 1973.

Hoffmann's X725, "Humor concerning adultery"; X725.3, "Wife's adultery in absence of husband"; and X725.5, "Infidelity exposed" are relevant.

62. Collected in 1973 by Marla Crider from Marion Crider, Greenland, Arkansas. The informant is the brother of the collector and is the manager of a grocery store that had, at the time of collection, been in his family for eighty years. Marla Crider says, "Marion is a great joketeller. Some you can tell in mixed company, a lot of them you can't. When people come in the store, they enjoy Marion's sense of humor."

X137, "Humor of ugliness."

63. Collected in 1961 by Margaret E. Hulse from an unidentified man at a store in Caverna, Missouri, who called it "a story about the Depression days." A once popular story in jokebooks, this item is rarely found in such sources today. It is, however, among the 640 jokes included in Isaac Asimov's *Treasury of Humor*, p. 361, a collection of Asimov's favorite jokes. W153, "Miserliness."

64. Collected in 1982 by Mary Camron from Della Horton, Big Flat, Arkansas. Camron, a high school student at the time, called this a ghost story even though there is no mention of a ghost in the text. The tale is given as a variant of the corpse sits up in coffin/on the cooling board complex in Lynwood Montell, *Ghosts Along the Cumberland*, p. 204, and he cites parallels in Richard M. Dorson, *American Negro Folktales*, and John A. Lomax, *Adventures of a Ballad Hunter*. In both Dorson, pp. 329–30, and Lomax, pp. 182–83, the scare element is prevalent, whereas in the present example it is the humorous element that dominates. In the same spirit as the Horton text are the examples in *Anecdota Americana* (1934), p. 152; B.A. Botkin, *A Treasury of American Anecdotes*, pp. 13–14, which is taken from Allan M. Trout's *Greetings From Old Kentucky*, p. 114; Loyal Jones, *Minstrel of the Appalachians*, p. 187; Isaac Asimov, *Treasury of Humor*, pp. 360–61; and Willard Scott, *Down Home Stories*, p. 83. Motif E1, "Person comes to life," is the most relevant motif.

65. Collected in 1973 by Marla Crider from Virgil Bradshaw, Greenland, Arkansas. Bradshaw is Crider's uncle and, according to Crider, "his knack for telling jokes is incredible. When he was a small boy, he used to sit around and make up jokes. He never goes a day without telling someone a joke." Apparently Bradshaw has a large stock of jokes, for he told a number of them to Crider. Milton Wright, writing in *What's Funny—And Why* (1939), p. 51, gives a version of this joke which he calls an example of the married-life joke which "is rooted firmly in the belief that if love is blind, marriage is an eye-opener." In other words, Wright considered this an old, time-tested joke fifty years ago.

T250, "Characteristics of wives and husbands," and W100, "Unfavorable traits of character."

66. Collected in 1973 by Marla Crider from Virgil Bradshaw, Greenland, Arkansas. For information about Bradshaw see the notes to text 65. This is another item that is occasionally found in modern jokebooks such as Bennett Cerf's *The Sound of Laughter*, p. 116.

J1701, "Stupid wife."

67. Collected in 1973 by Marla Crider from Irene Guadalajara, Fayetteville, Arkansas. Crider says, "With a name like Guadalajara, you wouldn't think she was my aunt, would you? Well, she is and a lot of fun to have around. She married Manuel Guadalajara who was from Caracas, Venezuela. She met him when she worked in Tulsa and he was attending the University of Tulsa, Oklahoma, getting a Ph.D. in Petroleum Engineering. Aunt Irene carries out the tradition of the Bradshaw family by being a great joke teller."

J1701, "Stupid wife," and J1730, "Absurd ignorance," apply. Guadalajara's text bears some resemblance to type 1339A, "The fool is unacquainted with sausages."

68. From the Max Hunter Collection, Greene County Public Library, Springfield, Missouri. No informant data available. T70, "The scorned lover," is the closest relevant motif.

69. From the Max Hunter Collection, Greene County Public Library, Springfield, Missouri. Recorded in 1971 from a handwritten notebook of jokes kept by a Springfield man. The general section of motifs T200–T299, "Married Life," is relevant.

70. Collected in 1971 by Joe Lindsey from H.R. "Rip" Lindsey, Fayetteville, Arkansas. For information about H.R. Lindsey see the notes to text 31. This is Aarne-Thompson type 1443, "The Pillow too High," a tale that dates back at least to 1906, for Thompson reports hearing it in Kentucky in that year where it was reported as a true happening about a local character. In a 1955 festschrift for German folklorist Will-Erich Peuckert, Kurt Ranke reports a German version. In *Anecdota Americana* (1934), p. 154, a "Massachusetts youth" spends the night with "a freshman at an Eastern University," and, to assure her "of his irreproachable probity" places a bolster between them. Generally, it is one of the girl's parents who places the object between them. Often, as in Legman, vol. 1, p. 123, this is a traveling salesman joke. Legman (vol. 1, p. 124) suggests that ultimately this item can be traced back to ancient legends of the Arthurian and Tristan and Isolde cycles.

Hoffmann gives this motif number X729.1.2.

71. Collected in 1977 by Earnest Eugene Seward from Junior Debow, Batesville, Arkansas. Debow was born August 15, 1925, at Chinquapin, Arkansas, and spent his first extended stay away from home in 1946 when he was drafted into the U.S. Army Air Corps. Debow has four children who, at the time of the collection, ranged in age from 23 to 32. Since 1946 Debow has traveled throughout most of the United States and, according to Seward, "has collected stories and jokes from most every place he has been." Although he has had a variety of jobs, including working on a Mississippi River riverboat, working for a tire company, and being a truck driver, at the time of the collection Debow had been a member of the Batesville Fire Department for several years. A gregarious person, Debow is also well known among his co-workers as a joketeller. The present tale is a version of an item that turns up regularly in modern jokebooks such as Bennett Cerf's *The Sound of Laughter*, p. 98.

Hoffmann's X725, "Humor concerning adultery," is relevant.

72. Collected in 1973 by Marla Crider from Bill Yoes, Greenland, Arkansas. At the time Yoes was U.S. Postmaster at Greenland and, apparently, was a very jolly person. Crider says, "He is one of those people that turns red all over when he laughs. He stays red a good deal of the time. He's a jolly guy that loves to tell a good joke."

There is no motif that is an exact parallel, but J1700, "Fools," and J1730, "Absurd ignorance," are implied.

73. From the Max Hunter Collection, Greene County Public Library, Springfield, Missouri. Recorded in 1971 from a handwritten book of jokes kept by a Springfield man.

J2200, "Absurd lack of logic—general," and J2214, "Absurd generalization from particular incident."

74. From the Max Hunter Collection, Greene County Public Library, Springfield, Missouri. Recorded in 1971 from a handwritten notebook of jokes kept by a Springfield man. A version given in Vance Randolph, *Hot Springs and Hell*, p. 17, has a girl of "about fifteen" getting married to a man who "looked like he was pretty near seventy." According to Randolph (p. 180), the same joke is in an anonymous 1890 booklet, *New Yarns and Funny Jokes*, p. 38; Mody C. Boatright, *Folk Laughter on the American Frontier*, p. 105; and a 1949 article by Stuart Gallacher in *Michigan History*. A version also appears in W.L. Gross, *Good Stories for All Occasions*, pp. 30–31. Also see the text in James N. Tidwell, *A Treasury of American Folk Humor*, p. 412. The "shotgun wedding," such as described here, does not often appear in Ozark jokes. X700, "Humor concerning sex," is the closest relevant motif.

Foolish

75. Collected in 1982 by Mary Camron from Leonard Horton, Big Flat, Arkansas. Camron was collecting material for a high school project when she interviewed Horton. She provided an accurate text but told nothing else about Horton. See a text from a black informant reprinted in Richard Walser, *Tar Heel Laughter*, pp. 133–34. Also compare the story "Joe Learning to Drive" in Frank B. Rowlett, Jr., *Say . . . Have I Told You?*, pp. 22–23. See also the comments in the notes for text 48.

J1730, "Absurd ignorance."

76. Collected in 1964 by Robin Jordan from Lee Parker, Goshen, Arkansas. For information about Parker see the notes to text 12. Versions of this mock children's story appear in Gershon Legman, vol. 2, p. 914, and in Johnny Lyons, *Joking Off #2*, pp. 98–99. Legman suggests that there is really only one son, and the story merely presents the two sides of his character. In other words, this is how he really is, and how he wishes he were able to be. Parker's text is both "cleaner" and longer than most versions.

Thompson's general section U100–U299, "The Nature of Life—Miscellaneous Motifs," is appropriate.

77. Collected April 25, 1977, by Laneal Altom and Chris Jackson from Neal Crow, Cave City, Arkansas. Crow, born near Cave City, May 15, 1912, is well known throughout much of the Arkansas Ozarks because of his role as the squatter in the Arkansaw Traveller Folk Theatre, an outdoor theater near Hardy, Arkansas. Since 1967, when the theater opened, Crow has played the squatter for thousands of tourists each summer and is very proud of the fact that he has never missed a performance. Every year he digs sassafras roots that are used in tea served at the Traveller Theatre. At one time he earned his living as a janitor at the Independence County Courthouse in nearby Batesville but has retired from that occupation. He still continues to run a small farm of 120 acres on which he grows a few crops and raises some livestock. Very fond of fishing and coon hunting, he keeps a pack of twelve to fifteen dogs; one of his hounds usually has the part of "Old Blue" at the theater. One of the achievements Crow is proudest of is that he has never been heavily in debt. The most he has ever owed is $350.

Crow is a very outgoing person who loves to visit with anyone who comes to his house. He has a large number of yarns he enjoys telling, many of them hunting and fishing stories, but with a few older narratives also in his repertoire. For these reasons he is frequently sought out by persons looking for "local color" and by folklore students at Arkansas College in Batesville, Altom and Jackson being two of the latter. Although the tale given here sounds like something that might be included in one of the books of the nineteenth-century Southwestern humorists, I have been unable to find any parallels in such writings. The general idea of Crow's narrative is quite old, as the narratives related in Paul Oppenheimer, *A Pleasant Vintage of Till Eulenspiegel* (1515), pp. 90–93, 116–17; *The Jests of Scogin* (1626), pp. 96–97; and *Merie Tales of the Mad Men of Gotham* (1630), pp. 17–19, indicate. (The last two booklets are reprinted in W. Carew Hazlitt, *Shakespeare Jest-Books*, Scogin in vol. 2, Gotham in vol. 3, and it is those printings that are cited here.)

78. Collected in 1973 by Marla Crider from Edna Henbest, Fayetteville, Arkansas. At the time of collection Henbest was a resident of Hillcrest Towers, apparently a senior citizens' residence. Crider noted that Henbest was a very good joketeller and, despite her seventy-six years, a very active person who kept busy working as County Coordinator of the Council on Aging, a national organization.

79. Collected in 1973 by Marla Crider from Ricky Medlock, Fayetteville, Arkansas. At the time of collection Medlock was a junior at the University of Arkansas and an outstanding basketball player who achieved All-American status as a freshman. From Cave City, Arkansas, Medlock was, according to Crider, "usually quiet, and shy" but, she also noted, "he can tell some funny jokes."

This story is a favorite of modern jokebook compilers. Compare the versions in A. Monroe Aurand, *Wit and Humor of the Pennsylvania Germans*, p. 21; J.M. Elgart, *Over Sixteen*, p. 113; Bill Yates, *Forever Funny*, p. 14. Vance Randolph includes a version in *Hot Springs and Hell*, p. 53, collected from a Mrs. Ann Miller of Aurora, Missouri, who heard it from relatives in Crane, Missouri, in 1947.

J1700, "Fools."

80. Collected in 1974 by E.W. Lee from John Townsley, Calamine, Arkansas. I have heard several people, both inside and outside the Ozarks, tell about experiences with vintage cars that were unable to go up a hill forward, although no deception was involved. For example, my grandmother told me about such an experience my grandfather had in western North Carolina in about 1910 with a Ford. Townsley worked part-time for the American Lead and Zinc Company in Calamine and, apparently, had a large fund of narratives, many of which were of a humorous nature.

81. Collected sometime between 1965 and 1970 by E.W. Lee from Jack Krepps, Cave City, Arkansas. Krepps was thirty years old in 1974 when this collection was written up. This tale seems to be a variation on a so-called urban legend about a driver who finds his car has been dented in his absence. A note is found on the windshield with the message, "The people who see me writing this note think I am giving you my name and address, but I'm not."

82. Collected in 1977 by Earnest Eugene Seward from Nolan Garrett, Locust Grove, Arkansas. Garrett, born November 21, 1950, at Batesville, Arkansas, lived in Locust Grove, a small community about ten miles south of Batesville, at the time of collection. His family has lived in the immediate vicinity for several generations; Garrett himself never traveled farther away than Little Rock (approximately one hundred miles) until he started driving a truck for a Batesville company. At the time of collection he was still employed in that job. Garrett was a gregarious person who was locally noted as a good joketeller. Seward recorded a number of jokes from him, several of them being "dirty."
J1700, "Fools," and J1742, "The countryman in the great world."

83. Collected in 1977 by Earnest Eugene Seward from Nolan Garrett, Locust Grove, Arkansas. For information about Garrett see the notes to text 82. J1730, "Absurd ignorance."

84. Collected March 1983 by W.K. McNeil from Julie Kelley, Big Flat, Arkansas. For information about Kelley see the notes to text 55. Relevant motifs are J1730, "Absurd ignorance," and J1732, "Ignorance of certain foods."

85. Collected March 1983 by W.K. McNeil from George Vickers, Big Flat, Arkansas. For information about Vickers see the notes to text 25b. The local character who is always looking for a handout from his friends is a familiar figure in most communities. A man addicted to tobacco but who never seems to have any of his own is primarily encountered in American folk tradition.

86. Collected November 1982 by W.K. McNeil and George West from Elisha Honeycutt, Big Flat, Arkansas. Honeycutt was another of the sixth-graders interviewed on video camera (see the notes to text 7b). This is motif J1761, "Animal thought to be object," an item of long-standing popularity in the Ozarks, being reported from Kirbyville, Missouri, over one hundred years ago. The story was printed a number of times by the late Ozark folklorist Vance Randolph. For examples, see his *Funny Stories About Hillbillies*, p. 11, and *Hot Springs and Hell*, p. 152. Also see the latter book, p. 272, for a list of other printings.

87. Collected March 1983 by W.K. McNeil from George Vickers, Big Flat, Arkansas. For information about Vickers see the notes to text 25b. Motif J1742, "The countryman in the great world," seems to apply here because the humor derives from the fact that the main character is unfamiliar with a practice found in an area outside his home region.

88. Collected November 1982 by W.K. McNeil and George West from Toby Treat, Big Flat, Arkansas. For information about Treat see the notes to text 7b. Perhaps the most famous story about being ignorant of bananas is one in which the man throws away the fruit and eats the peel, and as a result finds bananas bitter. The present joke, however, is a close second. A favorite with vaudeville entertainers sixty to eighty years ago, it is somewhat noteworthy as being the first joke told on *The Grand Ole Opry* by Sarah Ophelia Colley Cannon, who is better known as Minnie Pearl. Compare the story titled "Harold's Train Ride" in Frank B. Rowlett, Jr., *Say Have I Told You*, pp. 36–37.

J1730, "Absurd ignorance," and J1732, "Ignorance of certain foods."

89. Collected in 1973 by Marla Crider from Virgil Bradshaw, Greenland, Arkansas. For information about Bradshaw see the notes to text 65.

Hoffmann's X749.5.4, "Double entendre and extended verbal misunderstandings."

90. Collected in 1973 by Marla Crider from Gordon Bradshaw, Farmington, Arkansas. Bradshaw was one of Crider's uncles; she referred to him as her "country" uncle. She likened him to her grandfather, noting that he was "mild-tempered and full of remarks." Crider considered him "a delight to be around."

J1730, "Absurd ignorance."

91. From the Max Hunter Collection, Greene County Public Library, Springfield, Missouri. Recorded in 1971 from a handwritten book of jokes kept by a Springfield man. This joke, or some variation of it, has been popular for many years, being one of the standbys of many vaudeville and professional country comics. It is, of course, a mock children's story for it is clear that it is adults, not children, who are speaking. As told by most people it is a buffoon, not a child, that delivers this pun.

Hoffmann's X749.5.6, "Puns."

92. Collected in 1971 by Joe Lindsey from H.R. "Rip" Lindsey, Fayetteville, Arkansas. For information about H.R. Lindsey see the notes to text 31.

J1730, "Absurd ignorance," and Hoffmann's X716, "Humor concerning defecation and breaking wind."

93. Collected in 1971 by Joe Lindsey from H.R. "Rip" Lindsey, Fayetteville, Arkansas. For information about H.R. Lindsey see the notes to text 31.

J1730, "Absurd ignorance," and J1732, "Ignorance of certain foods."

94. Collected in 1971 by Joe Lindsey from H.R. "Rip" Lindsey, Fayetteville, Arkansas. For information about H.R. Lindsey see the notes to text 31. The joke is double-edged because of the circumstances of the Depression when many farmers quite likely could be described in terms similar to those the agent used in depicting the billygoat. Basically, though, it is bureaucrats who are made fun of here. Compare the story in Bennett Cerf, *The Sound of Laughter,* p. 289.

The general category J1750–1849, "Absurd misunderstandings," applies here.

95. Collected in 1971 by Joe Lindsey from H.R. "Rip" Lindsey, Fayetteville, Arkansas. For information about H.R. Lindsey see the notes to text 31.

J1742, "The countryman in the great world," is implied here.

96. Collected in 1964 by Robin Jordan from Lee Parker, Goshen, Arkansas. For information on Parker see the notes to text 12. In *Isaac Asimov's Treasury of Humor,* pp. 350–51, several similar jokes are given. Asimov suggests that jokes "in which the women are awarded the last word" are relatively small in number because women do not participate in joketelling sessions as fully as men—an interesting thesis but one that is unproven and, in my view, improbable. It seems likely that women do engage in joketelling sessions but such sessions have certainly not been as frequently considered by the relatively small number of joke scholars as have those of men. Legman, vol. 1, pp. 128–29, gives several similar jokes.

J1702, "Stupid husband," and Hoffmann's X725, "Humor concerning adultery."

97. Collected December 1962 by Bill Knowles from Darrell Knowles, Mountain Home, Arkansas. For information about Darrell Knowles see the notes to text 8. The present joke has appeared in a number of recent jokebooks such as Bennett Cerf, *The Sound of Laughter,* p. 194.

Hoffmann's J1731, "The city person ignorant of the farm."

98. Collected in 1959 by Gene H. Brooks from Fred Starr, Fayetteville, Arkansas. For information about Starr see the notes to text 61. The joke told here has been printed widely in the twentieth century in both jokebooks and folklore collections. Some of its numerous printings include James Schermerhorn, *Schermerhorn's Stories,* p. 187; J. Frank Dobie, *A Vaquero of the Brush Country,* pp. 35–38; James W. Blakley, *Tall Tales,* p. 54 (which is different from most versions in that the man asks "What's time to a cow?"); Leewin B. Williams, *Master Book of Humorous Illustrations,* pp. 398–99: George Milburn, *The Best Rube Jokes,* p. 15, and *The Best Yankee Jokes,* p. 13; Peggy Edmund and Harold Workman Williams, *Toaster's Handbook,* p. 447; Lewis Copeland, *The World's Best Jokes,* p. 59; Powers Moulton, *2500 Jokes for All Occasions,* p. 211; Stetson Kennedy, *Palmetto Country,* p. 235; James Masterson, *Arkansas Folklore,* p. 392; Bennett Cerf, *Try and Stop Me,* p. 175, and *The Sound of Laughter,* p. 285; B.A. Botkin, *A Treasury of American Folklore,* p. 570, and *A Treasury of American Anecdotes,* p. 101, a reprint from Vance Randolph's *Funny Stories About Hillbillies;* Francis Leo Golden, *Laughter Is Legal,* p. 229; *Willard Scott's Down Home Stories,* p. 128 (which differs from most versions in that the man asks "What's a hen's time worth?"); and Vance Randolph, *Hot Springs and Hell,* p. 116. Randolph's informant heard the tale in the 1920s and no known text can be traced farther back, but the story most likely predates that era.

99. Collected in November 1962 by Bill Knowles from Jane Smith, Calico Rock, Arkansas. Smith was one of Knowles's former teachers. According to Knowles, "she had this story from her father who, she said, was a great storyteller, and when the family would all get together his brothers, sisters, and nephews around the fire at night he would tell stories that his father and grandfather had told him." Thus, Smith apparently told these stories as much because they were part of her family heritage as for their humor.

J1700, "Fools."

100. Collected in December 1962 by Bill Knowles from a Mr. Estes, Forty-Four, Arkansas. Apparently, he told Knowles several other narratives but this is the only one recorded, Knowles says, "He told me a few short stories but the one I liked best goes like this." This is a version of type 1687, "The Forgotten Word," a tale that has been more frequently reported from Europe than from the United States. Known in the Scandinavian countries, Germany, Russia, Hungary, India, Japan, and England, it has also been reported from Canada, Cuba, Puerto Rico, and, of course, several of the United States. Some representative texts appear in Joseph Jacobs, *More English Fairy Tales,* pp. 211–14; Richard Chase, *Grandfather Tales,* pp. 130–35; and Leonard W. Roberts, *South from Hell-fer-Sartin,* p. 142.

J2671, "The forgetful fool"; J2671.2, "Fool keeps repeating his instructions so as to remember them"; and Thompson's D2004.5, "Forgetting by stumbling."

101. Collected in 1959 by Gene H. Brooks from Fred Starr, Fayetteville, Arkansas. For information about Starr see the notes to text 61.

J1730, "Absurd ignorance."

102. Collected March 1983 by W.K. McNeil from George Vickers, Big Flat, Arkansas. For information on Vickers see the notes to text 25b. The ignorance here is of certain legal formalities involved with homesteading. Relevant motifs are the general one J1730, "Absurd ignorance," and the more particular J1742, "The countryman in the great world."

103. From the Max Hunter Collection, Greene County Public Library, Springfield, Missouri. Recorded in 1971 from a handwritten book of jokes kept by a Springfield man. Another of the numerous mock children's stories in which dialogue is given an added degree of innocence because of being placed in the mouths of children. Indeed, in this case much of the humor would be lost if the words were put in the mouths of adults.

Hoffmann's X711, "Humor concerning the breasts," and X749.5.6, "Puns."

104. From the Max Hunter Collection, Greene County Public Library, Springfield, Missouri. Recorded in 1971 from a handwritten book of jokes kept by a Springfield man.

J1700, "Fools."

105. From the Max Hunter Collection, Greene County Public Library, Springfield, Missouri. Informant data not available.

J2210, "Logical absurdity based upon certain false assumptions."

106. From the Max Hunter Collection, Greene County Public Library, Springfield, Missouri. Recorded in 1971 from a handwritten book of jokes kept by a Springfield man. This is an example of a bull, or Irish bull as they are sometimes called, which is an absurd and illogical mistake in statement. The origin of the term "bull" for this type of humor is obscure, but it first became popular in the early seventeenth century, one of the earliest collections of this sort of material being in *John Taylor's Wit and Mirth: Chargeably Collected out of Taverns. Ordinaries. Innes, Bowling-Greenes and Allyes, Ale-houses, Tobacco-shops, Highwayes, and Water-passages. Made up, and fashioned into Clinches, Bulls, Quirkes, Yerkes, Quips, and Jerkes, Apothegmatically bundled up and garbled at the request of old John Garretts Ghost* (1630). John Garrett was a well-known jester. The first serious study of such jokes was Maria Edgeworth and Richard Lovell Edgeworth's *Essay on Irish Bulls* (1801). According to John Wardroper, *Jest upon Jest,* p. 97, the term possibly had its origin in a joke about the Sieur Gaulard that came into English some time before 1620. In that yarn the "bull-speaker said he saw someone riding 'a-horseback on a cow,' and the Gaulard original was improved upon with the reply, 'That's a bull'—which then became a catch-phrase applied to all such unwittingly ludicrous turns of phrase." Perhaps so, but it seems just a little too good to be true. For some other examples of bulls see the annotated edition of *On a Slow Train Through Arkansaw,* pp. 45–47.

J2200, "Absurd lack of logic—general."

107. Collected in 1973 by Marla Crider from Mitchell Crider, Fayetteville, Arkansas. The informant was the collector's father. Marla notes, "Daddy never really has time to tell jokes, but when he does he gets excited right in the middle of them and usually tells the punch line." A former grocery store manager and U.S. Postmaster in Greenland, Arkansas, Mitchell Crider was retired at the time of collection.

J1730, "Fools," and J1730, "Absurd ignorance."

108. Collected in 1959 by Gene H. Brooks from Fred Starr, Fayetteville, Arkansas. For information on Starr see the notes to text 61. For some reason Brooks did not transcribe the narrative as related by Starr but merely summarized. This is a variation on X1211(c), "Cats which are hard to kill."

109. Collected in 1977 by Chris Jackson and Laneal Altom from Neal Crow, Cave City, Arkansas. For information on Crow see the notes to text

77. This is a widely traveled yarn that has been printed numerous times during the past century. Often it is told as a numskull tale not associated with any particular ethnic or racial group. It is found in the following publications: Marshall Brown, *Wit and Humor*, pp. 125–26; J.B. McClure, *Entertaining Anecdotes*, p. 63; W.A. Clouston, *The Book of Noodles*, pp. 14–15; Melville D. Landon, *Wit and Humor of the Age*, p. 494; Arthur Palmer Hudson, *Humor of the Old Deep South*, p. 452; Arthur Huff Fauset, *Folklore from Nova Scotia*, p. 61; Lewis Copeland, *The World's Best Jokes*, p. 16; F. Meier, *The Joketeller's Joke Book*, p. 306; Lewis and Faye Copeland, *10,000 Jokes, Toasts and Stories*, p. 747; Powers Moulton, *2500 Jokes*, p. 327; Richard M. Dorson, *Negro Folktales in Michigan*, p. 183; and Vance Randolph, *Hot Springs and Hell*, p. 41. According to Randolph, p. 195, Bennett Cerf published it in a syndicated column in 1962 as a new story, with a Boy Scout background. Ronald L. Baker, *Jokelore*, p. 126, includes a version in which the Irishmen specifically call the lightning bugs fireflies. Although both terms refer to the same insect, few texts use the word "firefly."

J1759.3, "Numskull thinks lightning bugs are mosquitoes carrying lanterns to find victims," and X621*, "Jokes about the Irish."

110. Collected in 1964 by Robin Jordan from Lee Parker, Goshen, Arkansas. For information on Parker see the notes to text 12. This is possibly the best known joke about Scotsmen and their stereotypical parsimoniousness, but surprisingly it hasn't appeared frequently in print. Its first American publication, apparently, was in *Anecdota Americana*, pp. 112–13, that version concluding with the line "I was trying to get your attention after the first loop, when the wife fell out." A shorter version in Larry Wilde's *Complete Book of Ethnic Humor*, p. 225, concludes with the Scotsman saying, "I almost did speak when my wife fell out." In a version given in Julius Alvin, *Totally Gross Jokes*, vol. 2, p. 12, the Scotsman says, "There was one time you almost had me." When asked to explain he answers, "When my wife fell out."

X600, "Humor concerning races or nations."

111. Collected in 1971 by Joe Lindsey from H.R. "Rip" Lindsey, Fayetteville, Arkansas. For information on H.R. Lindsey see the notes to text 31. "Pood" is, of course, a euphemism for breaking wind.

X600, "Humor concerning races or nations," and Hoffmann's X716, "Humor concerning defecation and breaking wind."

112. Collected in 1977 by Earnest Eugene Seward from Nolan Garrett, Locust Grove, Arkansas. For information on Garrett see the notes to text 82. This joke has been told, minus the Polish connection, on such country music shows as the syndicated *Hee Haw* TV program. A version collected from a deputy sheriff in Terre Haute, Indiana, March 1982, is given in Ronald L. Baker, *Jokelore*, pp. 140–41. In his *The Types of the Polack Joke*, William Clements assigns this motif E5.7.1, "The Polish Tracker."

113. Collected in 1958 by James McClain Stalker from Jean Crouch, Newark, Arkansas. Stalker says, "Mrs. Crouch is an attractive young lady who is a friend of long standing. She has a family heritage rich in tales and enjoys telling them very much." The story given here is about her great-grandfather, Captain George Rutherford, and is probably told as much because it is considered part of family and local history as for its humor.

K1810, "Deception by disguise"; K1870, "Illusions"; and K1889, "Other illusions."

114. Collected in 1964 by Robin Jordan from Lee Parker, Goshen, Arkansas. For information on Parker see the notes to text 12. Robert Love Taylor (1850–1912) was twice governor of Tennessee, from 1887 to 1891 and 1897 to 1899. During his long public career he was also a United States congressman and a United States senator. Known as "fiddling Bob" or the "fiddling governor" because he was skilled as an old-time fiddler, Taylor used his talents in that regard to project an image of himself as a down-to-earth country boy. In 1886 he gained a degree of notoriety nationally when, in the so-called "War of the Roses," he campaigned against his older brother Alfred, who was known as Alf. A selection of Bob Taylor's stories and sayings are given in B.A. Botkin, *A Treasury of Southern Folklore,* pp. 276–78. Samuel Porter Jones (1847–1906) was one of the more famous revivalists in late nineteenth- and early twentieth-century America. An Alabama native, he gained considerable following in Tennessee and other southern states and in a sense left a lasting impression in the Volunteer State. The Ryman Auditorium, longtime home of the famous country music show *The Grand Ole Opry,* was originally built as the Union Gospel Tabernacle for Jones. It is, of course, not impossible that the debate mentioned here took place, but no documentation of it has been found.

X599.1*, "Jokes on politicians" and Hoffmann's X749.5.6, "Puns."

115. Collected in 1973 by Marla Crider from Mitchell Crider, Fayetteville, Arkansas. For information about Mitchell Crider see the notes to text 107. The present joke has been widely reprinted appearing in, among other places, the following books: J. Gilchrist Lawson, *The World's Best Humorous Anecdotes,* p. 210; J.H. Johnson, Jerry Sheridan, and Ruth Lawrence, *The Laughter Library,* p. 122; George Milburn, *The Best Rube Jokes,* p. 19; Edmund Fuller, *Thesaurus of Anecdotes,* p. 334; Lewis and Faye Copeland, *10,000 Jokes, Toasts and Stories,* p. 522; B.A. Botkin, *A Treasury of New England Folklore,* p. 109, and *A Treasury of Southern Folklore,* p. 10; Alexander Wiley, *Laughing With Congress,* pp. 105–6; Louis Untermeyer, *A Treasury of Laughter,* p. 91; and Vance Randolph, *Hot Springs and Hell,* p. 120. Henry Spalding, *A Treasury of Irish Folklore and Humor,* p. 263, gives a version set during the Kennedy-Nixon presidential campaign in which the protagonist heckles Nixon. Although most versions use "horse thief," some others have "fool." One text quoted by Randolph (pp. 249–50) has the canvasser asking, "What if your father had been a bear and your mother a wildcat?" The voter answers, "A Democrat, I reckon, just like the rest of you." There are, of course, many possible explanations for the great popularity of this joke, but one is certainly its versatility; another is the opportunity it gives tellers to take a swipe at a group often held in low repute. In folk tradition politicians are generally distrusted and this joke provides occasion to air negative ideas about those who run for public office. Almost anything can be substituted for the phrase "horse thief." Either political party can be mentioned, but most often it is Republicans who are named. Those who favor that party might, however, use Democrats in the punch line. Also, as in the case of Randolph's informant, who in his village was in the minority as a Democrat, it provided an acceptable means for him to poke fun at his neighbors. He occasionally told this tale in a loud voice for the benefit of his fellow townspeople.

X599.1*, "Jokes on politicians."

116. Recorded in 1973 from memory by Marla Crider who heard it from her grandfather, Fred Bradshaw, Fayetteville, Arkansas, who had died several years earlier. According to Crider, "He lived with my family and me until his death. He was a very mild-mannered man with a dry sense of humor. People loved to be around him because he was coming up with some type of joke or saying. Grandpa was very special to me, because he taught me how to read and write when I was barely four years old. I was his pride and joy, and he never joked when it came to 'Papa's little girl.' I'm not the only one, though, that misses his wit and dry humor."

The general category WO-99, "Favorable traits of character," applies.

117. Collected in 1973 by Marla Crider from her aunt, Blanche Bradshaw, Farmington, Arkansas. A farmwife, Bradshaw also works, or did at the time of collection, in Food Services at the University of Arkansas, Fayetteville. Crider notes that "she is a very jolly lady and a great joketeller for a woman." This story is sometimes attributed to Mark Twain but I have been unable to find it in any of Twain's writings. In 1981, however, I did hear a stage impersonator of Twain use the story, referring to a different city. The same joke appears in a lengthier than usual version in *Isaac Asimov's Treasury of Humor*, p. 304. Asimov notes that any city could be utilized in the joke, and this versatility is undoubtedly one reason for its popularity.

118. Collected in 1973 by Marla Crider from Carolyn Crider, West Fork, Arkansas. Carolyn is Marla's sister-in-law and, according to Marla, "is a very happy-go-lucky person and jokes are part of her everyday life." Although this item sounds like jokebook fare I have been unable to find it in any such source. The closest relevant motif is Thompson's X350, "Jokes on teachers."

119. Collected in 1973 by Marla Crider from John Williams, Fayetteville, Arkansas. Williams was an insurance salesman who, apparently, was known among his friends as an inveterate joketeller. Crider notes, "He is forever telling jokes, some good and some not so good. He gets most of them from his clients. He is a very entertaining person to be around."

Thompson's X681, "Blason populaire."

120. Collected in 1971 by Joe Lindsey from his father, H.R. "Rip" Lindsey, Fayetteville, Arkansas. For information on H.R. Lindsey see the notes to text 31. This item has frequently appeared in jokebooks of which the following are representative: Lewis and Faye Copeland, *10,000 Jokes, Toasts and Stories,* p. 144; Josh Lee, *How to Hold an Audience Without a Rope,* p. 97; and Bennett Cerf, *The Sound of Laughter,* p. 287. It is also among the stories included in Vance Randolph, *Hot Springs and Hell,* pp. 17–18. Randolph got his text from one of his prize informants, Lon Jordan of Farmington, Arkansas, October 1941. Jordan was primarily known as a fiddler but he also told a number of traditional narratives to Randolph, including some that were "salty." Jordan said the joke given here was a very ancient tale, and so it may be. Even so, there are few printed references that predate the twentieth century. Randolph, p. 180, says the theme has often been used in fiction, citing two examples from *Esquire* magazine in the 1930s.

121. Collected in 1964 by Robin Jordan from Lee Parker, Goshen, Arkansas. For information about Parker see the notes to text 12.

122. From the column "Jimmie Wilson Opines," January 26, 1935. For information on Wilson see the notes to text 4.

J1250, "Clever verbal retorts."

123. From the column "Jimmy Wilson Opines," January 10, 1934. For information on Wilson see the notes to text 4.

X800, "Humor based on drunkenness."

124. From the Max Hunter Collection, Greene County Public Library, Springfield, Missouri. Recorded in 1971 from a handwritten notebook kept by a Springfield man. According to Melville D. Landon, *Kings of the Platform and Pulpit,* pp. 354–55, this is a story told by Mark Twain. Paul M. Zall, in *Mark Twain Laughing,* p. 20, quotes a version of the story attributed to Twain in an 1870 publication. Other versions of the story appear in George Korson, *Minstrels of the Mine Patch,* pp. 179–80; Leewin B. Williams, *Master Book of Humorous Illustrations,* p. 280; Nathan Ausubel, *Treasury of Jewish Folklore,* p. 339; Norman Lockridge, *Waggish Tales of the Czechs,* pp. 198–99; Mody C. Boatright, *Folk Laughter of the American Frontier,* pp. 27–28; and Vance Randolph, *Hot Springs and Hell,* pp. 41–42. Randolph's informant, Joe Ingenthron of Forsyth, Missouri, told him that "everybody in southwest Missouri knows this one." A closely related tale appears in B.A. Botkin, *A Treasury of American Anecdotes,* p. 14.

Interestingly, two different motif numbers are given this tale. Baughman lists it as J1499.7*(a) but Hoffmann gives it as J1641.

125. Collected in 1979 by George West from Dr. William Hudson, Jasper, Arkansas. For information on Hudson see the notes to text 2. This anecdote belongs to a group of tales that might be called "first-time stories." In a similarly humorous vein, one can hear in the Ozarks and other rural areas traditional jokes and personal incidents concerning the first time to see an automobile, to use an indoor toilet, to talk on the telephone, to see a picture show, to visit a big city, etc. The stories capture the comedy of these rites of initiation into "modern" living. This specific story has appeared, so I am told, in several jokebooks with a racial orientation. In these texts the porter is always black and it is unusual in that he gets the best of the white passenger. Hudson's text does not indicate the race of the porter, although the accent he uses in telling the story suggests the man is black. For Hudson, the story serves two purposes—one, it brings a laugh to listeners, or is intended to; and two, it commemorates an important event in his personal life, namely the outset of his professional career in medicine.

126. Collected in 1974 by E.W. Lee from Arthur Ward, Strawberry, Arkansas. Ward, born in 1902, was Lee's uncle, and earned his living primarily as a blacksmith, although he also worked in the sorghum mill. Lee noted that Ward "has been 'retired' most of his life in that he never worked much for a living; then again he never spent much either." The joke given here was one of the favorite stories of Vance Randolph, who said the incident took place in Siloam Springs, Arkansas, a small town in the extreme northwestern part of the state. It sounds to me like a traditional yarn that never happened except in someone's imagination. See a related tale in Irvin S. Cobb, *A Laugh a Day,* p. 13.

127. Collected in 1982 by Nancy Lee from Coy Harness, Big Flat, Arkansas. Lee was a high school student at the time she recorded this joke. Although this story sounds traditional I have been unable to locate an exact parallel. For a discussion of the difficulty Americans once had with false teeth see John Woodforde, *The Strange Story of False Teeth,* especially pp. 93–117.

128. Collected May 11, 1978, by Kathy Nicol from Jessie Hubert Wilkes, Cave City, Arkansas. For information on Wilkes see the notes to text 1. It is evident that many of Hubert's witty responses, of which he was rightly proud, are traditional jokes and tales. This particular yarn is often told on Kentuckians, who also come from a state with a bad reputation in some quarters. Despite this fact the story is not modern but dates back at least to the fifteenth century, for it was among the stories collected in the household of the Medici family by the poet and humanist Angelo Poliziano (1454–1494). Poliziano's manuscript of over four hundred humorous anecdotes was later titled *Bel Libretto* (Beautiful Little Book) and published by Ludovico Domenichi (1515–1564), a proofreader and historian who is now best remembered as the compiler of the largest collection of humorous anecdotes published in the sixteenth century. Poliziano's variant involves Piero de Medici and an official of Perugia. When Piero becomes irritated with the man's "foolish statements and asinine questions," another man calls Piero aside, saying, "Don't be too hard on him, Piero. I am sure that you, too, must have fools just like him in Florence." "Yes, we do," snapped Piero. "But we don't appoint them as officials." (Poliziano's text is given in Henry D. Spalding, *A Treasury of Italian Folklore and Humor*, pp. 54–55.)

In its present form the joke has appeared in several popular publications, most recently in Loyal Jones and Billy Edd Wheeler, *Laughter in Appalachia*, p. 127. Thompson's motif X350, "Jokes on teachers," is implied here but the joke is really about a state, for which there is no appropriate motif number. The general section of motifs X600–699, "Humor Concerning Races or Nations," is the closest relevant material.

129. Recalled in 1973 by Marla Crider, who heard it several years earlier from Fred Bradshaw, Fayetteville, Arkansas. For information on Bradshaw see the notes to text 116. Compare the related story in Richard Walser, *Tar Heel Laughter*, p. 147, in which a supposedly dead man returns. A man reading a newspaper is told "the dead has come to life!" to which he replies, "I'm damned sorry to hear it."

X300, "Humor dealing with professions."

130. Collected in 1971 by Joe Lindsey from H.R. "Rip" Lindsey, Fayetteville, Arkansas. For information on H.R. Lindsey see the notes to text 31. Two versions of this yarn appear in *Isaac Asimov's Treasury of Humor*, pp. 72–73, along with Asimov's note that it is one of those jokes that has several possible endings, all of which are meritorious. I was once told that this was a favorite joke of Stith Thompson's but he never indicated such was the case. It was, however, told about him probably because he was the person responsible for standardizing the type and motif indexes that are still used by comparative folklorists.

131. Collected in 1959 by Gene H. Brooks from Fred Starr, Fayetteville, Arkansas. For information on Starr see the notes to text 61. A very similar version of this story is given in *Isaac Asimov's Treasury of Humor*, p. 302. Starr's text is unusual in that it has two "city fellows" rather than the usual one. This is, of course, part of the "Arkansas Traveler" routine that has been popular throughout the United States since the second half of the nineteenth century. The earliest known printing of the extensive dialogue was from 1858 to 1860, but none of the material was original even then. Some of the humor was decades, even centuries old. Like Starr's text, most twentieth-century versions tend to reduce the long dialogue of the "original" to just a few questions. The numerous witty responses of earlier versions are reduced here to just one, the punch line. For a history of the "Traveler" see James R. Masterson, *Arkansas Folklore*, pp. 186–219.

J1250, "Clever verbal retorts: general."

132. Collected in 1959 by Gene H. Brooks from Fred Starr, Fayetteville, Arkansas. For information on Starr see the notes to text 61. According to Bill Adler, *Jewish Wit and Wisdom*, p. 38, French dramatist and novelist

Tristan Bernard (1866–1947), when asked about his opinion about life in the hereafter, responded: "With regard to the climate, I would prefer heaven; but with regard to the company I would give preference to hell." That quote is not included among the several attributed to Bernard in Clifton Fadiman, *The Little, Brown Book of Anecdotes,* pp. 56–58. It is among the anecdotes contained in Mark Twain's notebooks for May 1889 through August 1890, although abbreviated to "heaven for climate, hell for company!" See Paul M. Zall, *Mark Twain Laughing,* p. 49. Zall says Twain used it in a speech delivered in 1901, adding that it was also an anecdote that Twain's physician, a Dr. C.C. Rice, told about a favorite cigar maker. Compare also Thomas W. Jackson's best-selling jokebook *On a Slow Train Through Arkansaw,* p. 44, where one man says "that all we need in this country is a little more rain and a little better society." To which the other replies, "That is all that Hell needs." Starr's text which deals with sectional prejudice is unique among published versions.

133. Collected in 1959 by Gene H. Brooks from Fred Starr, Fayetteville, Arkansas. For information on Starr see the notes to text 61.
N100, "Nature of luck and fate."

134. Recalled September 9, 1975, by Howard C. Johnson, Paragould, Arkansas. Johnson was, at the time, sixty years old and heard this story "a great number of times" from his grandfather who used the narrative "to teach me not to waste time on trivial matters." Johnson was born near Charleston, Missouri, where his grandfather moved about 1905 from his home in Kentucky. The family ran a large farm that was tended primarily by black labor. The blacksmith shop on the farm was the setting of this story.
J1250, "Clever verbal retorts: general."

135. Collected sometime between 1965 and 1970 by E.W. Lee from John Townsley, Calamine, Arkansas. For information about Townsley see the notes to text 80.
X255*, "Jokes about merchants."

136. Collected in 1979 by W.K. McNeil from Jessie Hubert Wilkes, Cave City, Arkansas. For information on Wilkes see the notes to text 1. This story has been occasionally printed, most often told as a true story. Vance Randolph printed two versions of the tale, one in *Funny Stories from Arkansas,* p. 11, and another in *Hot Springs and Hell,* pp. 49–50. The latter was from fellow writer Nancy Clemens who heard it about 1930 in Cedar County, Missouri. B.A. Botkin, in *A Treasury of American Anecdotes,* p. 29, reprints Randolph's text from *Funny Stories from Arkansas.* In his comments on the Clemens text (p. 202), Randolph cites a *Saturday Review* article of 1954 that attributes the remark to a barefoot native of Mountain Home, Arkansas. He also quotes a 1958 *Ozark Guide* article in which a countryman delivers the lines to a tourist from Chicago.
J1250, "Clever verbal retorts: general."

137. From the Max Hunter Collection, Greene County Public Library, Springfield, Missouri. Recorded from a handwritten book of jokes kept by a Springfield man. Compare the following tale from Maximilian Schele De Vere's *Americanisms: The English of the New World,* p. 144:

> A schoolmaster in a public school in the interior of Pennsylvania was drilling his class in arithmetic. He said: "If I cut an apple in two, what will the parts be?" "Halves!" was the answer. "If I cut the halves in two, what would you call the parts?" "Quarters!" "If I cut the quarters in two, what will the parts be?" The answer was unanimous, "Snits!" *(Snits,* a colloquial form of *Schnitz,* meaning "to slice, cut, or chop," is a Pennsylvania German term for slices of dried fruit.)

138. From the Max Hunter Collection, Greene County Public Library, Springfield, Missouri. Recorded in 1971 from a handwritten book of jokes kept by a Springfield man.

J1100, "Cleverness."

139. Collected March 1983 by W.K. McNeil from George Vickers, Big Flat, Arkansas. For information on Vickers see the notes to text 25b. Hubert Wilkes of Cave City, Arkansas, also used to tell this story. According to Cyril Clemens in *Mark Twain's Jest Book,* p. 21, this incident happened to Twain when he did some out-of-season fishing in Maine. The Clemens version is reprinted in Paul M. Zall, *Mark Twain Laughing,* p. 179; Zall says it is also recounted as a true experience of H.L. Woods and a Colorado game warden in *After Dinner Stories and Repartee,* p. 38 (1908). According to Lowell Thomas, *Tall Stories,* pp. 99–100, the exchange took place between an old clam-spearer and eel-digger who did some duck hunting out of season and a game warden on Long Island. A version reported in Ray B. Browne, "A Night with the Hants," pp. 95–96, has the exchange taking place between Jim, a colored man who does some illegal squirrel hunting, and an Alabama game warden. Two Indiana versions are given in Ronald L. Baker, *Jokelore,* p. 90. In one a hunter has killed twenty quail and in the other he merely has a bag of sticks, rocks, and similar things he has found. This is, to my knowledge, the only version in which the protagonist has not actually acquired game illegally. Compare also Richard M. Dorson, *Negro Tales from Pine Bluff,* p. 270.

J1155.1.1*(b), "Hunter (or fisherman) meets stranger, tells him about all the animals, birds, or fish he has caught that day. The numbers are all above bag limits, or else the game is out of season. Finally the stranger asks: "Do you know who I am?" "No." "Well, I'm the game warden." "Do you know who I am?" "No." "Well, I'm the biggest liar in this county."

140. Collected May 11, 1978, by Kathy Nicol from Jessie Hubert Wilkes, Cave City, Arkansas. For information on Wilkes see the notes to text 1. This tale has the sound of the vaudeville stage about it, but I have been unable to locate it anywhere. Nevertheless, the punch line, with slight variations, is relatively common in oral tradition.

X1215.3, "Lie: small dog."

141. Collected May 11, 1978, by Kathy Nicol from Jessie Hubert Wilkes, Cave City, Arkansas. For information about Wilkes see the notes to text 1. This seems like an item that might be found in jokebooks but I have been unable to locate any exact parallels. Vance Randolph includes a number of tall tales about hunting dogs in *We Always Lie to Strangers*, pp. 124–30, but this one is not among them. Relevant motifs include X1215.13*, "Lie: remarkable dog: miscellaneous," and X1215.13*(a), "Hunter works dog so hard that he wears full-grown dog down to size of puppy by end of day's hunt."

142. Collected in 1973 by Bill Spurlock from John Williams, Ash Flat, Arkansas. Except for his name and place of residence no information is given about Williams. Compare this tale to that given in text 139.

X584, "Jokes about hunters."

143. Collected in 1959 by Gene H. Brooks from Fred Starr, Fayetteville, Arkansas. For information on Starr see the notes to text 61. It is hardly necessary to state here that people from Chicago are often the butts of Ozark humor, this story being an interesting reversal of the norm because the "foreigner" has the last word. In a version printed in Vance Randolph, *Funny Stories About Hillbillies*, pp. 3–4, it is a rural Missourian who is trying to sell his farm to a hillman from Arkansas. Randolph's text is reprinted in B.A. Botkin, *A Treasury of American Anecdotes*, p. 100. A version given in *Willard Scott's Down Home Stories*, pp. 121–22, doesn't specify where the event occurred, noting merely that the man involved was an old farmer who "had a reputation for being a particularly shrewd businessman."

X500, "Humor concerning other social classes."

144. Collected in 1959 by Gene H. Brooks from Fred Starr, Fayetteville, Arkansas. For information on Starr see the notes to text 61.

J1250, "Clever verbal retorts: general."

145. Collected in 1959 by Gene H. Brooks from Fred Starr, Fayetteville, Arkansas. For information on Starr see the notes to text 61. Relevant motifs include X1500, "Geography and topography"; X1530, "Lies about land (soil)"; and X1535*, "Remarkably poor country and poor soil."

146. Collected in 1959 by Gene H. Brooks from Fred Starr, Fayetteville, Arkansas. For information about Starr see the notes to text 61. Compare the distantly related tale given in Henry D. Spalding, *A Treasury of Irish Folklore and Humor*, p. 89.

J1250, "Clever verbal retorts: general," and K139, "Other worthless animals sold."

Religion

147. Collected in 1974 by F.W. Lee from John Townsley, Calamine, Arkansas. For information on Townsley see the notes to text 80. I have heard stories of a prank such as this one occurring in several Ozark communities during the years when such protracted meetings as that described here were common. One informant, in Fox, Arkansas, said that years ago these extended meetings were the main form of entertainment for local people. Unfortunately, they brought out the mischievousness in some pranksters who enjoyed playing tricks such as that recounted here. She told about a similar incident to that recounted here by Townsley that occurred in her community during the 1920s.

148. Collected in 1964 by Robin Jordan from Lee Parker, Goshen, Arkansas. For information about Parker see the notes to text 12. Here, as in many Ozark jokes about religion it is not really so much the preacher who is ridiculed as the church and its practitioners. Absurd ignorance of the type implied by motif J1742, "The countryman in the great world" is suggested here, but it is really not the backwoodsman, but his more civilized counterparts, that are made light of in this joke. J1738, "Ignorance of religious matters," applies.

149. Collected in 1973 by Marla Crider from Irene Guadalajara, Fayetteville, Arkansas. For information about Guadalajara see the notes to text 68. This item has appeared in a number of contemporary jokebooks such as Bennett Cerf, *The Sound of Laughter,* p. 166. This seems to be a modern adaptation of type 1833, "Application of the sermon." A variant form of that humorous tale appeared in *A C Mery Talys* (A Hundred Merry Tales) (c. 1525), the first jokebook printed in English. See the reprint by W. Carew Hazlitt in *Shakespeare Jest-Books,* pp. 75–76. Texts of that tale type are common in English and American tradition. Compare the related tale in Henry D. Spalding, *A Treasury of Irish Folklore and Humor,* p. 62.

X410, "Jokes on parsons."

150. Collected in 1973 by Marla Crider from E.W. Thornton, Fayetteville, Arkansas. At the time Thornton was a resident of Hillcrest Towers, apparently a residence for senior citizens. Treasurer of the Council on Aging and the Community Adult Center, Thornton also was, apparently, a cheerful person, for Crider notes "when I get depressed at the office, he is always telling a joke to cheer me."

X410, "Jokes on parsons."

151. Collected in 1973 by Marla Crider from E.W. Thornton, Fayetteville, Arkansas. For information on Thornton see the notes to text 150. I have been told that this story was told by Mark Twain, but I have been unable to find it in his writings. Paul M. Zall does not include it in *Mark Twain Laughing,* although he does have a related story, p. 114, taken from Alexander McD. Stoddardt, "Twainiana," *Independent* 68 (May 5, 1910): 961.

X410, "Jokes on parsons."

152. Collected November 24, 1978, by Ed and Judy Copeland from Roland Gillihan, Mountain View, Arkansas. Gillihan, a retired farmer and lay preacher in the Baptist church, was sixty-eight at the time of collection. The Copelands noted that he "is fairly articulate" and "although he is a religious man, he is not pious and he enjoys a preacher joke as much as the next man." The joke given here Gillihan heard from another preacher in 1965, at the Gaylor Church near Mountain View. This has been a popular American story for at least fifty years and has appeared in numerous jokebooks, including Martha Lupton, *Treasury of Modern Humor*, p. 344; Bertha Damon, *Grandma Called It Carnal*, p. 70, where it is set in New England; F. Meier, *The Joke Teller's Joke Book*, pp. 197–98; and Lewis and Faye Copeland, *10,000 Jokes, Toasts and Stories*, p. 697. In *Hot Springs and Hell*, p. 223, Vance Randolph refers to a Mexican Spanish text in English translation that was printed in the *New Mexico Folklore Record*, vol. 1, p. 29, but I have been unable to locate that text. Other versions are given in Alexander Wiley, *Laughing With Congress*, pp. 214–15; B.A. Botkin, *A Treasury of New England Folklore*, p. 172; J. Mason Brewer, *The Word on the Brazos*, pp. 9–10; Alben W. Barkley, *That Reminds Me*, p. 39; B.A. Botkin, *A Treasury of American Anecdotes*, p. 121 (a reprint of Barkley's text); Vance Randolph, *Hot Springs and Hell*, p. 84, which was collected in December 1938 from Lew Bearden, Branson, Missouri, who claimed it was commonly told in Taney County, Missouri (where Branson is located) as early as 1900. A version in *Willard Scott's Down Home Stories*, p. 49, is unusual in that the minister is designated an Episcopalian; the denomination of the preacher is usually not given.

153. Collected November 24, 1978, by Ed and Judy Copeland from Roland Gillihan, Mountain View, Arkansas. For information on Gillihan see the notes to text 152. A shorter version of this joke appears in Daryl Cumber Dance, *Shuckin' and Jivin'*, p. 51. It was written down by Dance on October 2, 1974, because the informant, who lived in Richmond, Virginia, refused to let her tape any of his jokes that could be interpreted as derogatory of the church. In that text church members pour whiskey into the punch being served at a party. The preacher is unaware of the "spiking" and consumes the punch in great quantity, afterwards while praying he says, "God, bless the cow that gave this milk." Essentially the same text as that recorded by the Copelands appears in Mody C. Boatright, *Folk Laughter on the American Frontier*, p. 153. According to volume 2 of *Twainiana*, issued by the Mark Twain Association of America, Mark Twain told a similar yarn about a "great American temperance orator" who was tricked by the chairman of a meeting at which he was speaking. The chairman put rum into the glass of milk the orator requested. After downing the glass the speaker exclaimed: "Gosh! What cows!" This text is reprinted in Paul M. Zall, *Mark Twain Laughing*, pp. 172–73.

X410, "Jokes on parsons," and X800, "Humor concerning drunkenness."

154. Collected November 25, 1978, by Ed and Judy Copeland from Bob

Stewart, Mountain View, Arkansas. Stewart, a sawmill operator, was forty-five years old at the time of collection. Born and raised in Mountain View, Stewart has worked in the timber business most of his life. The Copelands characterized him as "fairly articulate" and speaking "with a slow, hillbilly drawl" and having a dry sense of humor. They further noted, "He is at his best when he tells anecdotes about his travels through the boondocks of Stone County in search of timber to make into whiskey barrel tops." The tale Stewart related to the Copelands is a version of type 1738*, "The dream: all parsons in hell," a tale that is widely known in America. The narrative most often concerns preachers or lawyers but sometimes is told on others, such as wealthy people. According to J.H. Johnson, Jerry Sheridan, and Ruth Lawrence in *The Laughter Library*, p. 209, the story was told by Abraham Lincoln. In *Lincoln Talks*, p. 21, Emanuel Hertz says that Lincoln told it in a tavern where he was spending the night after a long trip across country in the coldest kind of weather. He was to appear in court the next day and told the yarn about lawyers. A related story about preachers was published in a London jestbook, *A Legacy of Fun by Abraham Lincoln* (1865), an anti-Lincoln publication compiled from American jokebooks, newspapers, and English jestbooks. It is doubtful, however, that Lincoln ever uttered the story because many of the items seem to be merely old stories to which his name has been attached. The version of this story is reprinted in Paul M. Zall, *Abe Lincoln Laughing*, p. 50.

Emelyn Gardner credits the yarn to the evangelist Lorenzo Dow (see *Folklore from the Schoharie Hills*, p. 38), but it undoubtedly predates Dow. The tale is also sometimes attributed to Ulysses S. Grant. It has also been a favorite item in jokebooks such as the 1903 *On a Slow Train Through Arkansaw* (see the annotated edition, p. 84). Texts given in J. Mason Brewer, *The Word on the Brazos*, pp. 90–92, and Daryl Cumber Dance, *Shuckin' and Jivin'*, p. 46, clearly indicate that it is common in Afro-American folk tradition. Other versions appear in Marshall Brown, *Wit and Humor*, pp. 61–62; Melville D. Landon, *Wit and Humor of the Age*, pp. 417–18; Robert Hays Cunningham, *Amusing Prose Chap-Books*, p. 349; B.A. Botkin, *A Treasury of New England Folklore*, p. 162; *A Treasury of American Anecdotes*, p. 187 (a reprint of the Gardner text); Alfred Williams, *Round About the Upper Thames*, p. 41; Mody C. Boatright, *Folk Laughter of the American Frontier*, p. 151; Vance Randolph, *Hot Springs and Hell*, p. 57; and Loyal Jones and Billy Edd Wheeler, *Laughter in Appalachia*, p. 41. The Jones and Wheeler text is unusual in that it is set in the first person. Compare the distantly related story "Hell at the Local Level" in Richard Walser, *Tar Heel Laughter*, pp. 211–12.

155. Collected November 24, 1978, by Ed and Judy Copeland from Roland Gillihan, Mountain View, Arkansas. For information on Gillihan see the notes to text 152. In a version of this yarn reported in Arthur Huff Fauset, *Folklore from Nova Scotia*, p. 98, the little boy is the preacher's son and the agreement is between the two, the reward is to be an apple pie. A sweet potato pie is the promised reward in a version included in J. Mason Brewer, *The Word on the Brazos*, pp. 102–3.

X410, "Jokes on parsons."

156. Collected in 1977 by Earnest Eugene Seward from Nolan Garrett, Locust Grove, Arkansas. For information on Garrett see the notes to text 82. Two versions of this tale appear in Loyal Jones and Billy Edd Wheeler, *Laughter in Appalachia*, pp. 34–35, 39.

X410, "Jokes on parsons."

157. Collected November 25, 1978, by Ed and Judy Copeland from Bob Stewart, Mountain View, Arkansas. For information on Stewart see the notes to text 154. A very similar text to this is given in Mody C. Boatright, *Folk Laughter on the American Frontier*, p. 151. A related text from Tennessee appears in Loyal Jones and Billy Edd Wheeler, *Laughter in Appalachia*, p. 34. Another similar yarn from Missouri is given in Vance Randolph, *Hot Springs and Hell*, p. 4. A whole series of similar items containing the punch line "The Lord done ruined me," or something to that effect, is discussed by Randolph, p. 170.

X410, "Jokes on parsons."

158. Collected November 27, 1978, by Ed and Judy Copeland from Lee Jeffery, Mountain View, Arkansas. Jeffery, a retired farmer, is a direct descendant of one of the first settlers in his area of the Arkansas Ozarks. An avid hunter and fisherman, Jeffery once worked as a guide for trout fishermen on the White River. The Copelands said, "He probably knows the woods of Izard and Stone Counties as well as anyone." At the time of the collection Jeffery was sixty-seven years old.

A similar text appears in Mody C. Boatright, *Folk Laughter on the American Frontier*, p. 151. Another version is given in Ralph Steele Boggs, "North Carolina White Folktales and Riddles," *Journal of American Folklore* 47 (1934): 315. Jeffery's narrative is a version of type 1841, "Grace before meat," which can be traced back at least to the early nineteenth century and is probably much older. Versions have been reported from Finland, Estonia, Livonia, Sweden, Ireland, and the former Serbocroatian states, in addition to the United States.

159. Collected November 27, 1978, by Ed and Judy Copeland from Lee Jeffery, Mountain View, Arkansas. For information on Jeffery see the notes to text 158. Jeffery heard this joke in the 1940s at a pool hall in Calico Rock, Arkansas, a town about twenty-five miles north of Mountain View. An Alabama version, from a preacher, appears in Ray B. Browne, "A Night with the Hants," p. 98.

X410, "Jokes on parsons."

160. Collected in 1978 by Ed and Judy Copeland from Bill Whitfield, Mountain View, Arkansas. The Copelands failed to supply any information about Whitfield other than his name and place of residence. They did note that he said he heard the present joke about 1930 in Mountain View. James Schermerhorn, *Schermerhorn's Stories*, p. 92, gives the story essentially as recorded here, as does Vance Randolph in *Hot Springs and Hell*, p. 136. Most other printed versions have a glass, rather than a cup, and often a Negro preacher is involved. See, for example, E.V. White,

Chocolate Drops from the South, pp. 69–70. Interestingly, two texts from African-American informants from Richmond, Virginia (see Daryl Cumber Dance, *Shuckin' and Jivin',* pp. 51–52) do not mention the race of the protagonist. In *Laughing with Congress,* pp. 16–17, Alexander Wiley credits the joke to Fred Vinson, one-time Chief Justice of the United States Supreme Court from Kentucky.

X410, "Jokes on parsons," and X800, "Humor based on drunkenness."

161. Collected November 18, 1978, by Ed and Judy Copeland from Jim Whitfield, Mountain View, Arkansas. Whitfield, a tire dealer, was fifty-eight years old at the time of the collection. The Copelands noted, "He has a good sense of humor and enjoys hearing and telling a good joke. Jim only has a fourth-grade education, but he is considered by many to be one of the few truly honest men left in Stone County. In his business he meets and talks to people from all walks of life, including the tourists. Jim will take time out from his work to have a drink and swap stories with you." Whitfield said he heard the story given here in the 1930s from his father. Vance Randolph includes in *Hot Springs and Hell,* pp. 152–53, a text almost identical to this one. He collected it in 1930 from a Pittsburg, Kansas, native who heard it in Phelps County, Missouri, three decades earlier. In *Wit and Humor,* Marshall Brown, pp. 258–59, gives a variant in which a stranger asks "Is this store closed?" The storekeeper says, "Go to blazes with your conundrums." In *Thesaurus of Anecdotes,* p. 310, Edmund Fuller has a minister ask a sick man, "Do you know Who died to save you?" to which the patient replies, "Is this a time for conundrums?" Randolph, p. 273, refers to another version in which a preacher asks the question of a dying pauper in the County Hospital. The man replies, "To hell with your damned riddles. Can't you see I'm sick?" See also Vance Randolph, *Funny Stories About Hillbillies,* p. 9. Compare the very distantly related joke given in Paul M. Zall, *Mark Twain Laughing,* p. 42.

J1738, "Ignorance of religious matters."

162. Collected November 18, 1978, by Ed and Judy Copeland from Jim Whitfield, Mountain View, Arkansas. For information on Whitfield see the notes to text 161. Whitfield heard the story given here in his tire shop in 1977. This is a variant of a widely told tale concerning sexual misadventures being related to a minister or priest by a young girl, a yarn that has been traced back to the eighteenth-century French erotic poet, Alexis Piron. It was later retold by Francois de Neufchateau, at the time of the French Revolution. The original protagonists were a nobleman and a "pretty young girl," its casting in anti-clerical form is a relatively recent development. The history of this narrative is traced in Legman, vol. 1, pp. 36–37, and is discussed again in the same volume, p. 419. See also the closely related text in Daryl Cumber Dance, *Shuckin' and Jivin',* pp. 57–58. In the exact form given by Whitfield the joke seems previously unreported in folklore collections. Most likely it also appears in some contemporary jokebooks but, if so, I have been unable to locate it in such sources.

X410, "Jokes on parsons."

163. Collected in 1978 by Ed and Judy Copeland from Troy Atchison, Mountain View, Arkansas. Atchison, a horse trader and former timber cutter and bootlegger, was sixty-six years old at the time of the collection. The Copelands noted, "He travels all over Stone County buying and selling horses and cattle. He enjoys a practical joke, and will go to great lengths to set one up. He has been involved in some of the classic practical jokes around Mountain View. He probably knows as much as anyone in the county what they are saying and thinking in the boondocks. He is considered one of the more colorful characters around town." The joke given here Atchison heard at a Mountain View sale barn in 1970. Another version of this tale appears in Ray B. Browne, "*A Night with the Hants*," pp. 101–2.

X410, "Jokes on parsons."

164. Collected November 15, 1978, by Ed and Judy Copeland from Buster Decker, Mountain View, Arkansas. Decker, sixty-eight at the time of the collection, ran a popular pool hall in Mountain View for several years, his place being a frequent gathering site for many local wales. Decker heard the story recorded here from one of his customers about a year prior to the collection by the Copelands. The joke is relatively common in African-American tradition, texts being given in Edward C.L. Adams, *Nigger to Nigger*, pp. 223–24; J. Frank Dobie, *Tone the Bell Easy*, pp. 36–37; Philip Sterling, *Laughing on the Outside*, p. 123; and Daryl Cumber Dance, *Shuckin' and Jivin'*, p. 72. Compare also Dance, pp. 71–72, and the song "The Preacher and the Bear," a hit in 1904 and again in 1947 when revived by Phil Harris, which tells essentially the same story.

X410, "Jokes on parsons."

165. Collected in 1973 by Marla Crider from Irene Guadalajara, Fayetteville, Arkansas. For information on Guadalajara see the notes to text 67.

X410, "Jokes on parsons."

166. Collected February 1969 by Stephen Sanders from Ed Ruff, Morrilton, Arkansas. Ruff, fifty-three years old at the time of the collection, was the co-owner of Morrilton Packing Company, an organization he had worked for approximately forty years. All of Ruff's formal education was in Catholic schools and he was a devout member of the Church. Although he did not "approve" of jokes such as that recorded here Ruff did know several. Sanders believes this is a Catholic joke "because Catholics observe Lent much more religiously than any Protestants do." A version of this joke printed in Julius Alvin, *Totally Gross Jokes*, vol. 2, p. 26, has the situation reversed. An Irish girl marries her fiancé two weeks before Easter but finds her husband unresponsive on their wedding night. When he tells her he can't because "it's Lent," she asks "To whom and for how long?"

Hoffmann's X749.5.4, "Double entendre and extended verbal misunderstandings."

167. From the column "Jimmie Wilson Opines," January 26, 1935. For information on Wilson see the notes to text 4.

X459, "Miscellaneous jokes about preachers," and X800, "Humor based on drunkenness."

168. Collected in 1961 by Margaret E. Hulse from her husband, who had it from Alvin Green, a farmer living near Pea Ridge, Arkansas.

X410, "Jokes on parsons," and X800, "Humor based on drunkenness."

169. Collected in 1973 by Marla Crider from E.W. Thornton, Fayetteville, Arkansas. For information on Thornton see the notes to text 146. Compare the text called "Liars" in *Willard Scott's Down Home Stories*, p. 39.

170. Collected in 1973 by Marla Crider from E.W. Thornton, Fayetteville, Arkansas. For information on Thornton see the notes to text 150.

X410, "Jokes on parsons."

171. Collected in 1973 by Marla Crider from Carolyn Crider, West Fork, Arkansas. For information on Carolyn Crider see the notes to text 118.

X410, "Jokes on parsons."

172. Collected in 1973 by Marla Crider from John Williams, Fayetteville, Arkansas. For information on Williams see the notes to text 119.

X410, "Jokes on parsons," and X459, "Miscellaneous jokes about preachers."

173. Collected in 1979 by W.K. McNeil from Melvin Anglin, Berryville, Arkansas. For information on Anglin see the notes to text 7. The text given here plays on religious stereotypes, good-natured fun being aimed at itinerant preachers of old who relied on the goodwill of local folks (and sometimes their own fast-talking) for food and other necessities. The term "Holy-Rollers" is a derogatory nickname Ozarkers apply to any religious groups whose meetings are characterized by extreme emotionalism and physical agitation. The Primitive Baptists are a small sect of Baptists organized in 1835 that preach a strong belief in predestination. Most of their clergy have little formal training, the call to preach being of primary importance. In the South, large numbers of Scotch-Irish immigrants who brought a Calvinistic tradition with them became Primitive Baptists. The double-shovel plow that Anglin mentions is a plow that makes two furrows at one time, one of the main implements used by pioneer farmers.

The Anglin text is unusual in that the protagonist is initially identified as just a candidate seeking election to public office. Then, the listener suddenly learns he is also a preacher, and it is as a preacher that he becomes the butt of the joke. A Kentucky text is given in Loyal Jones and Billy Edd Wheeler, *Laughter in Appalachia*, pp. 32–33, has Methodists, Presbyterians, and Baptists singled out for innuendo. A variant form in

Mody C. Boatright, *Folk Laughter of the American Frontier,* p. 152, reprinted from the Galveston News Anecdote Contest of 1902, ridicules the same denominations, although the mother and daughter discover that the preacher is a "Hardshell Baptist" when they find a flask of liquor in his saddlebags. In "Anecdotes from the Brazos Bottoms," *Publications of the Texas Folklore Society* 13 (1937): 100–1, A.W. Eddins prints a very similar yarn in which a young couple agree to provide room and board for one of the ministers who will be presiding at a camp meeting. The man of the house finds that he will have to be gone, so he gives his wife instructions on how to provide for the preacher. If he is a Presbyterian she is to put the new Bible on the table, a fire in the fireplace, and leave the man alone. If a Baptist she is to put a pitcher of water, the sugar bowl, a spoon and a quart of rock and rye on the table. If he is a Methodist then she is to send her husband a telegram because she is too "good-looking a woman to trust with any Methodist preacher."

X410, "Jokes on parsons," and X459.2*, "Entertaining the preacher."

174. Collected November 15, 1978, by Ed and Judy Copeland from Walter Whitfield, Mountain View, Arkansas. Whitfield, a farmer, was sixty-eight years old at the time of the collection. Whitfield lives in a log cabin that was built in the 1840s, which doesn't have electricity and, in many respects, is the same as it was over a hundred years ago. The Copelands said, "Walter has a grade school education and is fairly articulate. He enjoys a good yarn and will spin some himself. He has been very little affected by the twentieth century, and lives at his own slow, easy pace. He has a strong sense of history about Stone County." Ed Cray in "The Rabbi Trickster," *Journal of American Folklore* 77 (1964): 341, says that this is one of the most widely known of the rabbi trickster tales. Popular both with Jews and non-Jews, it has been printed in numerous joke collections, including Richard M. Dorson, "Jewish-American Dialect Stories on Tape," in *Studies in Biblical and Jewish Folklore,* pp. 145–46; S. Felix Mendelsohn, *Let Laughter Ring,* p. 37; Elsa Teitelbaum, *An Anthology of Jewish Humor and Maxims,* p. 356; *Isaac Asimov's Treasury of Humor,* p. 340; Blanche Knott, *Truly Tasteless Jokes* V, p. 88; Ronald L. Baker, *Jokelore,* p. 153; and in the anonymous and unpaginated *World's Best Irish Jokes.* In the latter the repartee takes place between a rabbi and an Irish priest but usually the nationality of the priest isn't mentioned. The Whitfield text is unusual in that four people are present during the conversation; generally it occurs with only two persons. It is notable, however, that only the rabbi and the priest take part in the conversation.

175. Collected November 20, 1978, by Ed and Judy Copeland from Carl Long, Mountain View, Arkansas. Long, sixty-six years old at the time of the collection, was a disabled farmer. The Copelands noted that Long "has no education and cannot read or write. He is not considered a religious man, but he is highly respected in the community." A version of this story involving a Baptist preacher who wants to show his amazing powers to church members attending his revival announces his plan to walk on water in J. Mason Brewer, *The Word on the Brazos,* pp. 46–47. An Evansville, Indiana, version collected in 1969 appears in Ronald L. Baker, *Jokelore,* p. 152. Baker, p. 228, says another version is given in Richard Edward Buehler, "An Annotated Collection of Contemporary Obscene Humor from the Bloomington Campus of Indiana University," p. 164. Buehler's study was an M.A. thesis submitted at Indiana University in 1964. Another version appears in Blanche Knott, *Truly Tasteless Jokes IV,* p. 91.

X410 "Jokes on parsons."

176. Collected in 1971 by Joe Lindsey from H.R. "Rip" Lindsey, Fayetteville, Arkansas. For information on H.R. Lindsey see the notes to text 31. This tale is popular both with members of the Society of Friends (Quakers) and non-members alike. It is one of the stories told by North Carolina singer-guitarist Arthel "Doc" Watson; his version appears on *Doc Watson on Stage* (Vanguard VSD-9/10). Another text is found in William Haughton Sessions, *More Quaker Laughter,* p. 76. The Lindsey text is unusual in that it gives the cow a reason beyond sheer stubbornness for being difficult.

X410, "Jokes on parsons," is implied, although the story really deals more with the actions of a religious group than of an individual minister.

177. From the Max Hunter Collection, Greene County Public Library, Springfield, Missouri. Recorded in 1971 from a handwritten book of jokes kept by a Springfield man. The Salvation Army was an outgrowth of English evangelist William Booth's (1829–1912) East London Revival Society, organized in 1865. Booth, a former Wesleyan Methodist preacher, founded the Army in 1878, featuring in its program informal preaching and outdoor evangelistic meetings that featured brass bands. Theologically conservative, the Army stressed sin, redemption, and growth in holiness, its main emphases today. Introduced into the United States in 1880, the Salvation Army at first met great criticism from many organized churches but eventually the opposition waned.

178. Collected May 1969 by Stephen Sanders from Ed Ruff, Morrilton, Arkansas. For information on Ruff see the notes to text 166. A version of the present joke is reported in Daryl Cumber Dance, *Shuckin' and Jivin',* pp. 117–18, in which the incident occurs on the campus of Virginia Union University, Richmond, Virginia. Another version in Blanche Knott, *Truly Tasteless Jokes,* pp. 67–68, fails to specify the race of either nun. Ruff's text is unusual in that it specifies an "integrated" cast of characters; the Negro one in true stereotypical fashion is much more knowledgeable about sex than the white nun. The joke is, then, in a sense, both anti- Catholic and anti-Negro.

X665*, "Jokes about Negroes," and X691.2.1*, "Unusual sexual capacity of Negro," is implied.

179. Collected spring 1966 by Stephen Sanders from his mother, Mrs.

Jo Sanders, Rogers, Arkansas. At the time of the collection Mrs. Sanders was forty-seven years old and working as a secretary at Daisy Manufacturing Company in Rogers. The collector noted that his mother "had attended Draughon's College in Muskogee, Oklahoma. She was raised in a very staunch Protestant home, and is a member of the Christian Church."

Hoffmann's X458, "Jokes on religious women," is the closest relevant motif.

180. Collected May 1969 by Stephen Sanders from Ed Ruff, Morrilton, Arkansas. For information on Ruff see the notes to text 166. Sanders says "the theme of this joke is very common." Often the story is merely about the unsatisfiable female, as in Legman, vol. 1, p. 359, but it is easily applicable to almost any woman, especially to those, like nuns, who are bound by oath to not engage in sexual intercourse. Also see Legman, vol. 1, p. 262.

181. Collected May 1969 by Stephen Sanders from Ed Ruff, Morrilton, Arkansas. For information on Ruff see the notes to text 166. In a version given in Julius Alvin, *Totally Gross Jokes,* vol. 2, p. 66, the young nun asks, "Will that keep me from getting pregnant?"

Hoffmann's X458, "Jokes on religious women," and X732.7, "Humor concerning rape."

182. Collected March 1969 by Stephen Sanders from Ed Ruff, Morrilton, Arkansas. For information on Ruff see the notes to text 166. Sanders says this story "demonstrates the feeling that many non-Catholics have about the pecuniary interests of priests and the Catholic Church in general." In *Isaac Asimov's Treasury of Humor,* pp. 336–37, a version of this joke is given, along with a commentary suggesting that the meaning of jokes such as this have changed, as far as Asimov is concerned, over the years. He notes that when he was young, "I lived right across the street from a Catholic church, and I had a vague fear of it and its priests, though I delivered papers to them and they went out of their way to be pleasant to me. The fear has long since disappeared, I am glad to say. A certain diffidence in the presence of nuns lingered longer, but that too is now gone." These remarks indicate that at one time Asimov may have told the story for the same reason Sanders offers in explanation of the yarn's popularity.

X410, "Jokes on parsons."

183. Collected May 1969 by Stephen Sanders from Ed Ruff, Morrilton, Arkansas. For information on Ruff see the notes to text 166. Sanders says this joke "is especially good because to non-Catholics, the Catholic Church seems to be surrounded by a mystery which is more apparent than real. This mystery breeds misunderstanding which broadens the gap between Catholics and other faiths." Perhaps so, but it seems to me that this joke is popular because it has a very good, unexpected ending and because it plays on stereotypes of beatniks—an earlier generation's hippies. Beatniks were said to have an aversion to bathing.

This is clearly a variant of J1738, "Ignorance of religious matters," for which Baughman suggests a new type, 1833B.

Heaven and Hell

184. Collected December 1962 by Bill Knowles from Darrell Knowles, Mountain Home, Arkansas. For information on Darrell Knowles see the notes to text 8. Compare the story given in Richard Walser, *Tar Heel Laughter,* pp. 199–200. W152, "Stinginess," and X597*, "Jokes about new arrival in heaven."

185. Collected April 13, 1979, by Jim Bird from J. Bill Summers at Inn of the Ozarks Restaurant near Eureka Springs, Arkansas. Bird notes that Summers "drives a tour bus for Grayline Tours and in between points of interest when there is a lag, he likes to tell this joke." Eureka Springs is one of those towns that has from its inception been tourist-oriented; in the late nineteenth century when it was founded it was known as a health resort. In recent years it has become known as an arts and crafts center.

X597*, "Jokes about new arrival in heaven," and Thompson's Q172, "Reward: admission to heaven," seem applicable, although all of the references Thompson includes refer to European myths or exempla.

186. Collected May 1969 by Stephen Sanders from Carla Reames of Fort Smith, Arkansas. At the time of the collection Reames was twenty-five years old and a senior English major at the University of Arkansas. Sanders notes that "Carla was raised in a Catholic home and attended Catholic schools, including college, until she entered the University of Arkansas. Carla has several relatives who are priests and nuns." About the text given here the collector says, "It is a pun making fun of people who get into heaven by praying the rosary. Praying the rosary asks for the intercession of the Virgin Mary and prayers to God."

K2371.1, "Heaven entered by a trick," and Thompson's Q172, "Reward: admission to heaven."

187. Collected in 1973 by Marla Crider from Bill Yoes, Greenland, Arkansas. For information on Yoes see the notes to text 72. Thompson's F81, "Descent to lower world of dead (Hell, Hades)."

188. Collected December 1962 by Bill Knowles from Darrell Knowles, Mountain Home, Arkansas. For information on Darrell Knowles see the notes to text 8. Gershon Legman, vol. 2, p. 944, calls this "the most popular joke told at the present time in America." It appeared in *Anecdota Americana,* vol. 2, in 1934, and Legman says he has personally collected over 140 versions of it in a forty-year period. One variant form of the joke—that which ends with the punch line "Don't make waves"—has become a proverb or catch-phrase, although many of those using it are unaware of the joke. Legman sees the joke as a conscious assessment of the human condition. The "Don't make waves" variant is found in *Isaac*

Asimov's Treasury of Humor, p. 331, and the version given here appears in Ethelyn G. Orso, *Modern Greek Humor,* p. 108.

Thompson's E755.2.7, "Devils torment sinners in hell," and F81, "Descent to lower world of dead (Hell, Hades)," are applicable.

Drinking, Gambling, and Other Vices

189. From the column "Jimmy Wilson Opines," January 4, 1934. For information on Wilson see the notes to text 4. X800, "Humor based on drunkenness," and Z20, "Cumulative tales."

190. Collected May 1969 by Stephen Sanders from Ed Ruff, Morrilton, Arkansas. For information on Ruff see the notes to text 166. According to Sanders, "The joke makes fun of the way confessionals look in the Catholic Church. They do, in fact, look like rest rooms." This was merely one of several jokes Sanders collected from Ruff, the father of a friend, all of them dealing in some way with the Roman Catholic Church. Versions of this joke have been published in various popular jokebooks, such as Blanche Knott, *Truly Tasteless Jokes,* p. 70, and Julius Alvin, *Gross Jokes,* p. 77.

X800, "Humor based on drunkenness," and Hoffmann's X716, "Humor concerning defecation and breaking wind."

191. From the Max Hunter Collection, Greene County Public Library, Springfield, Missouri. Recorded in 1971 from a handwritten jokebook kept by a Springfield man. X800, "Humor based on drunkenness."

192. Collected in 1964 by Robin Jordan from Lee Parker, Goshen, Arkansas. For information on Parker see the notes to text 12. Relevant motifs include B200, "Animals with human traits"; B210, "Speaking animals"; B211, "Animal uses human speech"; and X800, "Humor based on drunkenness."

193. Collected in 1973 by Marla Crider from E.W. Thornton, Fayetteville, Arkansas. For information on Thornton see the notes to text 150. X800, "Humor based on drunkenness," is the closest relevant motif.

194. Collected in March 1983 by W.K. McNeil from George Vickers, Big Flat, Arkansas. For information on Vickers see the notes to text 25b. A version of this tale collected in Evansville, Indiana, in March 1970 from an eighteen-year-old male apprentice butcher, is given in Ronald L. Baker, *Jokelore,* p. 74. Older versions of this joke are given in Legman, vol. 1, p. 668, and vol. 2, p. 201. The former, taken from *Anecdota Americana,* dates from the 1920s while the latter was collected in 1937 in Minneapolis, Minnesota. Both omit the feature of the husband's drinking, the joke instead focusing on a wife's attempts to win back her husband's love. The humor comes from the overtones of prostitution and fake-adultery as a sort of marital spice. Legman, vol. 1, p. 668, suggests that this form of the joke has passed out of common use because prostitution of the classic kind alluded to in the joke has disappeared in America since World War II, owing to the financial and sexual emancipation of women in the past forty years. In other words, alcoholism has replaced fake-adultery in this one joke.

J1485, "Mistaken identity"; J1766, "One person mistaken for another"; and X800, "Humor based on drunkenness."

195. As remembered by Margaret E. Hulse in 1961. She originally heard the story several years earlier when she and her husband, a career military man, were living in France. She explains the circumstances of her first hearing this yarn. "A group of Non-Commissioned Officers and their wives were visiting at the N.C.O. Club at Chinon Engineer's Depot near Chinon, France. When they learned that we were from the Ozarks, one fellow told this story that he said happened to him when he was in this part of the country." Despite the man's claim, this is just another traditional yarn that has been infrequently reported in folklore collections. Versions are given in Henry D. Spalding, *A Treasury of Irish Folklore and Humor,* p. 149, where it is suggested that the joke explains how the feud between the Martins and the Coys started. The Martins and the Coys are fictitious southern mountain clansmen who were the protagonists of a 1936 popular song written by Al Cameron and Ted Weems. In *Willard Scott's Down Home Stories,* p. 130, the tale takes place in the mountains of North Carolina with the confrontation being the classic one between the city slicker and the mountaineer. In Loyal Jones and Billy Edd Wheeler, *Laughter in Appalachia,* pp. 71–72, it is set in Kentucky, the principals being two mountaineers. The man who produces the moonshine is "about seven feet tall" and is picked up while hitchhiking.

X800, "Humor based on drunkenness."

196. Collected in 1973 by Marla Crider from Gordon Bradshaw, Farmington, Arkansas. For information on Bradshaw see the notes to text 90.

X800 "Humor based on drunkenness."

197. Collected in 1982 by Kenneth Pemberton from J.D. Sutterfield, Big Flat, Arkansas. No other information supplied about Sutterfield. A variant of this story was told by Abraham Lincoln as a true story on one John Moore of Blooming Grove, Illinois. Lincoln claimed that Moore told the story on himself. As Lincoln related the joke it concerned an occasion when Moore became inebriated and fell asleep in his cart. The steers were left to find their way home on their own. During the trip they struck a stump or root which loosened their yoke making it possible for them to run away. When Moore awoke the next morning he said, "If my name is John Moore, I've lost a pair of steers; if my name ain't John Moore, I've found a cart." See Paul M. Zall, *Abe Lincoln Laughing,* p. 138. Despite Lincoln's claim this joke is a jestbook favorite that appeared in print numerous times since the seventeenth century. Its earliest known printing is in Thomas Young's *England's Bane: or the Description of Drunkenness,* a temperance tract issued in 1617. It was among the jests included in Louden's *Almanack for 1786* (see Robert K. Dodge, *Early American*

Almanac Humor, p. 16), which may be its earliest American printing.

Sutterfield's text is unusual in that it deals with gambling rather than drinking and that the protagonist is an anonymous generic figure rather than one who is specifically named. The closest relevant motif is Thompson's Q381, "Punishment for gambling."

198. Collected in 1973 by Marla Crider from Gordon Bradshaw, Farmington, Arkansas. For information on Bradshaw see the notes to text 90.

W111, "Laziness."

199. Collected May 11, 1978, by Kathy Nicol from Jessie Hubert Wilkes, Cave City, Arkansas. For information on Wilkes see the notes to text 1. Applicable motifs include W111, "Laziness," and Thompson's Q321, "Laziness punished."

200. Collected May 11, 1978, by Kathy Nicol from Jessie Hubert Wilkes, Cave City, Arkansas. For information on Wilkes see the notes to text 1. Baughman assigns this type 1951, "Is Wood Split?" and also cites it as motif W111.5.10.1. It is very well-known in North America, being previously reported from Ontario, Maine, New York, New Jersey, Pennsylvania, South Carolina, Texas, and Indiana, in addition to Arkansas. Perhaps its most recent prior publication is in Ronald L. Baker, *Jokelore*, p. 85. Compare the version given in Richard Walser, *Tar Heel Laughter*, p. 127. The most common American form is the one used by Hubert here. Other versions have the lazy man asking if wood is split before he accepts it as a gift, while in others he asks if rice is cooked. Apparently this yarn is unknown in Europe, for Thompson cites only Baughman's references.

Eerie Humor
201. Collected January 11, 1978, from Nadine Bonds, Fox, Arkansas, by Kathy Nicol. Nicol was doing fieldwork for a film on tall tale tellers in the Arkansas Ozarks (the movie was later released as *They Tell It For the Truth*) and was particularly interested in finding female narrators of tall tales. She had little success with her quest, although she did turn up a few women, such as Bonds, who knew some humorous stories such as the one included here. This is a very widely known narrative that Thompson lists as type 1791, "The Sexton Carries the Parson." In European versions thieves steal a sheep or turnips. A lame parson has himself carried by the sexton. The latter hears the thieves in the cemetery cracking nuts and thinks it is the devil cracking bones. With the parson on his back he comes upon the thieves who, thinking it is their companion with a sheep, call out, "Is he fat?" The sexton answers "Fat or lean, here he is." Bond's version is typical of most American texts in that it is two boys dividing walnuts, rather than sheep thieves. Known throughout Scandinavia, the British Isles, Europe, India, the West Indies, and, of course, the United States, this story is at least as old as the medieval *Thousand and One Nights* and appears in most medieval and Renaissance tale collections. Its widespread popularity is partly due to its versatility. A teller can insert whatever he wants to be counted, and various versions have the walnuts

used here, or hickory nuts, fish, pawpaws, sweet potatoes, or corn, but almost anything that is countable could be used. Undoubtedly the punch line in which one of the people doing the counting says to the other "You take that one and I'll take this one" or "We'll get them two at the gate" is also partially responsible for its popularity. The absurd misunderstanding, no matter what form, is a perennially popular feature of folk tales and it helps the story's popularity.

For other versions see Richard Walser, *Tar Heel Laughter,* p. 126 (a text printed in the Raleigh, North Carolina, *News and Observer,* April 15, 1951), Arthur Huff Fauset, *Folklore from Nova Scotia,* pp. 104–5, and my own *Ghost Stories from the American South,* p. 129. The applicable motif is X424, "The devil in the cemetery."

202a. Collected in 1977 by Earnest Eugene Seward from Junior Debow, Batesville, Arkansas. For information on Debow see the notes to text 71. The present text is, of course, a variant form of the "on the cooling board" narratives and is a joke popular in both black and white tradition. A version set in Salisbury, North Carolina, is given in Walser, pp. 205–6 (taken from J. Mason Brewer, *American Negro Folklore,* 1968) and Daryl Cumber Dance gives a version collected March 5, 1975, in Richmond, Virginia, in *Shuckin' and Jivin',* pp. 48–49.

J1769.2, "Dead man is thought to be alive," and Thompson's K1885, "Dead made to appear alive."

202b. Collected in March 1983 by W.K. McNeil from George Vickers, Big Flat, Arkansas. For information on Vickers see the notes to text 25b. The frontier custom of staying up all night with the dead person is still practiced in many communities in the southern mountains and elsewhere in the United States. Related stories appear in Lynwood Montell, *Ghosts Along the Cumberland,* pp. 202–3; Ray B. Browne, *"A Night with the Hants,"* p. 165; Daryl Cumber Dance, *Shuckin' and Jivin',* p. 29; and Richard M. Dorson, *American Negro Folktales,* pp. 329–30. This particular humorous story has also been reported from Nova Scotia, Pennsylvania, and native Americans. Usually the dead man is hunchbacked or deformed in some way making his body a more likely candidate for drawing up. This story is generally told as a true experience rather than as a funny but fictitious tale. Nevertheless, the element of humor seems to be the main reason it is recalled.

J1769.2, "Dead man is thought to be alive," and Thompson's K1885, "Dead made to appear alive."

203. Collected May 4, 1978, by Kathy Nicol from Jessie Hubert Wilkes, Cave City, Arkansas. For information on Wilkes see the notes to text 1. The most popular motif in this narrative is one that is well-known among both blacks and whites in the United States but rare in other parts of the world. Baughman assigns this the number J1495.1, "Man runs from actual or from supposed ghost." It has been collected from black informants in New Jersey, South Carolina, and Florida, and from whites in New Jersey, Florida, Indiana, Wisconsin, Iowa, and Arkansas. A version from

Tennessee, which fails to identify the racial background of the informant, appears in my *Ghost Stories from the American South,* pp. 131–32. This particular narrative is probably even more widespread in the United States than collections indicate, because most American folklore collections have focused on a relatively small portion of the country. Apparently, the yarn is unknown in Europe, or at least hasn't been reported there, because Thompson cites only Baughman's references. It is of interest that Wilkes called this story, which he had from an aunt, a fairy tale.

In most versions of this yarn the protagonist encounters a headless corpse or one that is incomplete in some way. Often the ghost is carrying its head under its arm and the man running from the ghost outraces a rabbit. In several texts the ghost is a cat who talks to the man and later chases him, although in the Tennessee text included in my book of ghost stories the animal merely provides a prelude to the real action. The Wilkes text is unusual in that the ghost is a complete corpse. E422.1, "Body of living corpse" is a relevant motif.

204a. Collected in 1964 by Robin Jordan from Lee Parker, Goshen, Arkansas. For information on Parker see the notes to text 12. The item given here is a version of what may well be the most popular joke in Ozark folk tradition, the reason it is represented here by three texts. Generally, as in Vance Randolph, *Hot Springs and Hell,* p. 8, the man who falls in the grave is intoxicated, a feature missing from all three of the versions given here. Sometimes the action is assigned to two Negroes who some informants think of as inferiors and, thus, capable of actions such as those detailed here. In white stereotypes of blacks the latter are often highly superstitious, making them even more believable than the main characters involved in a narrative such as that given here. The Parker text, which is far longer than the other two, suggests a more accomplished narrator or, at least, one who takes greater time with his tales, elaborating by adding greater detail.

According to the *Arkansas Gazette,* May 21, 1953, the story is one credited to evangelist Billy Graham. Another version, from a black in Plum, Texas, is given by G.M. Williams in *Publications of the Texas Folklore Society* 29 (1959): 168. Randolph's informant told it as a true story that happened in the 1930s in Barry County, Missouri. Many informants suggest that it is a true story, but this may be for effect as much as for historical accuracy.

X828*, "Drunk person falls in open grave with humorous results."

204b. Collected in 1959 by Gene H. Brooks from Fred Starr, Fayetteville, Arkansas. For information on Starr see the notes to text 62. For a discussion of this joke see the notes to text 204a.

Bibliography of Works Cited

Aarne, Antti, and Stith Thompson. *The Types of the Folktale: A Classification and Bibliography.* Helsinki: Folklore Fellows Communications 184, 1961.

Adams, Edward C.L. *Nigger to Nigger.* New York: Charles Scribner's Sons, 1928.

Adler, Bill. *Jewish Wit & Wisdom.* New York: Dell Publishing Co., Inc., 1969.

Alvin, Julius. *Gross Jokes.* New York: Kensington Publishing Corp., 1983.

———. *Totally Gross Jokes: Volume II.* New York: Kensington Publishing Corp., 1983.

Anecdota Americana: Five Hundred Stories for the Amusement of the Five Hundred Nations That Comprise America. New York: Nesor Publishing Company, 1934.

Arpad, Joseph J. "The Fight Story: Quotation and Originality in Native American Humor." *Journal of the Folklore Institute* 10 (1973): 141–72.

Asimov, Isaac. *Isaac Asimov's Treasury of Humor: A lifetime collection of favorite jokes, anecdotes, and limericks with copious notes on how to tell them and why.* Boston: Houghton Mifflin Company, 1971.

Aurand, A. Monroe. *Wit and Humor of the Pennsylvania Germans.* Harrisburg, Pennsylvania: Aurand Press, 1946.

Ausubal, Nathan. *Treasury of Jewish Folklore.* New York: Crown Publishers, 1948.

Baker, Ronald L. *Jokelore: Humorous Folktales from Indiana.* Bloomington: Indiana University Press, 1986.

———. *Hoosier Folk Legends.* Bloomington: Indiana University Press, 1982.

Barkley, Alben W. *That Reminds Me*. Garden City, New York: Double-day & Co., 1954.

Baughman, Ernest W. *Type and Motif Index of the Folktales of England and North America*. The Hague, The Netherlands: Mouton & Co., 1966.

Baum, Paul F. "The Three Dreams or 'Dream Bread' Story." *Journal of American Folklore* 30 (1917): 378–410.

Blakley, James W. *Tall Tales*. Franklin, Ohio: Eldridge Entertainment House, Inc., 1936.

Boatright, Mody C. *Folk Laughter on the American Frontier*. Gloucester, Massachusetts: Peter Smith, 1971. Reprint of a work originally published in 1949.

Boggs, Ralph Steele. "North Carolina White Folktales and Riddles." *Journal of American Folklore* 47 (1934): 289–328.

Botkin, B.A. *Lay My Burden Down: A Folk History of Slavery*. Chicago: The University of Chicago Press, 1968. Reprint of a work originally issued in 1945.

——. *A Treasury of American Anecdotes: Sly, Salty, Shaggy Stories of Heroes and Hellions, Beguilers and Buffoons, Spellbinders and Scapegoats, Gagsters and Gossips from the Grassroot and Sidewalks of America*. New York: Random Houss, 1957.

——. *A Treasury of American Folklore*. New York: Crown Publishers, 1944.

——. *A Treasury of New England Folklore*. New York. Crown Publishers, 1947.

——. *A Treasury of Southern Folklore*. New York. American Legacy Press, 1984. Reprint of a work originally issued in 1949.

Brewer, J. Mason. *The Word on the Brazos: Negro Preacher Tales from the Brazos Bottoms of Texas*. Austin: University of Texas Press, 1976. Reprint of a work originally issued in 1953.

Brown, Frank C. *The Frank C. Brown Collection of North Carolina Folklore*. General Editor Newman Ivey White. Durham: Duke University Press, 1952–1964. Seven volumes.

Brown, Marshall. *Wit and Humor*. Chicago. S.C. Griggs & Co., 1880.

Browne, Ray B. *"A Night with the Hants" and Other Alabama Folk Experiences*. Bowling Green, Ohio: Bowling Green University Popular Press, no date given.

Brunvand, Jan Harold. *The Study of American Folklore: An Introduction.* New York. W.W. Norton & Company, Inc., 1968.

Campbell, Marie. *Tales from the Cloud Walking Country.* Bloomington: Indiana University Press, 1958.

Cerf, Bennett. *The Sound of Laughter.* New York: Bantam Books, Inc., 1972. Reprint in paperback of a work originally issued in hardback in 1970.

——. *Try and Stop Me.* New York: Simon & Schuster, 1944.

Chase, Richard. *American Folk Tales and Songs.* New York. The New American Library of World Literature, Inc., 1962. Reprint of a work originally issued in 1956.

——. *Grandfather Tales.* Boston. Houghton Mifflin Co., 1948.

Clements, William M. *The Types of the Polack Joke.* Bloomington, Indiana: Folklore Forum Bibliographic and Special Series 3, 1969.

Clouston, W.A. *The Book of Noodles.* London: Elliot Stock, 1888.

Cobb, Irvin S. *A Laugh a Day Keeps the Doctor Away: His Favorite Stories as Told by Irvin S. Cobb.* Garden City, New York: Garden City Publishing Co., Inc., 1923.

Copeland, Lewis. *The World's Best Jokes.* New York. Blue Ribbon Books, 1936.

—— and Faye Copeland. *10,000 Jokes, Toasts and Stories.* Garden City, New York: Garden City Publishing Co., 1946.

Cray, Ed. "The Rabbi Trickster." *Journal of American Folklore* 77 (1964): 331–45.

Cunningham, Robert Hays. *Amusing Prose Chap-Books, Chiefly of Last Century.* London: Hamilton, Adams & Co., 1889.

Damon, Bertha. *Grandma Called It Carnal.* New York: Simon & Schuster, 1938.

Dance, Daryl Cumber. *Shuckin' and Jivin': Folklore from Contemporary Black Americans.* Bloomington: Indiana University Press, 1978.

De Vere, Maximilian Schele. *Americanisms: The English of the New World.* New York: Johnson Reprint Corporation, 1968. Reprint of a work originally issued in 1871.

Dobie, J. Frank. *Tone the Bell Easy.* Austin: Texas Folklore Society Publications 10, 1932.

———. *A Vaquero of the Brush Country.* Dallas: The Southwest Press, 1929.

——— and Mody C. Boatright. *Straight Texas.* Austin: Texas Folklore Society Publications 13, 1937.

Dodge, Robert K. *Early American Almanac Humor.* Bowling Green, Ohio: Bowling Green State University Popular Press, 1987.

Dorson, Richard M. *America Begins: Early American Writing.* Bloomington: Indiana University Press, 1971. Reprint of a work originally issued in 1950.

———. *American Folklore.* Chicago: The University of Chicago Press, 1959.

———. *American Negro Folktales.* Greenwich, Connecticut. Fawcett Publications, Inc., 1967.

———. *Jonathan Draws the Long Bow.* Cambridge, Massachusetts. Harvard University Press, 1946.

———. "Maine Master Narrator." *Southern Folklore Quarterly* 8 (1944): 279–85.

———. *Man and Beast in American Comic Legend.* Bloomington: Indiana University Press, 1982.

———. *Negro Folktales in Michigan.* Cambridge, Massachusetts. Harvard University Press, 1956.

———. *Negro Tales from Pine Bluff, Arkansas, and Calvin, Michigan.* Bloomington: Indiana University Press, 1958.

Dundes, Alan. *Mother Wit from the Laughing Barrel: Readings in the Interpretation of Afro-American Folklore.* Englewood Cliffs, New Jersey: Prentice-Hall, Inc., 1973.

Edmund, Peggy, and Harold Workman Williams. *Toaster's Handbook, Jokes, Stories and Quotations.* New York: H.W. Wilson Co., 1938.

Elgart, J.M. *Over Sixteen.* New York: Grayson Publishing Corp., 1951.

Fadiman, Clifton. *The Little, Brown Book of Anecdotes.* Boston: Little, Brown and Company, Inc., 1985.

Fauset, Arthur Huff. *Folklore from Nova Scotia.* New York: American Folklore Society Memoirs 24, 1931.

————. "Negro Folk Tales from the South." *Journal of American Folklore* 40 (1927): 213–303.

Fuller, Edmund. *Thesaurus of Anecdotes*. New York: Crown Publishers, 1942.

Gardner, Emelyn Elizabeth. *Folklore from the Schoharie Hills, New York*. New York: Arno Press, 1977. Reprint of a work originally issued in 1937.

Gerlach, Russel. *Immigrants in the Ozarks: A Study in Ethnic Geography*. Columbia and London: University of Missouri Press, 1976.

Golden, Francis Leo. *Laughter Is Legal*. New York: Pocket Books, Inc., 1953.

Gross, W.L. *Good Stories for All Occasions and How to Tell Them*. New York: Greenwich Book Publishers, 1959.

Halpert, Herbert. "John Darling, a New York Münchausen." *Journal of American Folklore* 57 (1944): 97–106.

Hand, Wayland D., and Jeannine E. Talley. *Popular Beliefs and Superstitions from Utah Collected by Anthon S. Cannon*. Salt Lake City: University of Utah Press, 1984.

Harris, Joel Chandler. *Uncle Remus and His Friends*. Boston: Houghton Mifflin Co., 1892.

Hart, Fred H. *The Sazerac Lying Club: A Nevada Book*. San Francisco: Henry Keller & Co., 1878.

Hawkins, Jim. *Jokes from Black Folks*. Garden City, New York: Doubleday and Company, 1973.

Hazlitt, W. Carew. *Shakespeare Jest-Books*. New York: Burt Franklin, no date given. Reprint of a work originally issued in 1864. Three volumes.

Hertz, Emanuel. *Lincoln Talks: An Oral Biography*. New York: Bramhall House, 1986. Reprint of a work originally issued in 1939.

Hoffmann, Frank. *Analytical Survey of Anglo-American Traditional Erotica*. Bowling Green, Ohio: Bowling Green University Popular Press, 1973.

Hughes, Langston, and Arna Bontemps. *The Book of Negro Folklore*. New York: Dodd, Mead and Company, 1958.

Hudson, Arthur Palmer. *Humor of the Old Deep South*. New York: Macmillan Co., 1936.

Hurston, Zora Neale. *Mules and Men.* New York: Harper & Row Publishers, Inc., 1970. Reprint of a work originally issued in 1935.

Jackson, Thomas W. *On a Slow Train Through Arkansaw.* Edited by W.K. McNeil. Lexington: The University Press of Kentucky, 1985. Annotated reprint of a work originally issued in 1903.

Jacobs, Joseph. *More English Fairy Tales.* London: David Nutt, 1894.

Johnson, Clifton. *What They Say in New England and Other American Folklore.* New York: Columbia University Press, 1963. Reprint of a work originally issued in 1896.

Johnson, J.H., Jerry Sheridan and Ruth Lawrence. *The Laughter Library.* Indianapolis: Maxwell Droke, Publisher, 1936.

Jones, Loyal. *Minstrel of the Appalachians: The Story of Bascom Lamar Lunsford.* Boone, North Carolina: Appalachian Consortium Press, 1984.

—— and Billy Edd Wheeler. *Laughter in Appalachia: A Festival of Southern Mountain Humor.* Little Rock: August House, Inc., 1987.

Kennedy, Stetson. *Palmetto Country.* New York: Duell, Sloan & Pearce, 1942.

Kitchens, Ben Earl. *Tomatoes in the Tree Tops: The Collected Tales of Harry Rhine.* Florence, Alabama: Thornwood Book Publishers, 1982.

Knott, Blanche. *Truly Tasteless Jokes.* New York: Ballantine Books, 1982.

——. *Truly Tasteless Jokes IV.* New York: Pinnacle Books, Inc., 1984.

——. *Truly Tasteless Jokes V.* New York: Pinnacle Books, Inc., 1985.

Korson, George. *Minstrels of the Mine Patch: Songs and Stories of the Anthrocite Industry.* Hatboro, Pennsylvania: Folklore Associates, Inc., 1964. Reprint of a work originally issued in 1938.

Landon, Melville D. *Wit and Humor of the Age.* Des Moines and Chicago: Western Publishing House, 1883.

——. *Kings of the Platform and Pulpit.* Chicago: The Werner Co., 1900.

Lawson, J. Gilchrist. *The World's Best Humorous Anecdotes.* New York: George H. Doran Co., 1923.

Lee, Josh. *How to Hold an Audience Without a Rope.* Chicago and New York: Ziff-Davis Publishing Co., 1947.

Legman, Gershon. *Rationale of the Dirty Joke: An Analysis of Sexual Humor.* New York: Grove Press, Inc., 1968.

————. *No Laughing Matter. Volume Two of Rationale of the Dirty Joke: An Analysis of Sexual Humor.* New York: Bell Publishing Company, 1975.

Lockridge, Norman. *Waggish Tales of the Czechs.* Chicago. Candide Press, 1947.

Lomax, John A. *Adventures of a Ballad Hunter.* New York: The Macmillan Company, 1947.

Lupton, Martha. *Treasury of Modern Humor.* Indianapolis: Maxwell Droke, Publisher, 1938.

Lyons, Johnny. *Joking Off #2.* Toronto and New York: Paperjacks Ltd., 1987.

McClure, J.B. *Entertaining Anecdotes from Every Available Source.* Chicago: Rhodes and McClure, 1880.

McNeil, W.K. "Folklore from Big Flat, Arkansas. Part II: Folk Narratives." *Mid-America Folklore* 11 (1983): 1–20.

————. *Ghost Stories from the American South.* Little Rock: August House, Inc., 1985.

Masterson, James R. *Arkansas Folklore.* Little Rock: Rose Publishing Co., Inc., 1974. Reprint and retitling of a work originally issued in 1942.

Meier, F. *The Joke Teller's Joke Book.* Philadelphia: Blakiston Co., 1944.

Mendelsohn, S. Felix. *Let Laughter Ring.* Philadelphia: Jewish Publication Society of America, 1941.

Milburn, George. *The Best Rube Jokes.* Girard, Kansas: Haldeman-Julius Publishing Co., no date given.

————. *The Best Yankee Jokes.* Girard, Kansas: Haldeman-Julius Company, no date given.

Montell, William Lynwood. *Ghosts along the Cumberland: Deathlore in the Kentucky Foothills.* Knoxville: The University of Tennessee Press, 1975.

Moulton, Powers. *2500 Jokes for All Occasions.* Garden City, New York: Blue Ribbon Books, 1946.

"O'S," Mr. *The World's Best Irish Jokes.* New York: Castle, 1983.

Oppenheimer, Paul. *A Pleasant Vintage of Till Eulenspiegel: Born in the Country of Brunswick. How he spent his life. 95 of his tales.* Middletown, Connecticut: Wesleyan University Press, 1972.

Orso, Ethelyn G. *Modern Greek Humor: A Collection of Jokes and Ribald Tales.* Bloomington: Indiana University Press, 1979.

Owen, Jim. *Jim Owen's Hillbilly Humor.* Cassville, Missouri. Privately printed, 1970.

Owen, Mary Alicia. *Voodoo Tales: As Told Among the Negroes of the Southwest.* New York: G.P. Putnam's Sons, 1893.

Parsons, Elsie Clews. *Folk-lore of the Sea Islands, South Carolina.* Philadelphia: American Folklore Society Memoirs 16, 1923.

Patai, Raphael, Francis Lee Utley and Dov Noy. *Studies in Biblical and Jewish Folklore.* Bloomington, Indiana: American Folklore Society Memoirs 51, 1960.

Puckett, Newbell Niles. *Folk Beliefs of the Southern Negro.* Chapel Hill: The University of North Carolina Press, 1926.

Ramsay, John M. *Dog Tales: Collected mainly from the oral tradition of the Southern Appalachians.* Berea, Kentucky: Kentucke Imprints, 1986; reprint August House, 1988.

Randolph, Vance. *Funny Stories About Hillbillies.* Girard, Kansas: Haldeman-Julius Publishing Co., 1944.

———. *Funny Stories from Arkansas.* Girard, Kansas: Haldeman-Julius Publishing Co., 1943.

———. *Hot Springs and Hell and other Folk Jests and Anecdotes from the Ozarks.* Hatboro, Pennsylvania: Folklore Associates, 1965.

———. *Ozark Magic and Folklore.* New York: Dover Publications, Inc., 1964. Reprint and retitling of a work originally issued in 1947.

———. *Ozark Mountain Folks.* New York: Vanguard Press, 1932.

———. *Sticks in the Knapsack and other Ozark Folk Tales.* New York: Columbia University Press, 1958.

————. *We Always Lie to Strangers: Tall Tales from the Ozarks*. New York: Columbia University Press, 1951.

Rattlehead, David. *The Life and Adventures of an Arkansaw Doctor*. Philadelphia: Lippincott, Grambo & Co., 1851.

Reaver, J. Russell. *Florida Folktales*. Gainesville: University of Florida Press, 1987.

Ring, Bill. *Tall Tales Are Not All From Texas*. No place of publication or date of publication given.

Roberts, Leonard W. *South from Hell-fer-Sartin: Kentucky Mountain Folk Tales*. Berea, Kentucky: The Council of Southern Mountains, Inc., 1964. Reprint of a work originally issued in 1955.

Rowlett, Frank B., Jr. *Say . . . Have I Told You?* Radford, Virginia: Commonwealth Press, Inc., 1975.

Sale, John B. *A Tree Named John*. Chapel Hill: University of North Carolina Press, 1929.

Schermerhorn, James. *Schermerhorn's Stories*. New York: George Sully & Co., 1928.

Scott, Willard. *Willard Scott's Down Home Stories*. Indianapolis: The Bobbs-Merrill Company, Inc., 1984.

Sessions, William H. *More Quaker Laughter*. York, England: William Sessions Limited, 1974. Reprint and revision of a work originally issued in 1967.

Smith, Grace Partridge. "Tall Tales from Southern Illinois." *Southern Folklore Quarterly* 7 (1943): 145–47.

Sonstein, Shelli. *The Thoroughly Tasteful Dirty Joke Book*. New York: Stein and Day, Publishers, 1984.

Spalding, Henry D. *A Treasury of Irish Folklore and Humor*. Middle Village, New York: Jonathan David Publishers, Inc., 1978.

————. *A Treasury of Italian Folklore and Humor*. Middle Village, New York: Jonathan David Publishers, Inc., 1980.

Sterling, Philip. *Laughing on the Outside: The Intelligent White Reader's Guide to Negro Tales and Humor*. New York: Grosset and Dunlap, 1965.

Taliaferro, Harden E. *Fisher's River (North Carolina) Scenes and Characters*. New York: Arno Press, 1977. Reprint of a work originally issued in 1859.

Teitelbaum, Elsa. *An Anthology of Jewish Humor and Maxims*. Edited by Abraham Burnstein. New York: Pardes Publishing House, 1946.

Thomas, Lowell. *Tall Stories: The Rise and Triumph of the Great American Whopper*. New York: Harvest House, 1945. Reprint of a work originally issued in 1931.

Thompson, Harold W. *Body, Boots & Britches: Folktales, Ballads and Speech from Country New York*. New York: Dover Publications, Inc., 1962. Reprint of a work originally issued in 1939.

Thompson, Stith. *The Folktale*. New York. Holt, Rinehart and Winston, Inc., 1946.

———. *Motif-Index of Folk Literature*. Bloomington and London: Indiana University Press, 1966. Reprint and revision of a work originally issued from 1955 to 1958. Six volumes.

Tidwell, James N. *A Treasury of American Folk Humor*. New York: Crown Publishers, Inc., 1956.

Trout, Allan M. *Greetings from Old Kentucky*. Louisville. Courier-Journal, 1947.

Tryon, Henry H. *Fearsome Critters*. Cornwall, New York. Idlewild Press, 1939.

Untermeyer, Louis. *A Treasury of Laughter*. New York. Simon & Schuster, 1946.

Walker, Warren Stanley. "Dan'l Stamps: Tall Tale Hero of the River Country." *Midwest Folklore* 4 (1954): 153–60.

Walser, Richard. *Tar Heel Laughter*. Chapel Hill: The University of North Carolina Press, 1974.

Wardroper, John. *Jest Upon Jest: A Selection from the Jestbooks and Collections of Merry Tales published from the Reign of Richard III to George III*. London: Routledge and Kegan Paul, 1970.

Welsch, Roger L. *Shingling the Fog and Other Plains Lies*. Lincoln: University of Nebraska Press, 1972.

———. *A Treasury of Nebraska Pioneer Folklore*. Lincoln: University of Nebraska Press, 1966.

White, E.V. *Chocolate Drops from the South.* Austin, Texas: E.L. Steck Co., 1932.

Whitney, Annie Weston, and Caroline Caufield Bullock. *Folk-lore from Maryland.* New York: American Folklore Society Memoirs 18, 1925.

Wilde, Larry. *Larry Wilde's Complete Book of Ethnic Humor.* New York: Bell Publishing Company, 1984. Reprint of a work originally issued in 1978.

Wiley, Alexander. *Laughing With Congress.* New York: Crown Publishers, 1947.

Williams, Alfred. *Round About the Upper Thames.* London: Duckworth & Co., 1922.

Williams, Leewin B. *Book of Humorous Illustrations.* New York and Nashville. Abingdon-Cokesbury Press, 1938.

Woodforde, John. *The Strange Story of False Teeth.* London. Routledge and Kegan Paul, 1983. Reprint of a work originally issued in 1968.

Wright, Milton. *What's Funny And Why: An Outline of Humor.* New York: Harvest House, 1939.

Yates, Bill. *Forever Funny.* New York: Dell Publishing Co., 1956.

Zall, Paul M. *Abe Lincoln Laughing: Humorous Anecdotes from Original Sources by and about Abraham Lincoln.* Berkeley: University of California Press, 1982.

————. *Mark Twain Laughing: Humorous Anecdotes by and about Samuel L. Clemens.* Knoxville: The University of Tennessee Press, 1985.